The
Heddon
Legacy

A Century of Classic Lures

Bill Roberts
& Rob Pavey

cb

COLLECTOR BOOKS

A Division of Schroeder Publishing Co., Inc.

Front cover: #100 Dowagiac Minnow in Second box, circa 1905; Jeanette Hawley box and bait, circa 1905; Night-Radiant Moonlight box and bait, circa 1910; Heddon "hand-carved" Stick Frog, circa 1897; Dowagiac Perfect Surface Casting bait, circa 1902; Dowagiac No. 2, circa 1902.

Back cover: Dowagiac Underwater, circa 1903; Dowagiac Underwater and box, circa 1902; #150 Dowagiac Underwater, circa 1904; #300 Heddon Surface, circa 1905.

Cover design: Jim Blaylock, Beth Summers
Book design: Melissa J. Reed
Photography: Jim Blaylock

COLLECTOR BOOKS
P.O. Box 3009
Paducah, Kentucky 42002-3009
www.collectorbooks.com

Copyright © 2002 by Bill Roberts and Rob Pavey

The current values in this book should be used only as a guide. They are not intended to set prices, which vary from one section of the country to another. Auction prices as well as dealer prices vary greatly and are affected by condition as well as demand. Neither the authors nor the publisher assumes responsibility for any losses that might be incurred as a result of consulting this guide.

Searching For A Publisher?

We are always looking for people knowledgeable within their fields. If you feel that there is a real need for a book on your collectible subject and have a large comprehensive collection, contact Collector Books.

Contents

James Heddon: August 28, 1845 – December 7, 1911

*I*ntroduction & Acknowledgments

It is difficult, almost humbling, to begin the task of telling a story that has impacted so many lives over the past century. James Heddon and his children, Charles and Will, established what became an empire. Tracing the progress of this unique family and their contributions to recreation is like trying to piece together the very fabric of America's angling history.

It is true that fishing in various forms has existed since prehistoric times, and some lures and flies were used in England and Scotland long before wooden surface baits made their barely noticed debut in the 1890s. But plug-casting nonetheless remains as uniquely American as any pastime before — or since.

The Heddons didn't make the first lure. But they made the best lures. And they were the first to see the vast potential that the fishing tackle industry offered. Their background in science and agriculture helped them understand the largemouth bass — the angler's most hallowed quarry. Their experience in publishing and politics aided their efforts to promote and market their products. And their well-traveled worldliness offered the family the best perspective from which to unite fishing tackle with the people who wanted and used their products. They emerged early on as the industry's unchallenged leader. No one else even came close to catching up. And no one ever will.

Today, looking back over a century of classic lures produced by James Heddon and his long line of dedicated successors, it is easy to see why this company's lures are the hands-down favorite among collectors. The products changed with the times, and the evolution of Heddon baits mirrored closely the many changes in science, engineering, and American culture.

The chapters that follow have a multitude of intentions. Our hope is that the biographical sections will give you a flavor of what it was like to be a Heddon in the early years of the tackle industry. The reference chapters cover the array of lures, reels, boxes, and paperwork made by Heddon, and there are many photos of the wonderful advertising campaigns that lured anglers to the products that caught the fish.

We also need to acknowledge the many people whose patience, hard work, and willingness to share information helped make this book possible. One of those people is award-winning photographer Jim Blaylock from Augusta, Georgia, whose artistic talent and tireless dedication behind the lens and editing board made this book a reality.

Others to whom we are greatly indebted include Don and Joan Lyons of the National Heddon Museum in Dowagiac; Chuck Heddon of Florida, grandson of Will Heddon; former Heddon sales manager Lanny West, now a senior PRADCO executive; retired Heddon general manager Trig Lund; noted Heddon scholar Bill Sonnett; author and Heddon historian Clyde Harbin; Michael Sinclair, author of a fine book on Heddon rods; Museum of Fishing director Bill Stuart of Florida; and fellow Heddon collectors John Romero, Joe Stagnitti, Bruce Dyer and Dudley Murphy.

Read on — and enjoy!

James Heddon: The Man Before the Lures

Imagine a time, in the evolution of America, when there were no fishing lures, no reels, and no angling in the form we envision today. Imagine a world before James Heddon, and imagine how different our world might be today had this remarkable man not opened his eyes and gulped his first faltering breaths of life one summer morning long ago.

James Heddon was born on August 28, 1845, in the Genesee Valley area of western New York. The Civil War was many years away and much of the history of our nation was unwritten and unforeseen. Looking back today, it is almost unbelievable how fate, luck, and happenstance guided this family to their place in history. Heddon's father — a bearded immigrant who had moved with his parents to the United States from Devonshire, England, in 1831 — was himself an entrepreneur of sorts, whose drive and ingenuity helped spawn the work ethic that allowed the Heddons to create a family dynasty.

The ancestral home of the Heddon family was in Devonshire, England, where a farmer named Thomas Heddon bore a son, Richard Heddon, who ultimately moved to the United States. The farm was called "Huxtable" and still exists today.

When James was barely 5 years old, his parents, Richard and Elizabeth Tuttle Heddon, moved from New York to the Keeler Township area of southwest Michigan. James, an introspective only child, never seemed to mind growing up in a home without siblings. He enjoyed his rural childhood surroundings and soon learned to appreciate the outdoors. One of his childhood companions was a cousin, W.H. Tuttle, who would recall many years later that — as children — he and young James helped make maple sugar and syrup together, at the Tuttle family farm. The boys also hunted squirrels, fished together, and shared boyhood fantasies of someday becoming Indian fighters and trappers out West.

In 1860, when James was 15, the family finally settled in Dowagiac, a few miles away from the Keeler area. Richard resumed farming — a trade he had learned in New York from his father, Thomas Heddon. Richard also began raising bees and producing honey — a popular industry in that part of the country in the mid-1800s. The establishment of Richard's apiary in 1869 laid the foundation for a successful and profitable venture that would later involve his son James. More importantly, however, the beekeeping business would generate the capital that enabled the Heddons to create new businesses, one of which was destined to become an empire.

The town of Dowagiac, by the way, traces its origins to the 1830s, when a water-powered mill began to attract residents and commerce. The community was

Richard Heddon, James Heddon's father, was born in England in 1818 and moved to New York in 1831. The family moved to Michigan a few years later, where Richard's interest in farming later led his only son to explore beekeeping.

named for a word the Potawatomi Indian tribe used to describe "many fishes." Nearby, and aptly named, was Dowagiac Creek, the waterway dammed to create the mill that helped give birth to the town. The railroad's arrival in the late 1840s cemented the community's role in local commerce, and by the late 1870s, the settlement of Dowagiac had become incorporated into a full-fledged city, albeit a small one. The correct pronunciation is "Doe-wah-gee-ack." There are many incorrect pronunciations, too.

Young James, who throughout his life preferred to be called Jim, grew up in a busy household. His father Richard held a variety of intriguing occupations and offices, including sales associate for a basket factory, fire inspector, Dowagiac's mayor, the city's tax collector from 1877 to 1881, a member of the local school board in the early 1880s, and in his later years, a landlord who rented, bought, and sold properties.

As tax collector, Richard Heddon sometimes showed great compassion and generosity by using his own money to help needy citizens out of a bind. He was once quoted in a local newspaper as saying that taxes could be paid more easily if less of the citizenry's money was spent on tobacco, cigars, and "bad whiskey." Richard Heddon, born in 1818, died in 1900, when he was 82 years old, according to newspaper accounts. His death came just seven months after the death of his wife Elizabeth, who was 88. Both are buried in Dowagiac.

James, meanwhile, evolved with the same entrepreneurial spirit as his father and grandfather. He learned beekeeping from his father, and later from his father-in-law, Charles Hastings, whose daughter Eva was married to James on February 13, 1869. Hastings willingly took on his new son-in-law as an apprentice, and by 1870, Heddon launched his own beekeeping enterprises using the many lessons he had learned.

James followed in his father's footsteps in many other respects, serving as Dowagiac's mayor in 1888 and 1889. During that period, he was credited with helping to establish important, progressive improve-

James Heddon's father, Richard, held occupations that included fire inspector, mayor, and tax collector. In his later years, he was a landlord who rented, bought, and sold properties, as evidenced in this 1888 real estate ad bearing his name.

This is the only known photo of James Heddon's wife, Eva, taken in Chetek, Wisconsin, in 1913.

ments in Dowagiac, including a city water system and an electrification plant in which he held a financial interest. Those improvements set the stage for economic development that would follow in later years, including the famous Round Oak stove factory, which — with almost 1,000 workers — was the town's dominant employer by the turn of the century.

James also entered the world of newspaper publishing, having acquired the weekly *Dowagiac Times* in early 1887. Serving as editor of the newspaper offered Heddon an outlet for his prolific and often eloquent writings. He offered strong opinions and coverage of local issues, focusing heavily on business and politics. He tended to favor the Democratic Party in his views, enjoyed lengthy debates over politics, and was in demand as a speaker on topics of the day.

He was also a member, as was his father before him, of the Dowagiac Liberal League, an organization established in the 1870s to encourage debate and thought on issues such as religion and philosophy. Heddon's newspaper editorials were scathing and to-the-point. He never hesitated to go for the jugular on political issues in which he believed. But he also preached fairness and hard work.

Heddon's sharp wit and strong personality carried over into his demanding work ethic, and his face almost always carried a serious — if not stern — countenance. He was thin, almost gaunt, with a receding hairline and moustache that almost appeared too large for his slender face. He would awaken well before dawn to begin the tasks of the day, never wanting to waste a moment. He was a voracious reader, always wanting to learn everything he could about any topic that interested him. And there were many topics that interested him.

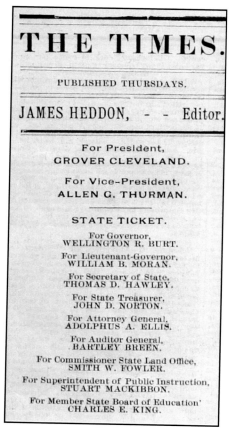

Above and right: James Heddon acquired the weekly Dowagiac Times *in 1887. Serving as editor offered Heddon an outlet for his prolific and often eloquent writings, and taught him the power of marketing and publicity. His name is visible on the masthead of these early papers.*

Heddon's newspaper office, and later his fishing tackle business, was located in downtown Dowagiac, which had a modern water system and electrification, both attractive assets for a pre-1900 town. This early view is of Front Street.

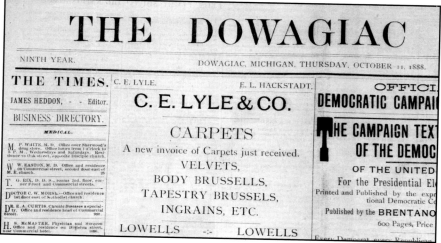

Beekeeping had become a major agricultural industry by the late 1800s, and Dowagiac was centered in bee country. James Heddon often transported his hives with wagons drawn by horses cloaked in white cloth to keep them from being stung and bolting.

By the mid-1880s, Heddon's beekeeping business was booming and the Heddon School of Apiary was established to groom future beekeepers with the best practices and equipment of the day. The demand for his instruction was so great that many prospective students were turned away. Heddon's 1884 application brochure for admission to the classes offers a glimpse into the demands placed upon the students, and some insight into Heddon's disciplined, no-nonsense personality:

> I will give you a short outline of what will be expected of you... Do not come here for any purpose except to learn the art of beekeeping. Do not come out of curiosity. Do not come to form new acquaintances. Do not come for the sake of leaving home. Do not come to study any other theme but apiculture. Do not come to write letters, enter new correspondence or to answer those neglected in the past. If you do your duty, by me, and to yourself, you will have no time for anything of the kind. It will be my endeavor to make this the most profitable half-year of your life.

Heddon demanded loyalty and dedication from his students and others with whom he interacted as a professional. He also wrote prolifically about topics that aroused his passion. In 1885, his detailed book, *Success in Bee-Culture as Practiced and Advised by James Heddon,* was published, and drew worldwide acclaim. He began to invent and manufacture his own products to improve the production and packaging of honey. He also served as president of the American Beekeepers Association and authored many periodical articles on the topic, often referring to himself as "Uncle Jimmy."

The Heddon Hive, patented on September 29,

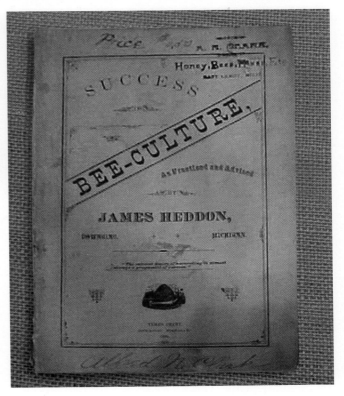

In 1885, Success in Bee-Culture as Practiced and Advised by James Heddon was published, and drew worldwide acclaim. Heddon was president of the American Beekeepers Association at that time. This rare example of Heddon's book was found in Australia.

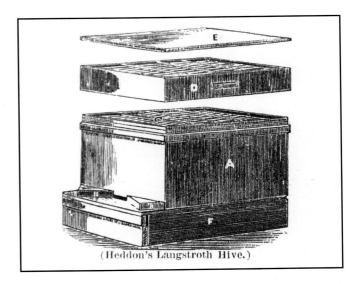

(Heddon's Langstroth Hive.)

The Heddon Hive, patented on September 29, 1885, had a removable frame that enabled the combs inside to be reversed. This feature was important to Heddon, who had learned through study that bees fill the top portions of their combs with honey, and being able to reverse them allowed them to be filled more completely and uniformly.

Heddon's honey jars are made of clear glass and embossed "Jas. Heddon Dowagiac Michigan" with the word "HONEY" in the top of the jar. Only two specimens of this rare jar are known to exist, one of which is owned by the Heddon family.

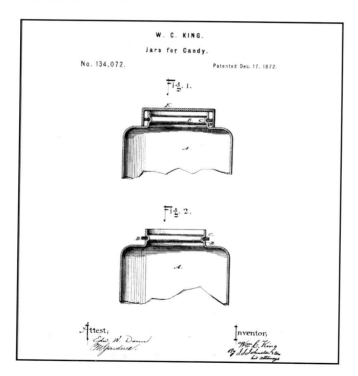

The base of the Heddon honey jar is embossed with the patent date of December 17, 1872, which was registered to a William C. King of Pittsburgh. All Heddon honey jars are very rare. The relationship between Heddon and King is unclear.

1885, with the issuance of Pat. No. 327,268, was Heddon's effort to improve upon a design already popular with apiarists everywhere. Its features included a raised base to retard dampness and a bottom board much wider than the base frame, which offered the bees a "landing pad" with easy access to the hive. Its honey board had perforations large enough to allow the worker bees to enter, but too small to enable the queen to pass through the opening and lay eggs.

The hive also had a reversible frame attached by wooden screws that enabled the combs inside the hive to be reversed. This particular feature was important to Heddon, who had learned through years of observation and study that bees tend to fill the top portions of their combs with honey, and being able to reverse them allowed them to be filled more completely and uniformly.

Heddon also had his own peculiar brand of honey jars, which are quite rare today. The attractive vessels include an embossed glass lid with a beaded rim. Inscribed around the circle is JAS. HEDDON DOWAGIAC. MICH. with the word HONEY in the center. By 1879, Heddon was advertising and selling his "Heddon Brand Apiary Supplies" to broad markets, and printed 3,000 flyers that year in efforts to secure new buyers. The catalogs were 20 pages apiece and by 1885 had grown to 32 pages. Even today, the Heddon strain of honeybees remains a popular hybrid.

By 1879, Heddon was advertising and selling his "Heddon Brand Apiary Supplies" to broad markets, and printed 3,000 flyers that year in efforts to secure new buyers. The catalogs were 20 pages apiece and by 1885 had grown to 32 pages.

In 1895, James Heddon was profiled in a journal titled *ABC of Bee Culture*, written by A.I. Root, and aptly described as one of the world's foremost authorities on the honey-producing insects. The author's characterization of this remarkable man also illustrates the underlying kindness and generosity that were often hidden beneath a relentless work ethic:

He credits his capital, amounting to thousands, entirely to the aid of the little busy bee. His apiaries have some years contrived between 500 and 600 colonies. Mr. Heddon is slight and wiry

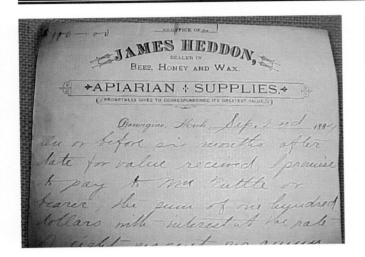

James Heddon, "Dealer in Bees, Honey and Wax" used this letterhead during the late 1800s as his beekeeping business prospered. This notation is in Heddon's own handwriting.

This photo of James Heddon appears in ABC of Bee Culture, just a few years before the famous man entered the fishing tackle industry. Heddon was a serious man and rarely was he photographed with a smile.

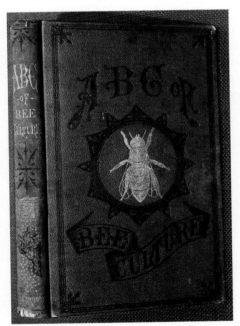

In 1895, James Heddon was profiled in a journal titled ABC of Bee Culture, written by A.I. Root, and aptly described as one of the world's foremost authorities on the honey-producing insects. Only world-renowned apiarists were included in this work.

in figure, below the medium size, of sandy complexion, and intensely nervous in temperament. This nervous tendency leaves its strong impasse on his writings, and more importantly, on his speaking. To that, and to the state of health resulting from it, may perhaps be attributed to a fierceness in controversy, especially in his earlier writings, that would hardly allow one to give him credit for the affability that he really possesses.

Heddon also was a family man, who raised his three children with the same vigor with which he approached his broadening business ventures. Will

James Heddon and his wife, Eva, had three children: Charles, born in 1875; Will, born in 1870; and Myra Heddon, born in 1873. This is the only known childhood photo of all three children. At the time this photo was taken, Charles was 11, Will was 16, and Myra was 13.

This early photo of Will Heddon was taken when the elder son was active in parachute jumping and balloon ascensions. Will made his fortune early on by establishing the Dowagiac telephone company and later selling it for a profit to the Bell conglomerate.

Heddon, born July 14, 1870, was the first child. A daughter, Myra Heddon, was born in 1873. On July 17, 1876, the last of the Heddon children, Charles, was born in Dowagiac and named for his grandfather, Charles Hastings. Although all three children were raised in the academic and political environment of their father, they developed fiercely independent personalities, interests, and lifestyles.

Will Heddon, as the oldest, grew up with an adventuresome spirit and a daredevil philosophy on life. He was handsome, almost dashing, according to some accounts, and had piercing blue eyes and a keen sense of humor. He loved to fish and hunt, and enjoyed riding and racing the high-wheeled bicycles of the day. By the time he was 20 years old, he was already in a management position at Dowagiac's electric lighting plant and had become fascinated with hot-air balloons and parachutes. None of the Heddon men had middle names or initials, but Will, at some point, added a "T." to his name, becoming widely known as W.T. Heddon in later years. No one knows what the "T" stood for.

Will also established the Heddon Telephone Company in Dowagiac, a profitable venture that was later sold to the Bell conglomerate. The company was organized in 1897 with Will and a partner named Dan White as the principals. At the time, their enterprise was the first competitor with the well-established Bell company. Will was quoted in a local newspaper as saying the operation began

with about 150 telephones and a 200 capacity switchboard. Heddon's company also offered rates of $12 per year, compared with Bell's seemingly exorbitant annual fees of $36. "We prospered far beyond our expectations," Will Heddon told a reporter a year later.

Will soon became manager of a larger phone company in nearby Kalamazoo, and eventually sold the entire operation to Bell. The wealth he accumulated through such ventures enabled him to make an important loan to his father a few years later that would cement the Heddon name in American history.

Despite his success as an entrepreneur and his independent nature, Will's thirst for adventure was never muzzled by his role as a businessman and manager. According to the May 12, 1892, edition of the *Dowagiac Republican*, a rival publication from that of the Heddons, Will made a parachute jump in Dowagiac from a hot-air balloon while a huge crowd looked on. It was, according to the article, the most spectacular such jump ever made, at least up to that point in history:

Will Heddon, the Boy Aeronaut, made a balloon ascension and parachute leap from the park in this city last Saturday that, without a doubt,

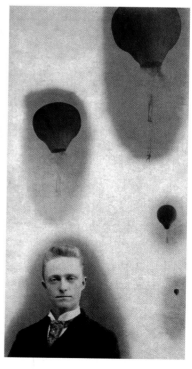

Balloon racing and parachute jumps were common in Dowagiac, due in part to the adventuresome spirit of the eldest Heddon son, Will Heddon. According to the May 12, 1892, edition of the Dowagiac Republican, *Will made a parachute jump from a hot-air balloon 400 feet off the ground while a huge crowd looked on.*

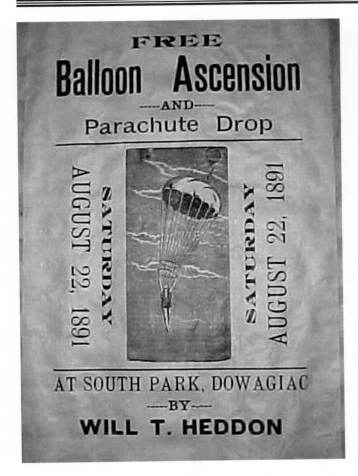

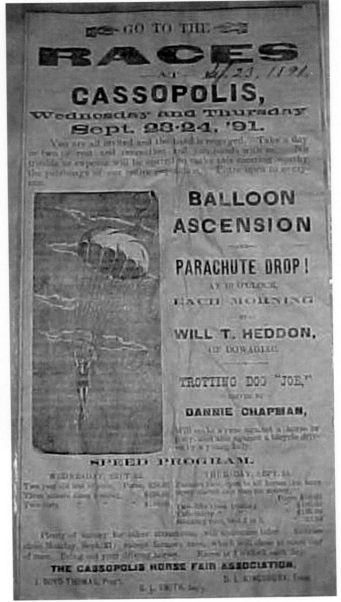

This rare flyer promoting one of Will Heddon's many balloon ascensions in Dowagiac is from the Heddon family scrapbook, and referred to an exhibition in 1891 in Dowagiac's South Park. Will Heddon made similar jumps that September, despite voluminous press coverage of the violent deaths of other parachutists in exhibitions elsewhere.

was the most successful ever made in this part of the country. One of the Baldwin Brothers of Quincy, Illinois, came here and made all the arrangements and sent him off in the finest kind of shape.

When about a mile in height, he struck a strong current of wind that appeared at first as though it would capsize the balloon. After ascending about a mile and a half, he cut loose from the balloon, shooting downward like a shot for about 400 feet, when the parachute opened up, bearing him downward very gracefully, landing near G.S. Wilbur's about three-fourths of a mile from his starting place.

Will's brother Charles was a different animal altogether. Younger, much quieter, and infinitely more conservative, Charles rapidly evolved into a responsi-

ble, dedicated, and capable businessman. He enjoyed quieter sports such as golf and shooting pool, both of which he mastered capably. At one time he held a world championship title in the amateur field of billiards, and he traveled extensively to participate in tournaments. He also organized The Recreation Company in Detroit, which was an entire city block devoted to billiard and bowling facilities. Charles, who also wrote poetry, was very close to his mother, Eva, and often dedicated his flowery prose to her.

Charles also was instrumental in establishing the Dowagiac National Bank, an institution with which he was involved throughout his entire life as vice president and director. He was knowledgeable about matters involving finance, and his opinions on such issues were valued by others in the community. Much later in his life, it would be written that Charles was a compassionate man who contributed heavily to charities and social service organizations, although he preferred to do so quietly and without thanks.

Charles lived almost his entire existence in Dowagiac and was very close to his father, having grown up in the surroundings of the apiary trade and the *Dowagiac Times* newspaper environment. He dropped out of school at an early age. As a teenager, Charles worked at the newspaper office for his father, who decided, when his son was just 19, that it was time to "buckle down" and become responsible. Charles suddenly found himself in charge of his father's paper, and soon thereafter realized that he possessed an aptitude and gift for writing, a trait likely inherited from his equally gifted dad.

In 1897, Charles founded a new publication, the *Dowagiac Daily News*, which was published in the same building — and with the same printing facilities — as the *Times*. The editorial staff at that time consisted of Charles, his father James, a gentleman named W.A. Stolley (about whom you will read much more later in this book), and a local citizen named Abner Moon. Their combination of intellect and wit earned a reputation for producing editorials so scathing that those writings would be described as "pungent" in Charles Heddon's obituary many decades later.

Charles's assumption of the duties of newspaper publishing enabled his father James to gradually withdraw from the daily rigors of the business. The year was 1898. Life had been both rewarding and successful. James continued to reap the benefits of his beekeeping enterprises and also was a respected newspaper publisher.

James Heddon, now 53 years old, had more free time on his hands than in previous years. His sharp mind began to ponder new things, as it always had whenever there was spare time. One of those new things was fishing. The best was yet to come.

Birth of a Legend:
The Splash Heard 'Round the World

The old mill, namesake of the "Old Mill Pond" where James Heddon made fishing history one sunny day in 1898, has long since been demolished. This early view of the now-famous structure shows what the pond must have looked like the morning Heddon whittled on a piece of wood while awaiting his fishing partner.

A few miles east of downtown Dowagiac, out past the railroad tracks and brick warehouses, is a place where the old highway bisects Dowagiac Creek. An ancient dam backs the water into a linear mill pond that meanders along miles of marshy shore. There are coves studded with lily pads and fragrant glades that harbor bullfrogs and waterfowl.

It is a place of great beauty — and great historical significance.

Like many gentlemen of his day, James Heddon often made the short journey to the pond to fish for largemouth bass that prowled the clear waters. A famous and oft-repeated legend holds that, on one particular day in 1898, he arrived at the designated spot early and was awaiting his fishing companions. To pass the time, Heddon whittled on a piece of wood, which grew smaller and smaller. He then tossed the whittled "plug" into the pond and was greeted with a resounding splash.

A bass lurking nearby had reacted to the action of wood upon water and attacked the floating object.

The hand-carved wooden frog (left) is from James Heddon's own hand. There is some evidence it was inspired by the cork frog (center) sold commercially around 1897 by Heddon's fishing friend, C.R. Harris of Manistee, Mich. The "broomstick frog" (right) is believed to be the earliest Heddon hand-carved frog, preceding the more lifelike specimen on the left.

Heddon, as the legend goes, knew instantly that he was onto something — and the idea for topwater lures was born. This story has a dozen or more subtle variations and has been told and re-told countless times over the many decades that have since elapsed.

Heddon often used family photos in early tackle catalogs. This picture, which appeared in 1922, shows Will Heddon's daughter Volta with a string of bass almost too large to hoist up for the camera.

It is generally accepted that there is, perhaps, a bit of folklore intermingled with the truth in this time-honored version of how the Heddon lures were conceived. It is also documented that floating artificial baits were in use elsewhere at or about the same time. Whatever the case, we do know that the veteran inventor set to work, gradually at first, and then with great enthusiasm, to carve wooden lures that could be outfitted with hooks and cast into the water in hopes of catching bass without the aid of live bait.

The idea worked quite well, and soon James Heddon's primitive wooden lures were increasingly in demand among his friends and associates. Heddon's first lures are believed to be his hand-carved, wooden frogs, of which only nine widely varying — but authen-

ticated — specimens have survived into present times. They were fashioned from red cedar or basswood and rigged with eyes made from hat pins. Hooks were hand-wrapped onto the wooden bodies and some featured bottle caps among their hardware. These frogs were never produced commercially but are said to be James Heddon's first experimental wooden baits. They were effective fish-catchers, too.

Many fragments of the Heddon story have surfaced over the years. Some accounts bolster the original legends, and some conflict with or even contradict the traditional stories of how the Heddon lures evolved.

One of the best testimonials to the origins of the Heddon company emerged when an outdoor writer named Sam Stinson set about in 1918 to trace the history of the fishing lure. His article, titled "Whence the Plug," appeared in the May 1918 edition of *The American Angler* magazine. Included was an interview with Charles Heddon, who discussed the circumstances that led his family to enter the fishing tackle industry and revealed that his father and grandfather had dabbled informally with wooden lures for almost half a century before entering the commercial manufacture of such products:

> *In saying that bait-casting was first practiced at that time, I make the exception that there were a few scattering anglers who devised their own equipment, and we seem to have authentic records that bait-casting was practiced earlier, but of course, these were very exceptional cases. My father first made wooden baits exclusively for his own use, originally having no intention of engaging in the art from a commercial standpoint. When asked who made the first wooden bait or plug, my father used to always exhibit two types of wooden minnows used by his grandfather in trolling for pickerel on Magician Lake, in this county, as far back as 1850 to 1855. It is safe to assume that wooden baits in various forms are as old as three quarters of a century.*

It is also possible, although purely conjecture at this point, that a frog lure being made at roughly the same time by C.R. Harris, a railroad employee from Mackinaw City, Mich., could have been the impetus for Heddon's earliest hand-made lures. Harris was making his cork frogs as early as 1896 and was granted a patent for his lure on August 24, 1897, a few months before James Heddon began making lures in Dowagiac.

Although little documentation exists from the early years, Will Heddon gave an intriguing account of the Harris Frog's relationship with his father many years later, in a 1927 interview with a reporter from the

Clermont Press in Florida. Clyde Harbin, a noted Heddon scholar and author of *Heddon Historical Footprints*, was the first to discover this very important bit of angling history. A portion of that interview, first published October 7, 1927, is reprinted below:

So far as we have been able to discover, the first artificial lure was made about 27 years ago by Charlie Harris, a dining car conductor on the Michigan Central (railroad). Harris' frog bait was made of cork. It was extremely buoyant and had a hook on each leg and a gang hook from the stomach. Harris used a crude rod about 6 feet in length and an equally crude reel with about a 10-pound-test soft line.

Frank Peak of Chicago, who operated a dancing school, came to Dowagiac with one of these frog lures. My father, who has now been dead 16 years, was a beekeeper, handled beekeeper's supplies, and wrote many articles for magazines about this industry. He was troubled with asthma and found that being on the water relieved him, so his friend, James Harley, who had been taught to cast by Peak, introduced him to fishing and artificial baits.

For some time they used the frog bait, but one day my father whittled out a "stick" on which he put gang hooks and on the front of the bait a bottle top which caused a spray. Being more slender it held the fish better, and soon his friends were asking him to make "sticks" for baitcasting, although the same principal had been in use by fly fishermen for many years.

It is quite possible, perhaps even likely, that the first "stick" baits with bottle tops on the front are the very same "broomstick style" handmade frogs that were found among the factory archives lures in the 1970s. Soon after the frogs, or perhaps even simultaneously with their production, came the rapidly evolving forerunners of the early commercial lures.

Heddon's "stick" lures eventually became the "Dowagiac Perfect Casting Bait," which today's collectors refer to as the classic "Slopenose." The crudely painted, no-eyed baits had a metal collar designed to give the lure more action as it was pulled through the water. It wasn't long before demand accelerated to the point that James Heddon considered manufacturing the lures as a commercial enterprise.

ANTELOPE HUNTERS — William A. Stolley and Will T. Heddon following an antelope hunting trip to Pine Bluffs, Wyoming in 1899. They had shot six antelope, "the last antelope brought to the original 1857 settlement of Grand Island, Neb." where Mr. Stolley was born, his father being one of the founders of Grand Island. Mr. Stolley came to Dowagiac to learn the bee business from James Heddon, one of the country's leading apiarists, maintained a close relationship with the Heddons, not only in the Heddon company but also the newspaper business. Will Heddon was the son of James Heddon and also associated with the Heddon Company for many years. The picture was loaned by Kirk Stolley, grandson of William Stolley. The latter lived at 612 Spruce Street where his son, William Richard Stolley and family now live.

Unlike his brother Charles, Will Heddon was an avid hunter who traveled wherever necessary to find game and good fishing. This 1899 photo was taken after Will Heddon and a friend, William A. Stolley, had been antelope hunting in Wyoming. Stolley later became a principal at the Heddon tackle company and is credited with several inventions.

The Dowagiac casting bait was the first commercial Heddon lure. This mint in the box specimen somehow survived for nearly a century without touching water. The beautiful picture boxes are highly sought by collectors. They are not common.

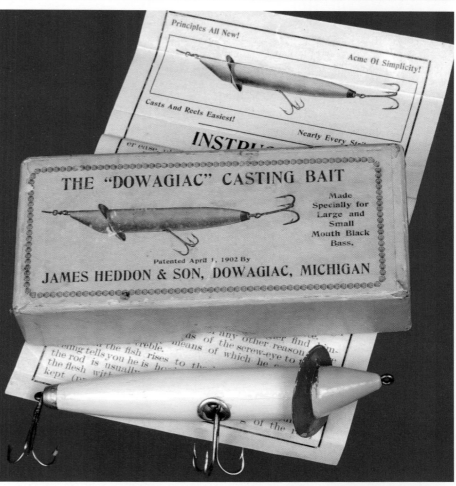

Although other artificial lures were beginning to appear on the market and various spoons and spinners had been around for more than two decades, James Heddon was fascinated with the aspect of topwater casting baits. He read extensively in efforts to learn more about the science and art of angling for the black bass. One of the resources he consulted — and scrutinized — was a 1900 copy of Dr. James Henshall's famous *Book of the Black Bass*.

The book, now owned by the National Heddon Museum in Dowagiac, still bears James Heddon's handwritten musings and notations in the margins. Of particular interest was a note that indicated Heddon's surprise that other anglers held neither knowledge of — nor appreciation for — topwater baitcasting: "These old roosters," he wrote, referring to the leading authorities on bass fishing, "know of no other surface bait — but the fly?"

Thus, it was time for Heddon to capitalize on what he knew and to take advantage of what others apparently didn't know!

In 1900, James Heddon borrowed $1,000 from his prospering son Will and used the capital to launch his lure business. He called the company James Heddon & Son, and laid out plans to make and sell his wonderful lures from his home at 303 Green Street in Dowagiac. For those important first few months, the lures were manufactured and painted in an upstairs room and — according to legend — baked dry in Mrs. Heddon's kitchen oven.

Supposedly, according to Heddon company history and folklore, the crackleback finish was later "invented" when lacquer was applied to a batch of lures and baked in the oven in efforts to make them dry faster. The lacquer "crackled" the paint, and the idea stuck. The era of lures made in the Heddon home was brief. The first permanent factory was established in 1902 on

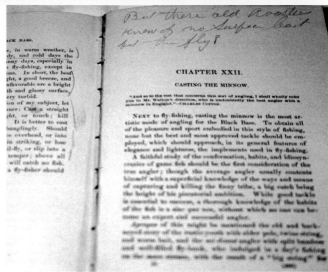

James Heddon's 1900 copy of Dr. James Henshall's famous Book of the Black Bass *includes Heddon's own handwritten notations expressing surprise that Henshall knew of no other topwater bait but the fly.*

The house where the first Heddon lures were commercially produced once occupied the lot at 303 Greene Street and later was moved to a rural farm a few miles from town. This is how the famous home looks today.

James Heddon fished often with his eldest son Will, who preferred testing and developing new lures in the field to the day-to-day operation of the company. Will loaned his father $1,000 to start the lure business. Their discussions while fishing together must have been fascinating! This Heddon family photo is from 1903, Taylor Creek, Ft. Pierce, Florida.

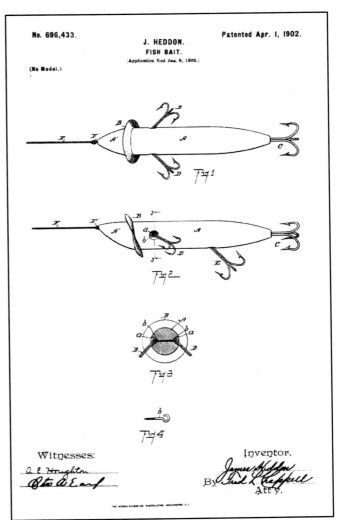

James Heddon, wanting to guard his method of attaching hooks in sunken cups, applied for a patent on January 9, 1902, and the request was made official on April 1, 1902 — a date that would appear on Heddon boxes for decades to come.

the second floor of the Phillipson Clothing Store building in downtown Dowagiac.

One of Heddon's first steps as a commercial fishing tackle dealer was to patent his method of attaching the hooks to his lures in sunken cups, so as to prevent them from tangling or damaging the lure's painted finish. James Heddon applied for that patent on January 9, 1902, and the request was granted by the U.S. Patent Office and made official on April 1, 1902, with the issuance of Pat. No. 696,433. A lawyer from Kalamazoo, Fred L. Chappell, assisted Heddon in acquiring the patent. That 1902 patent date would appear on Heddon boxes for decades to come.

Will Heddon, in that same 1927 interview with the *Clermont Press* in Florida, discussed his recollections of the rapid transition from hand-made baits to the factory products:

> *At that time I was employed by the Trouble Department of the Stromberg-Carlson Telephone Company and my brother, Charlie, was publisher of the* Daily News *in Dowagiac. The fishing tackle business began to develop so swiftly that both of us went into the line...*

Improvements were made over the original basswood plug that our father had made. First of these was fastening the hooks in a socket, which prevented them from catching on each other; and in a collar on the front of the bait, which assured it would travel with the hooks hanging down, rather than with a sidewise tendency.

With the patented features secured, the Heddons wasted no time launching their lures into commercial production. James Heddon, already a master of advertising and marketing, launched a campaign to sell his lures. The first known advertisements for the new baits appeared in the July 5, 1902 issue of *The Sportsman's Review*, followed soon afterwards by a similar ad in the August 1902 issue of *Field & Stream* magazine. Those ads advanced the slogan "Nearly Every Strike a Kill," and claimed the new baits would always float right side up without twisting lines or tangling the hooks. The ads also offered an "illustrated circular concerning the baits and the black bass in exchange for your address," but did not include a price for the lures.

There is little firsthand information preserved about the specifics of James Heddon's evolution as a tackle maker. But one account lends valuable insight into the goings-on at the Dowagiac mill pond in those years, especially as it relates to the extent of experimentation and change that occurred in the Heddon lures over a very short period of time. A 1974 article prepared for one of the Dowagiac newspapers includes a transcript of a letter sent to Dowagiac resident Richard M. Judd on May 2, 1953. The sender of this important information was Philip Johnson, who was born in the late 1800s at the "Wilderness Farm" on Rudy Road a few miles outside of town.

Johnson recounted his experiences as a fishing companion of James Heddon during the first year or two of Heddon's foray into the tackle industry. Johnson was an employee of the *Dowagiac Times* who later worked for a newspaper in Grand Rapids, Michigan. He died in the 1950s, a few years after the letter was written. Here's what he had to say:

I recall that in fall of 1902, Charlie Heddon rode out to our farm on his bicycle and told me that Whit Scattergood was leaving and he wanted me to act as city editor of the Daily News *and the* Weekly Times *... I know I was a lousy editor but I did the best I could. In those days there were no outside news services and I had to fill the paper up entirely with local happenings and boiler plate, of which we kept a good supply ...*

Jim Heddon was just fooling around with plugs for fish bait that fall, and for several days,

after I had put the paper to bed, I would drive him out to the mill pond with my horse and buggy and row a boat around the pond while he would flip various colored cedar plugs in the water to get the reaction of the fish to this kind of lure. He had plugs of every color of the rainbow and these experiments were really the start of the Heddon fish bait business.

There also was an article published in the June 4, 1902, issue of the *Dowagiac Times* that explained the business plans for the fledgling company, and the origins of its soon-to-be-famous products:

About two years ago, James Heddon, an enthusiastic sportsman of this city, began experiments along this line. He tested various kinds of casting baits, closely watching their operation as well as studying the habits and peculiarities of the wily bass, which led to the invention of the floating bait that wholly overcame the defects of other lures for this gamey, toothsome fish. It was thoroughly tested last year, and now it has the unanimous and enthusiastic endorsement of both dealers and baitcasters, as it intensifies the good qualities of other baits and eliminates their defects.

The article continued with the profoundly important news that "Mr. Heddon is now perfecting an underwater bait that is highly spoken of by experts who have seen and used it." The underwater bait, which we now know was the first Dowagiac Underwater (known to collectors as the "Underwater Expert") was said to be protected under the same patents granted to the design of the "Dowagiac Perfect Surface Casting Bait."

Perplexingly to some, the "Dowagiac Perfect Surface Casting Bait" almost always appeared in solid white with a blue head and a red painted collar. Such colors remained in production long after more modern finishes were perfected. The reasoning behind such decisions is revealed in an interview with James Heddon, conducted by *New York Sun* columnist Bob Davis, who fished with the great inventor in 1906 at Potato Lake in Wisconsin:

"Right there, I asked Uncle Jimmy (Heddon) why he had painted the nose of his first surface bait bright blue," Davis wrote.

"Pure deception," Heddon replied. "I wanted it to be the color of the sky, and thus invisible. The fish would then hit the white body which contains the hooks. An American invention applied to business."

"But what about the criticism that your bait is over-supplied with hooks?" Davis asked.

"National stupidity," Heddon replied. "A fish caught on a single hook is likely to take it into his gullet. The result is a dangerous wound from which he dies. The shape of my bait is such that a fish cannot swallow it. Thus all the wounds are limited to the lips, which are cartilaginous and without feeling. No lip wound is fatal. My bait is a benefactor to the fish family, not a threat."

James Heddon also wrote a column for *National Sportsman* magazine in which he related his experiments with — and opinions of — phosphorous baits designed to glow in the dark. Other companies, including Pflueger and the Moonlight Bait Company in nearby Paw Paw, Michigan, were experimenting with such finishes, but Heddon believed an all-white lure remained vastly superior:

> We often read of "phosphorescent baits." We read more about them in advertisements than in contributions of experience by anglers. Having gone through the phosphorescent experimental mill, it is a pleasure to relate to our brother anglers what has been our experience. A pure white surface will reflect more light than will come from a phosphorescent coating providing there is the least amount of light in the surrounding atmosphere.

> When a night is extremely dark – so dark that you can see practically nothing three feet off – the phosphorescent bait begins to show, but for no long distance, for we have never been able to notice any such attractions at any considerable distance as we get using very white lures when there is a little light in the atmosphere and consequently in the water.

> If the readers will try the phosphorescent bait, at the same time with the pure white, it is my word for it that the white bait will take preference.

Heddon began publishing catalogs for his lures starting in 1902. The business grew rapidly at that point, and changes were constant and perpetual as improvements were made with each successive batch of lures. Marketing campaigns were, for the most part, successful, although one particular photo, taken on the front porch of Heddon's home on May 21, 1902, stirred controversy.

The photograph showed 73 bass caught that day near Dowagiac. The fish are strung up along four ropes suspended between the porch columns of the Heddon house, and at least 26 early Dowagiac baits were hung at intervals between all the fish. That photo became an embarrassment to the Heddons when the editor of *Recreation* magazine wrote to James Heddon and his son Charles asking if it were true that they had caught and photographed 73 bass all taken the same day. Charles Heddon's unknowing response yielded the following dialog in the November 1902 issue of *Recreation*:

James Heddon preferred to be called "Uncle Jimmy" and frequently authored columns and articles in which he extolled the attributes of his Dowagiac lures. Heddon once told an outdoor writer why Slopenose baits had blue noses. "I wanted it to be the color of the sky, and thus invisible," he answered. Thus, the fish struck the hooked body of the lure. This 1911 photo is believed to be the last of Heddon before his death.

"I did catch 73 of the black beauties within a few hours. Thinking perhaps you would like to use a photograph, I am sending you one today," wrote Charles Heddon.

"No, I do not care to use the photograph," retorted the editor of *Recreation*, in the magazine's monthly "fish-hog" column. "If you had followed the usual method of fish-hogs and stood beside the string, I should then have been glad to print the picture, in order that decent men might recognize you when they saw you and shun you.

"The fish are not to be blamed for being photographed, and being dead and hung up they are like any other 73 dead bass," the *Recreation* editor continued. "It is safe to assume that these fish would average 2 pounds each or more, so it appears you destroyed 150 pounds of black bass, whereas no gentleman would care to kill more than 25 pounds in a day, at the most."

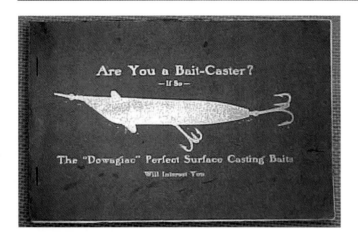

The first Heddon catalog, circa 1902, pictured the Slopenose on the cover with a black background and showed a beautiful lithograph of this famous lure inside. The lure was called "a relatively perfect creation" among surface baits.

Will Heddon was photographed in Mohawk, Fla., with this stunning string of bass in time to be included in the Heddon 1902 catalog. This is perhaps the earliest known angling photo of James Heddon's eldest son.

Although publicly derided over such wasteful angling, the publicity no doubt spurred many readers to scramble for the new Dowagiac baits, as many were sold that season. The company's catalog the following year, however, made it a point to show a different photo with 15 bass – not the piggish 73. And the caption this time pointed out that 12 other fish were caught on Heddon lures but released immediately. Finally, just to make sure no one could cry foul over such a bountiful catch, it was pointed out that the bass were caught by the "son of one of the most efficient game wardens in Michigan."

Advertising campaigns continued to unfold rapidly, as other tackle makers of the pre-1910 era began to experiment and market their own types of fishing lures.

These companies, including William Shakespeare and Pflueger, represented competition to the Heddons, who wasted no time in their efforts to become a leader in the industry.

The lineage of the first few years of commercially produced Heddon lures is confusing and difficult to sort out, in part because catalogs and lures sometimes changed within the years, instead of simply with each successive year. Bill Sonnett of Jackson, Michigan, is one of the best-known scholars of early Heddon history, and what follows are some of his observations gleaned from years of careful study and comparison.

Sonnett believes the first 1902 catalog was printed around May or June, coinciding with the appearance of Heddon lures in magazine ads. That all-important first catalog is the "one-lure" edition, which offers only the Dowagiac Perfect Surface Casting Bait. The first such lures were sold with "rimless" brass cups sunk into the hook sockets. Whenever one of these rare baits appears, you can be reasonably certain it is a lure from the first few *months*, rather than years, of Heddon's production.

By the end of June 1902, those rimless cups had been discontinued in favor of the more typical rimmed cups, and the Dowagiac Underwater lure, which we know as the "Underwater Expert," had already appeared. Six years later, the Heddons claimed they manufactured and sold 6,000 lures in 1902 alone. Only the first few batches of these were made with the rimless cups. Fewer than 10 such baits are known to exist in private collections today.

Sonnett also observed that the earliest illustrations of two- and four-hook Dowagiac Perfect Surface Casting Baits reveals that these illustrations were made using rimless cup baits as models. The finish on these early lures is very granular and almost chalky in texture. Some collectors have opined that the finish is little more than varnish mixed with white lead. Such paint finishes had vanished by the end of the 1902 season and were replaced with the typical white enamel that survives on many Heddon lures today.

Later in 1902, a second catalog, which we know today as the "three-lure catalog," was published by the Heddons. This catalog likely was published as early as July. The lures pictured were the two-hook Slopenose, which by this time had been renamed the "Dowagiac Expert Perfect Casting Bait," along with a four-hook Slopenose called the "Dowagiac No. 2," and finally, the "Dowagiac Underwater," the first of Heddon's many lures designed to sink beneath the surface. The first such Underwater featured a hanging belly weight that is absent on both 1903 versions that followed.

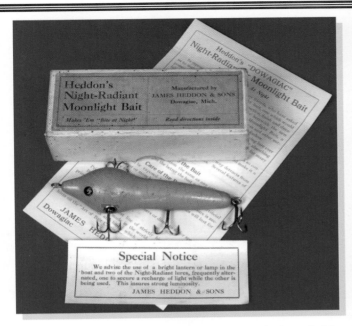

Despite having once claimed luminous night baits don't catch fish, Heddon came out with this very rare Night-Radiant Moonlight lure in 1910. Only a handful are known to exist.

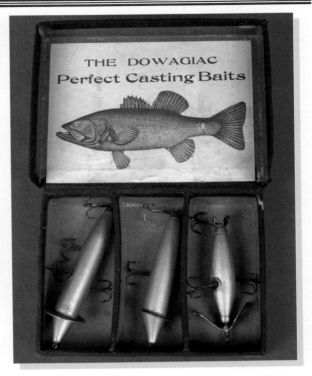

This trio of special-ordered aluminum finish Dowagiac lures dates to around 1904. The triple-compartment presentation box is hinged, and features an early fish logo and a velvety red bottom. Aluminum is a rare color finish on any Heddon lure.

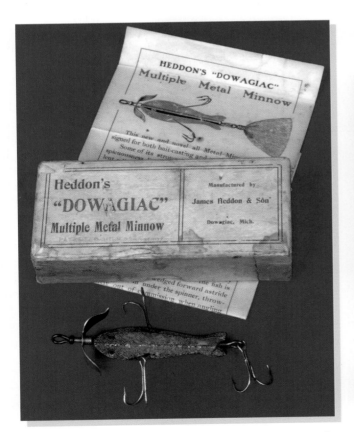

The Multiple Metal Minnow was patented in 1907 and was in the product line only briefly. It came in its own special box.

The Bucktail Surface Minnow, new for 1908, also came in its own special box. This example has a blue crackleback forehead and white enamel throughout.

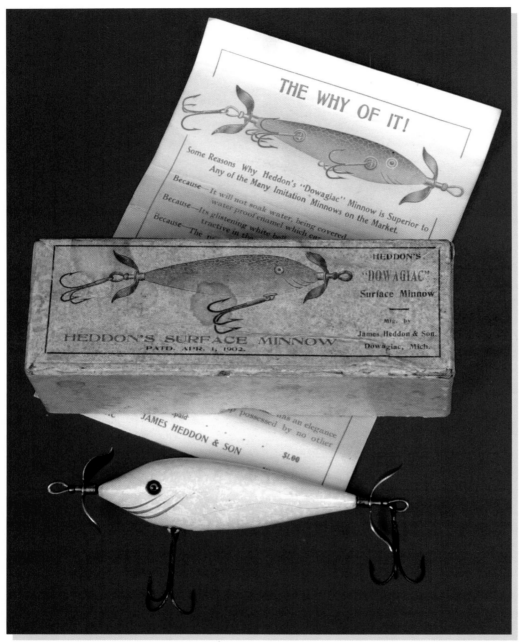

The Heddon 300 Surface Bait, first produced in 1905 as the "New Surface Minnow," went through a variety of changes over the years. The early models such as the one shown here have brass cup hardware and extra long sweeping gill-marks. The picture boxes are very rare.

"When the bait is being drawn through the water, at the speed imparted by the quadruple multiplying reel, the hooks (always two of them) are thrown, by the pressure of the water, up snugly against the body, thus being pressed almost entirely out of service and leaving but a small percentage of the catching capacity as compared with the trebles adjusted upon our plan."

Sonnett, after years of study, has pointed out that virtually all of the hanging belly weight Dowagiac Underwaters likely were produced in the summer and early fall of 1902. There are at least 13 known examples of this bait, all made within a few months of one another and in the same year, but they exhibit at least three specific stages of development, each with significant improvements over their predecessors in hardware. At one time, many collectors believed those variations represented different years. We now know the changes occurred in a matter of months.

The 1903 catalog opened with the statement, "This is the second season of the Dowagiac Baits. At the time of this writing, Jan. 31st, we have in process of manufacture 40,000 baits for this season's business, and we expect to sell them all." Indeed, it is likely they sold many, if not all of their baits, for the business con-

It is interesting to note, on page six of that important catalog, that Heddon included a diagram of his patented sunken-cup hook holding feature to illustrate its superiority over other commercial lures of the day. As a comparison, he also used an illustration of another early lure — the Aluminum Fish Phantom patented by Livingston Hinckley in 1897 — as an example of a lure with the typical "o-ring" fasteners that would hug the side of the lure when in motion, supposedly rendering it ineffective. The catalog claimed, in part:

Will and Laura Heddon fished together often and frequently experimented with new lure designs and reported the results back to Will's brother Charles, who ran the main factory in Dowagiac.

Laura Heddon shared her husband's enthusiasm for hunting and was a capable wingshooter as well as an angler. She also is found in frequent fishing poses, such as this one in which she wears a long skirt, white blouse, and sun hat.

tinued to expand, and plans were laid to add even more lures to the Heddon production line.

That 1903 catalog included important changes from the year before. The name "Dowagiac Expert Perfect Surface Casting Bait" was shortened to the more manageable "Dowagiac Expert," and the hanging belly weight was thereafter missing from the Dowagiac Underwater. Instead, a pair of tiny, internal belly weights were installed and a small, fixed tailpiece was added to create counter-torque that kept the lure from spinning in the water and twisting the line. The lure was also offered in two lengths — two and three inches — and an aluminum finish was added to supplement the basic enameled white. Sonnett has pointed out that the white lures were dipped, while the aluminum-finished baits show signs of being painted with a brush.

The next two years brought great changes to the Heddon line of fishing lures and to the tackle industry in general. In 1904, the important underwater minnows — the 100 and 150 — were introduced, as were the less expensive, no-eyed Killer underwater minnows. The Underwater Experts vanished forever.

One of the biggest problems with these underwater minnows was the spinning action that would tangle the line. Although earlier Underwater Experts featured the small fixed prop at the back of the lure to prevent spinning, it was later found — by copying the other manufacturers of the day — that the use of two

Will Heddon, who authored articles on angling and fishing tackle under the pen-name Billy Bass, was a frequent contributor to early sporting magazines. Much of his fishing experience was gained in Florida, where he first established a winter home in 1903.

SAYS BILLY, "YOU CAN ALWAYS GET A GOOD NAP UNDER AN AUTO"

25

This quaint cabin at the Jolly Palms Resort in Florida is where Will and Laura stayed in the winter of 1903 when many changes were in the works for the American fishing tackle industry.

equal-sized, counter-rotating props would prove much more effective.

Heddon initially derided such "two-prop" hardware in his first catalog, but quickly realized their value and necessity and followed in the footsteps of Pardee and Woods, who already made wooden minnows with equal-sized props fore and aft. These "Killer style" props emerged in 1903 and remained in the line for many years. It is also possible, or even likely, that the origin of the term "Dowagiac Expert" was a play on the success of F.C. Woods' Expert Minnow, which featured double props.

In 1905, the company again moved, this time to the much larger L.J. Pray Building at the intersection of Park Place and Front Street in downtown Dowagiac. The larger quarters offered the opportunity to add employees and expand operations with new and improved lines of lures.

During the next few years, the premium three- and five-hook Dowagiac minnows evolved through a series of hardware, hook hanger, and body style changes — each an improvement over its predecessor. Part of the reason for such rapid innovations and changes was the fact that Will Heddon and his wife Laura established a winter home in Minneola, Florida, in February 1903. Once there, they were less involved with the day-to-day operations of the company, but became infinitely more active in the development and testing of new and improved lures to be manufactured at the company's Dowagiac headquarters.

Florida, in those days, was sparsely populated, largely unexplored (at least by competent anglers) and literally packed with some of the biggest bass to ever strike a plug. Will wrote extensively of his fishing experiences in the many inland lakes and rivers, and his colorful accounts no doubt served to drum up even more business — both for Florida tourism and for the Heddon company. Will Heddon, who often wrote under the pen-name Billy Bass, described one of his more interesting adventures in an article published in the March 1904 issue of *Field & Stream* magazine. He was fishing, with a guide, in Taylor Creek near present-day Fort Pierce:

Without doubt, this was the first time a floating, artificial lure was ever introduced to these waters. About the fourth cast made, something took the bait, in the full sense of the term, for my No. 5 line readily parted company with the lure. Tying on another "white thing," as the paddler termed them, I proceeded to pound every likely spot. After a few moments, another fellow of unknown variety made a surge. In the twinkling of an eye another bait disappeared. Turning to the paddler, I inquired in the most unconcerned manner possible, "What kind of fish do you suppose those fellows are?"

"Small shark, I reckon," responded my assistant.

"No, but candidly, now," said I, "What do you think they are?"

"They sure be," said he.

"You don't mean a shark comes up in fresh water, do you?"

"This 'hain't fresh water; it's tide water, a right smart way up," said he.

After losing two more baits in the same manner, without the pleasure of even a fair glimpse of the thief, I made an extra long cast upstream, landing by a tuft of grass. Simultaneously a monster bass jumped halfway out of the water, taking the bait with him. There was but little room at this point in which to play him, it being the narrow part of the creek beset with roots and snags. Five times this big fellow leaped into the air, shaking the bait as a terrier shakes a captured rat, when coming straight for the boat, he passed like a flash, and another vigorous effort at throwing the hooks was made. This time, unfortunately, he came down upon the line taut, snapping it as a pipe stem.

Will's swashbuckling narration continues, describing how the bass continued to leap skyward, trying to dislodge the lure, even after the line had parted:

An hour later, upon returning from up the creek with fourteen beauties ranging from two to

(Above) This photo, snapped in June 1909 near Chetek, Wisconsin, shows dozens of largemouth bass and a trophy sized musky — all caught in a single day by Will and Laura Heddon. The picture appears on a postcard signed and mailed by Laura Heddon herself! The presumption is that they used only Dowagiac lures.

(Left) Will Heddon was rarely mentioned in Heddon tackle catalogs, but the elder Heddon son's early years in Florida helped produce classic lures like the Dowagiac 300 Surface lure and the 400 and 450 Killer baits.

In 1902, an editorial in Recreation magazine called Charles Heddon a "Michigan Razorback" (or fish hog) for catching and photographing 73 bass caught in one day on Dowagiac lures. Heddon responded by adding this conservation-minded request to the bottom of their early Expert boxes.

Protect and Perpetuate the Black Bass
By killing the big ones with a "Dowagiac" Bait and returning to the water all under one pound.

An early photo from Wisconsin shows yet another mess of bass that jumped at the Dowagiac Floating Bait. The picture, from a Heddon flyer, also shows rare 4-hook Slopenose lures!

CAUGHT WITH A DOWAGIAC
FLOATING BAIT
AT BIRCHWOOD WIS.
BEMIS PHOTO

Will Heddon and his young wife Laura moved to Florida in 1903 and established a home there. Although they had means, money, and large boats, they also camped together so they could fish in Florida's many unspoiled inland lakes. This photo was taken in 1904.

A little Bass trick played with a Dowagiac Minnow by Jeanette Hawley near Mohawk, Florida. She went out and caught this string before her husband was up. He "crawled out" just in time to use the camera. The Bass in this picture ranged in weight from 11 lbs 2 oz. to about 4 lbs.

Laura Heddon used the pen-name Jeanette Hawley in some of her many articles on baitcasting and bass fishing. The caption notes that these bass, including an 11-pound, 2 ounce monster, were caught while her husband was sleeping late!

six pounds, we saw him twice more repeat the effort. The next morning I saw a bass of the same apparent size, surely above fifteen pounds, leap into the air twice, trying to shake out a bait, about ten rods from where the above-described battle took place the day before.

The Heddon company's 1905 catalog, dated January 15 of that year, included many significant additions to the product line. The available lures included the 300 Surface Minnow, the Dowagiac 100, the 150, the 200, 400 Killer, and 450 Killer. A "new" rainbow finish was mentioned, and other colors listed included fancyback, plain white, aluminum, red, and copper.

On May 3, 1905, a large, full-page advertisement appeared in the *Dowagiac Times* announcing that the Onen Hardware Company of that city had arranged to purchase and sell all defective, or "second," Dowagiac baits at a reduced price. This ad would seem to validate the vintage of the extremely rare "Second" boxes bearing the Heddon name. The ad carried a headline stating: "WHILE THEY LAST: Genuine Dowagiac

The "Eclectic," a beautiful wooden motor yacht owned by the Heddons, was photographed on the St. Johns River in Florida in 1909. The family and their fishing companions often took the vessel on angling trips, towing a smaller boat behind them for use in the many inland bass waters.

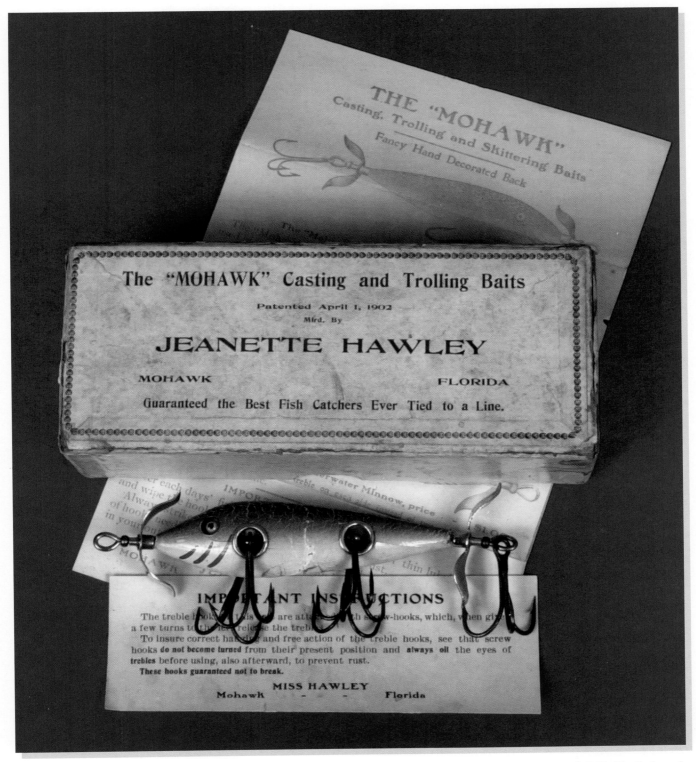

The Jeanette Hawley "Mohawk" minnows were marketed by Will and Laura Heddon in Florida for a few brief years around 1905. The finely made wooden minnows resembled Heddon's early high-forehead Dowagiac 150s.

Minnows at less than One-Half Regular Price," and carried the following announcement:

> Having purchased the entire stock of slightly marred or damaged "Dowagiac" baits of Messrs. James Heddon & Son, we are prepared to offer, while they last, the GENUINE DOWAGIAC MINNOWS at slightly less than one-half regular prices. They are going like hot cakes and will undoubtedly all be gone before the fishing season opens. Come while they last and stock your tackle box. These are not some of the many imitations of the "Dowagiac Minnows" but the genuine articles which are having such remarkable sales all over the United States.

Also by 1905, Will and Laura Heddon had begun to sell limited numbers of their own high-quality "Mohawk Casting and Trolling" lures from their home in Florida. The short-lived lures were sold under the name Jeanette Hawley, a pen-name under which Laura Heddon sometimes authored articles on angling and the outdoors.

The finely made minnows were similar to their Dowagiac counterparts and resembled the Heddon high-forehead wooden minnows. The lures came packaged in their own unique Hawley box, of which only two are known to have survived. The paperwork with these boxes showed three separate baits: the "Mohawk Surface Minnow," which resembles the Heddon 300 Surface bait; the "Mohawk Sinking or Underwater Minnow," which resembles the Heddon 150; and the "Mohawk Cracker," a very large, no-eyed underwater bait similar to Heddon's Killer lures.

Although only the 5-hook Hawley minnow has been found, it is also known that a 3-hook Mohawk minnow was offered as well. It was made from the same 5-hook body as the high-forehead, 150 style minnow. This hefty bait utilized the large cup hardware that appeared on the Heddon 175 Heavy Casting Minnow when it was first offered in 1906.

The Mohawk box instructions, from "Miss Hawley, Mohawk, Florida," offered the following information

Ready For the Overhead Cast.

Will Heddon, also known as "W.T.," was a frequent subject of photographs in early Heddon catalogs. This photo is from 1906 – 07. He was noticeably absent in later years, when brother Charles ran the company from Dowagiac and Will remained in Florida most of the year.

and advice about using and caring for these important lures:

> The Mohawk baits are manufactured under the patents of The Heddon Co., manufacturers of the celebrated "Dowagiac" Casting Baits, such alterations being made to adapt them to the successful taking of southern game fishes.
>
> The size, weight and special hook arrangement of the "Mohawk" surface minnow is the result of over two years of careful experimenting in the various waters of Florida and this lure is offered as the most killing artificial bait ever tied to a line.
>
> After each day's fishing, oil spinners with a drop of thin lubricating oil and wipe the hooks with an oiled rag to prevent rust. Always strike your fish as soon as he strikes the bait. Keep the points of hooks sharp. A small file is a handy tool and should be included in your outfit.

Will Heddon's love for fishing and hunting, and his decision to leave Dowagiac and participate in the fishing tackle business from afar, helped spur his brother Charles to join the company. Charles — through his experience in newspaper publishing and other ventures

Mr. Burton, of Martinsville, Indiana, and his largest catch of the season, taken on the "DOWAGIAC" Minnow at Trout Lake, Fla., in the winter of 1906.   Weights from 11 3-4 to 10 1-2 lbs.

(Above) This photo of bass taken on Heddon lures in Indiana appeared in the 1907 catalog, which claimed that Heddon minnows "are now known and used in almost every city and village in the United States."

(Right) The Heddon 1907 catalog includes beautiful color plates of the company's rapidly expanding product line. The catalog also shows "Jeanette Hawley," the only time Laura Heddon was pictured under her pen-name.

BOOK OF
**Heddon's "Dowagiac"
Minnows**
AND THE
Art Of Bait Casting
1907

— possessed a keen business and financial sense that helped continue the growth and expansion his father and brother had launched just a few years earlier.

In 1906, the Heddons opened a factory in Chetek, Wisconsin, mainly for the manufacture of high-quality cane rods. The family already owned property and a summer home there, with abundant fishing and hunting opportunities nearby. A famous rodmaker, George Varney of Poughkeepsie, New York, was brought on board to help launch the operation. Varney had previously worked with the famous H.L. Leonard Company, makers of exceptionally fine bamboo rods. Will Heddon was put in charge of the Chetek operation, which was described in detail in a story published in the November 2, 1906, editions of the *Chetek Alert* newspaper:

> The firm of Heddon & Co., manufacturers of fancy casting rods, and inventors of the famous "Dowagiac" baits, are now located in their building formerly owned by F.A. Southworth. All of their machinery has arrived and by January 1 they expect to have before the jobber a full line of samples. They do not do all the painting here, only what is known as the "fancy back," but are confident that this year's sales will by far outreach their output last year which was 120,000. They have booked for delivery by January first 200,000 minnows, which is no small output.
>
> They are now drying the bamboo which is shipped direct from Calcutta and by spring expect to have a full line of high class rods. In a former issue of the Alert, we stated that they make the best rod in the state, which is true, and to that we will add, the world, for Mr. Heddon being a practical black bass caster well knows the needs of every angler and surely he can see what is necessary to bring success along that line. As to the bamboo work, he has one of the world's best bamboo workers in the person of Mr. Varney, who through experience knows how the work should be done. These two points together convince us that the work is unexcelled. They do not make a cheap rod, the cheapest being $6.00, which is a stock rod. The work will be confined to rods ranging from $15 up.

Although designed mainly for the manufacture of rods, some wooden minnows also are believed to have been painted at the Chetek plant. These lures often appear in the "Killer" wooden minnow boxes that carry the important April 1902 patent date on the top, but make no mention of Heddon.

The *Chetek Alert* reported in 1906 that Laura Heddon and two other women "have already commenced work on Dowagiac lure painting" in the rooms above the nearby Carter's Store.

These lures could have included the round-bodied minnows that remain so steeped in mystery, but there is still a great deal of conjecture. Some historians believe the baits were actually made a few years later, and in Dowagiac, for sale to wholesalers like Edward K. Tryon and VL&A to repackage and sell under their own names.

However, we now know that the Chetek operation was under way for less than a year, and it is likely the Dowagiac lures that were painted in the rooms above Carter's Store were simply Heddon minnows — and that the other lures were manufactured elsewhere.

Despite the initial hoopla, and an apparently sizable investment, the Chetek factory was short-lived, and little is known about its apparent demise. Michael Sinclair, who researched the history of Heddon's rodmaking activities in his book, *Heddon: The Rod with the Fighting Heart*, theorized that perhaps a decision was made to consolidate all of the tackle manufacturing under one roof, which is ultimately what happened.

Also in 1906, we know where Heddon's boxes originated for the many lures that were now being made. An article titled "Bait Casting: By James Heddon" in the spring 1906 issue of *Northwestern Sportsman* includes the following discussion:

"Over in Elkhart, Indiana, which is only about twenty-five miles from the home of the writer, Dowagiac, Michigan, there is a businessman by the name of Barger. Mr. Barger is engaged in the paper box manufacturing, and makes good boxes, as we well know, being one of his customers."

Although it is unclear whether Barger also made the slide-top wooden boxes for which many early Heddon lures are well known, it is fairly certain that the early white pasteboard cartons originated in Elkhart. The Heddons also owned newspapers, however, and it is entirely possible — if not likely — that pre-1906 catalogs and perhaps box labels could have been produced in Dowagiac and affixed to boxes purchased elsewhere.

Several important new lures were added to the Heddon line in 1906 and 1907. The 1906 catalog, issued in February, carried the pledge, for the first time, that "all of the metal fittings used on Dowagiac Baits, including hooks, are nickel plated." The premium lures, such as the 100, 150, 175 and 300, are noted as being packaged in a wooden box.

Shown for the first time is the 175 "Heavy Casting Minnow," which is made for larger varieties of freshwater fish such as muskellunge and pike, and also for Florida gamefish such as the black bass. The Heavy Casting Minnow's colors were fancy back, rainbow, and white. The Killer is offered in red-white-red for the first time, and the use of numbers to denote paint codes also is introduced.

In February 1907, the new catalog included the Artistic Minnow (the No. 50), the No. 100, No. 150, the 175, and the 200. The catalog notes that the 200s are "packaged one each in strong wood box," although the authors are aware of no such box. The No. 300 is shown in three colors, and the weights of lures are denoted in pennyweight. It was also the last year for the 100, 150, 175, and 300 to be packaged in wooden boxes and the second year that the catalog contained color plates showing the beautiful lures.

By 1908, the company's name had been changed from James Heddon & Son to James Heddon & Sons, reflecting the fact that both Charles and Will Heddon were now a part of the daily operation of the business. Also in 1908, the business moved to its fourth home at 414 West Street, at its intersection with Telegraph Street, on the outskirts of Dowagiac. This location, with a sprawling, three-story building, had room for virtually unlimited expansions and would serve as the

The opening of the Heddon factory that still stands today was announced in the January 7, 1908, edition of the Dowagiac Times. "Its new home is a building of wood and sheet metal, three stories high with basement," the report said. There were 25 employees that year.

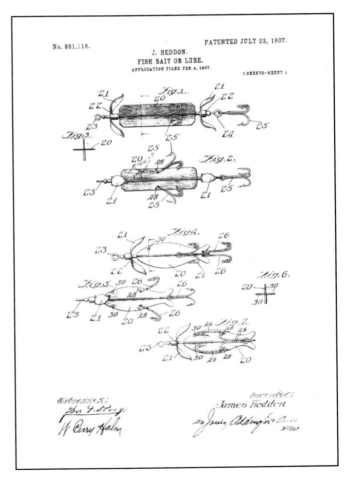

The Multiple Metal Minnow, a short-lived Heddon classic, was patented in 1907. The lure was offered in nickel finish and could be ordered in gold for a slightly higher price.

James Heddon established a rodmaking facility in Chetek, Wisconsin, in 1906, and Heddon used every opportunity to promote the quality cane casting, big game, and fly rods he planned to manufacture. Heddon rods remained in the product line many decades.

company's headquarters for many decades to come.

The new building, adjacent to what was once the city cemetery, initially employed 25 women and a handful of men. The January 7, 1908, edition of the *Dowagiac Times* tells of the official opening:

> *The bait factory has, for the past few years, occupied the entire of the two-story building at the corner of South Front and Park Place streets, known as the Pray building. Its new home is a building of wood and sheet metal, three stories high with basement.*
>
> *The rod factory, owned also by Messrs. Heddon & Son, which had been located at Chetek, Wisconsin, was moved here a few weeks ago and now occupies a portion of the building. The two industries will be operated independently.*

1. BEGINNING THE CAST. 2. OVER THE SHOULDER. 3. FORWARD FULL-ARM DRIVE.
4. DOING STUNTS WITH THE LURE. 5. DOES THE TRICK WITH A FIVE-FOOT ROD.

Laura Heddon's casting abilities earned her a national reputation among anglers, both male and female. This series of photos from an early catalog uses the angling pioneer to demonstrate the proper way to cast an artificial lure.

James Heddon often fished with son Will Heddon and Will's wife, Laura, whom the elder Heddon often referred to as the best "anglerette" on the continent. Laura was both an accomplished flycaster and bass angler and often promoted Heddon products.

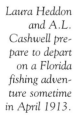

Laura Heddon and A.L. Cashwell prepare to depart on a Florida fishing adventure sometime in April 1913.

Although the authors are unaware of any 1908 catalogs, Heddon products were advertised in other publications. Thus, it is known that the new baits of that year included the No. 400 Bucktail Surface Minnow and the No. 500 Multiple Metal Minnow. Company history places that year's lure production at 250,000 baits — a record destined to be broken annually for many decades to come.

Sometime in the 1908 – 1910 era, Heddon backpedaled on his earlier disparaging comments on luminous baits and came out with the wonderful Night-radiant Moonlight Bait. This bulbous, four-hooks, glow-in-the-dark monster came packaged in its own special box with the James Heddon & Sons logo.

It is possible these lures were offered to compete with similar, but less sophisticated, lures being offered during the same time period by the then-fledgling Moonlight Bait Co. of nearby Paw Paw, Michigan. According to its accompanying literature, the lure was produced due to public demand and was useful primarily for fishing at night:

This early photo of James Heddon and sportswriter Bob Davis examining a giant salmon appeared a year later — in slightly amended form — as a line art drawing used for Field & Stream *magazine's 1913 fishing contest.*

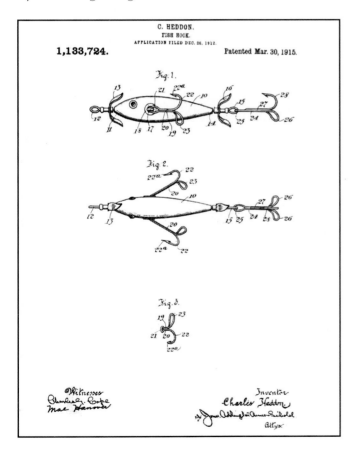

The famous "Dummy Double" hooks for the equally famous Heddon lure were patented in 1915.

Field&Stream PRIZE FISHING CONTEST
Grand Prize Landlocked Salmon, 1913

In response to requests from our many friends, who have asked us to make a Night-Radiant or Moonlight Bait, one which would possess the characteristics of high grade construction, finish and durability of the Dowagiac baits, we offer herewith the new Heddon's Dowagiac Night-Radiant or Moonlight bait, a surface or floating lure, designed for catching bass and other surface biting game fishes which are well known night feeders.

This bait is the strongest, self-radiant or self-glowing lure ever produced, being coated with a special preparation for absorbing either daylight or bright artificial light, radiating same when exposed at night. The constant use of it in daytime in no

The Heddon home at 303 Greene Street, which still stands today, is where James Heddon died in 1911. This early photo shows the house as it looked in that era. The identity of the child on the steps is unknown.

way detracts from the result at night or self-glowing properties. Several features of this bait are under our patent.

Other lures that soon appeared included the elegant No. 900 Swimming Minnow in 1910, and the No. 800 Swimming Minnow a year later. The fat-bodied 100 minnows appeared in 1911, and by this time virtually all Heddon baits were packaged and sold in cardboard boxes. The five-hook muskellunge minnow appeared in 1909, and the three-hook muskellunge minnow was first catalogued in 1911.

By spring of 1911, as the fishing season once again wound to its annual frenzy, things were good in Dowagiac, and the tackle industry thrived with the growing popularity of the sport. James Heddon, now 67 and in declining health, often recalled visits with his favorite son Will and fishing trips with his daughter-in-law Laura, whom the elder Heddon always described as a better "anglerette" than most men.

The February 1911 issue of *Field & Stream* magazine included a detailed account by *New York Sun* columnist and Heddon family friend Bob Davis, who had fished with the Heddon family the previous summer in Wisconsin. It was obvious that Davis held his friend in great esteem, for in closing, he related what he enjoyed most about the outing:

Even a trip into Wisconsin with the Heddons must alas come to an end. I stayed as long as I could and caught muskellunge and bass until I was wrist weary. Greatest perhaps of all pleasures were the hours I spent in the company of the philosoph-

ical Uncle Jimmy, whose soul is attuned to every hour in the twenty-four.

He is a tireless angler by day and a complete sleeper by night, his dreams being disturbed only by the longing for tomorrow — when he can take his rod and his favorite reel and fare forth to the lily pads. Whether the fish bite or not, Uncle Jimmy is the acme of good humor and his heart beats time to the sweep of the oars or the chug-chug of the motor boat bearing him to the good waters.

Soon afterwards, however, a chain of events unfolded that would change the Heddon company — and the fishing industry — forever. The same month

James Heddon's grave, surrounded by those of most other members of his family, is nestled in the city cemetery on the outskirts of Dowagiac.

that Davis' joyful account of fishing with the Heddons was published, James Heddon suffered a stroke back in his hometown. The *Dowagiac Times* had this to say:

"James Heddon suffered a stroke while at the office of a fellow businessman, James Harley. Mr. Harley had noticed there was something wrong with Mr. Heddon just before this, and was not surprised when the shock came. He is 65 years old and evidently as healthy as any man in the city of that age."

Heddon, already weakened by years of asthma, never recovered from the debilitating blow to his senses and spent the last months of his life in ill health and partly paralyzed. He died, quietly and in his own bed, at the family home at 303 Green Street, the morning of December 7, 1911.

A few days later, the *Dowagiac Times* described the funeral as simple, but so impressive as to make its simplicity both "fitting and perfect." Aside from the contingent of close friends asked to be pallbearers, only his wife and children attended.

A family friend, Fred Phillipson, had long ago been appointed by James Heddon to compose and deliver a eulogy if and when it became appropriate. Phillipson's comments traced the departed inventor's lifetime of achievements, his political and social contributions to his beloved town of Dowagiac, and his benevolence and kindness to everyone. His concluding remarks, in part, went like this:

We feel that in this hour, James Heddon has reached the loftiest heights of human achievement. He has lived a just, honest, truthful and useful life, and has enjoyed it best when germinating and disseminating some great truth. If there be a more exalted consummation of this, our sense of justice must be an abnormal one, and the highest fruition of any life must be in the imprint it leaves in the minds of the dear ones for good. Thus passeth James Heddon.

Heddon's fishing partner and friend, Bob Davis, was quite distressed to hear the sad news. He composed a few words into a telegraph, which he wired from New York on December 9, 1911, to the Heddon family. He asked that it be placed in his friend's hand:

TO: JAMES HEDDON, Dowagiac, Mich: – Goody bye, Uncle Jimmy, though you wore your name in water, it will remain indelible forever, and your memory will never fade. Your children will place this, my farewell, in your hand. Hold it until we meet again. BOB.

Davis' simple but loving farewell marked the end of an era in American fishing tackle history, but his words would prove to be a great prophecy as well, for the Heddon name would live on for many generations to come.

The Age of Competition: Heddon's Battle for Dominance

Charles Heddon, the younger of James Heddon's two sons, became president of the company in 1912, not long after James Heddon's death in December 1911.

James Heddon's death marked a turning point in the company's rise to prominence. His sons, Will and Charles, were now running the operation, and the company's name was changed in 1912 to James Heddon's Sons to reflect their father's loss.

The catalog that year included reels for the first time. The German silver, high-quality casting multipliers were an immediate hit in the market place and added revenue to the growing company's arsenal of top sellers. The earliest Heddon reels were actually the products of B.F. Meek & Sons, a well-known maker of the day. However, in addition to selling the Meek reels that first year, Heddon also marketed two of its own reels, which were manufactured for Heddon by the Meisselbach Company.

New lures that year included the wonderful No. 0 hexagonal wooden minnow, the No. 00 — its five-

hook counterpart — and the beautifully made No. 10 Light Casting Minnow, which featured a labor-intensive carved wooden tail.

Also in 1912, the first of the enduring "downward leaping bass" boxes emerged, and the logo, "All Genuine Dowagiac Minnows have 'Heddon Dowagiac' Stamped on the Spinners" appeared. The 1912 year also brought new changes to the famous 200 surface lure, the rapidly changing successor to the traditional "Slopenose" lure. The 1912 version of the 200, for example, introduced the three-flange collar, replacing the "pin" collar.

The next few years are truly the classic era in fishing tackle, and the Heddons introduced many of what have now become the most collectible and popular baits of all times.

The "Dummy Double" emerged in 1913, along with the classic No. 1300 Black Sucker. The Coast Minnow appeared that year, as did the 1400 "single hook minnow" that remains so elusive to collectors today. Ice decoys, advertised in 1912 and first catalogued in 1913, joined elegantly shaped and painted practice plugs and other new additions to the line.

Charles had assumed the role of president after his father's death, and Will Heddon gradually extended his withdrawal from the hands-on management of the

In 1919 – 1920, a second addition to the factory was completed, which included the transformation of a small house near the former city cemetery property into an office.

Although Charles Heddon remained in Dowagiac to supervise the lure factory, older brother Will (shown here in a 1920 family photo) traveled extensively and spent much of his time in Florida and Wisconsin.

company. Will Heddon, in his October 7, 1927, interview published by the *Clermont Press* in Florida, explained his role as a tester and creator of baits, but reiterated that the day-to-day business operations of the factory were left to his brother:

I first came to Florida (1903) the winter after our firm was founded (in 1902), going to Fort Pierce first, but hearing of the many lakes in this section, I came to Mohawk where I spent the winter at Charles Stokes' place with Harry Stokes, who was then pretty much of a boy, as guide. We fished in many lakes, tried out our pattern and color schemes, constantly adding to our line.

The factory soon outgrew itself until today it gives employment to from 175 to 200 people, with an annual production of more than 1 million baits. This is in addition to our complete line which includes rods, reels, lines, tackle boxes, stringers and dozens of items required by fishermen. Our product is sold all over the world.

We were constantly experimenting with new lures. Many of our friends develop lures which they think are successful and we always try them out thoroughly. Some of the models which we tried out and discarded as unpractical many years ago have been brought to life in later years and have proven our best items.

In our factory at Dowagiac we have a large cabinet in which are hundreds of lures which we have produced during the past quarter century, and to fishermen who visit our factory in Dowagiac this proves as interesting as our mechanical processes.

(Above) The Heddons maintained a beautiful home in Minneola, Florida, shown here in a 1918 family photograph made into a postcard. The note on the back was written by Laura Heddon to her siblings. "We leave Monday for Dowagiac," she wrote. "Then on to Chetek."

(Left) Laura Heddon often enjoyed fly-fishing for trout during the family's frequent visits to mountain waters in Michigan, Montana, and Wisconsin.

Long before becoming president of a major tackle chain, Charles Heddon had taken an interest in billiards and was an accomplished player.

1918 to testify as an expert witness in an important lawsuit in which Shakespeare successfully sued Pflueger, claiming their patented gem-clip style hook fastener had been inappropriately copied. The judge agreed with the plaintiffs, leaving the amount of damages as the primary issue to be resolved.

During his extensive testimony, Charles Heddon was asked a question about the origins of his father's company, and about the types of lures that represented the primary competition back in the early years. His response, in part, is reprinted below:

We found a wooden bait, of the underwater variety, with spinners, manufactured by a concern in Kent, Ohio. It occurs to me that it was Pardee & Co. Also a bait known as the "Expert," manufactured by the Woods Co. of Alliance, Ohio. I do not recall any others.

We are the largest manufacturers in the country of wooden baits. From the time we perfected our first underwater minnow, we anticipated, and later verified, that they (other tackle makers) would not prove in any way effective competitors for us, regardless of price, if our price was reasonably consistent with the prices of these baits.

Charles Heddon also addresses the primary competitive concerns in the first decade of the company's operation, noting that he was alarmed when other lure makers attempted to sell at lower prices that could dissuade anglers from buying Heddon's premium-priced lures. Shakespeare's less expensive "Rhodes" minnows were one example of such a tactic:

"They were made in substantially the same design as our own and were the nearest approximation to our goods in quality and possessed what we conceived to be the only other mechanically and commercially successful hook fastening, and were somewhat lower in price."

The Pfluegers also offered lower-priced minnows, he continued, and their salesmen often quoted retailers of the day prices that were well under Heddon's.

Will's life in Florida was a busy one, much like his father's and grandfather's before him. Will, or "W.T.," as he was sometimes known, had built his first Florida home in 1909 and another in 1915. Will Heddon also served as mayor of Minneola from 1933 to 1937 and was instrumental in establishing that city's public water system. In 1930, Will Heddon helped reorganize the city's State Bank to help preserve its solvency throughout the Great Depression. His wife, Laura Heddon, in addition to being an extraordinary and well-known angler, also served as mayor of Minneola in 1945.

The years up to and leading through the 1920s brought intense competition to what had become a very profitable American industry. Scores of smaller companies, many with quality products and useful innovations, emerged each season. Then there were the major competitors of the day, including Pflueger in Akron, Ohio; Shakespeare in nearby Kalamazoo, Michigan; the South Bend Bait Company in Indiana; and of course the always prolific Creek Chub Bait Company of Garrett, Indiana.

Battles raged over ideas, patents, and details as seemingly obscure as paint finishes and hook fasteners. Charles Heddon, as the top executive in the nation's leading fishing tackle company, was called upon in

Seymour's First Air Merchandise—Edward F. Maxon, right, is shown receiving the first merchandise delivered by air to Seymour almost 49 years ago from Mr. Fawcette, sales manager for James Heddon & Sons, fishing tackle manufacturers, Dowagiac, Mich., and Mrs. Charles Heddon following their arrival in the World War I single engine plane used by the Heddon company to advertise artificial fishing lures. The photo was taken by Platter & Company for the Seymour Daily Republican, and belongs to Maxon, now a resident of Chicago, who operated a pharmacy at Tipton and Chestnut streets at that time. Many local people took their first airplane ride in this plane which remained here three days.

49 Years Ago

First Air Merchandise To City Was Fishing Tackle

With air activity at Freeman Field, Seymour's modern municipal airport, now commonplace, it is interesting to note that the first air flight delivery of merchandise to Seymour was made almost half a century ago, with the plane landing in a field a short distance north of the present Freeman Field.

Three days before election day, in November, 1920, the first merchandise delivered to Seymour by air flight arrived in a World War I single engine biplane from James Heddon & Sons, of Dowagiac, Mich., fishing tackle manufacturers. The shipment came to Edward F. Maxon, operator of the Maxon Pharmacy at Tipton and Chestnut streets then. Accompanying the shipment were Mrs. Charles

manager for the Heddon company.

The visitors and the airplane remained here for three days, taking up passengers from the field which was the old Kasting circus grounds on Kasting Road south of present U. S. 50 near the west edge of Seymour. During that period, many "oldtimers" took their first airplane ride in the open cockpit biplane, which was used by Heddons to advertise their artificial fishing lures. The plane returned to Dowagiac on election day, 1920.

Amazed at Growth

Maxon, who retired in 1954 and is now 82 years of age, was in Seymour last week and was given a guided tour of the city. Following the tour, he

mour's industrial and residential growth, as well as the development of its school system.

Now a resident of Chicago, Maxon has always been a booster for Seymour and remembers all the older citizens, many of whom have passed away. He owned the former A. J. Pellens Drug Store, corner of Tipton and Chestnut streets, part of the site for the new Jackson County Bank, from 1916 to 1924. Among helpers in his drug store in 1918 were Dr. Durbin W. C. Day, John R. Wieneke, Bill Ross, and Marie Nichter.

Maxon left Seymour in 1923 and worked for Sunkist for 34 years, travelling in the United States and Canada. His guided tour here last week was his first of Seymour in 46 years, and Seymour's growth in that period impressed him great-

ly. While a druggist in Seymour, Maxon and the late Albert Walters tried to form a Chamber of Commerce. He built the Princess Theater next to his drug store on South Chestnut street and leased it to an amusement company.

Older residents remember "Maxon's Corner" as a source of hand-packed cartons of ice cream as there was no prepacked ice cream then. He sold out to the late Mr. and Mrs. Hiram Jones, who later moved the pharmacy to Chestnut street and St. Louis avenue selling it several years ago to Paul Vehslage.

Mr. and Mrs. Maxon had two sons born in Seymour. One is now a lawyer in Illinois and the other is with E. I. Dupont de Nemours and Co.

(Previous page)
Although the company was short-lived, it filled an important niche in aviation history before being relegated to the history books. The National Heddon Museum in Dowagiac has an extensive exhibit on the aviation company.

demand as a novelty, and were hired to offer rides and fly aerial shows at fairs, festivals, and holiday events.

On June 30, 1922, James Heddon's Sons issued a press release with the abrupt announcement that the aviation company would cease operations after a July Fourth celebration that year in Dowagiac. No explanation was offered, but company documents show that Charles Heddon made the formal request to dissolve the company during a September 15 meeting of the board of directors, who agreed without further comment.

The company's brief existence was formally dissolved when a certificate of dissolution was filed with the Secretary of State's office on December 9, 1922, thus ending a chapter in the history of American aviation.

And the Heddons returned their efforts to the business of making lures.

(Above) Workers assembled reels by hand in a special section of the factory.

(Left) Finishing work on Heddon rods was done by specially trained workers.

(Above) Many of the Heddon employees in the early 1920s were women. The workers here are installing hardware on Heddon lures before they were sent to a different part of the factory to be boxed and labeled.

(Left) Eyes and hardware were attached very carefully and by hand.

(Right) Each Heddon rod was hand-checked for balance and straightness before being packed for shipment to retailers.

(Left) This is perhaps the most famous of the factory photos. Notice all the boxed lures and packing crates. Outside the window, a Model T Ford is visible. This photo is believed to date to around 1924. How many lures can you count?

(Right) Rodmaking "stations" lined one wall in the rod section of the Heddon factory building.

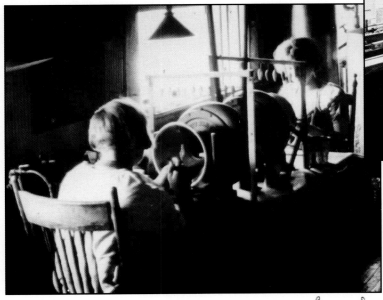

(Left) Exhaust fans used to ventilate the area where lures were spray painted and varnished were belt-driven and ran all day long.

The 1920s: Changes, Challenges, and Innovation

Although James Heddon's name endures as the patriarch of the company he created, his sons rightfully claimed credit for building the business to the levels it achieved. But there was no question that it was James Heddon, the initial founder and inventor, who instilled in his sons the love for fishing and the creative spirit that guided them to such success.

In an interview published in the July 1924 edition of *Sportsman's Digest*, Charles Heddon described for famed outdoor writer Robert Page Lincoln the impact that his late father had upon his early years as an angler and sportsman:

> In early childhood, when imagination was impressionable and warm, he taught me to love the beauty and sublime democracy of nature. He liberated me from the mental and physical fetters of the school-room and led me into the great cathedral of the outdoors. He taught me to interpret the symphony of the waterfall and the sublime dirge of chill November winds sighing the last requiem over leafless forests. Countless times when afield, I have seen him pause in silence to contemplate some pastoral scene, his eyes dimming with tears — an expression of the tender and poetic emotions, more intense and genuine than could possibly be voiced through the genius of the spoken word. As a sportsman, he pursued only feather and fin and it would have been impossible to his nature to have sought to fell the higher forms of our wildlife.

Charles continued, telling Lincoln that his late father realized little profit from the company he founded, and that James Heddon spent the final year of his life nearly bedridden and in poor health. Nonetheless, Charles told Lincoln, his father's status as the original inventor of the "Dowagiac" gave many anglers the impression that he remained alive and well "in the land of the living" for many years after his death.

During that same important interview, Charles also corroborated earlier assertions that the Heddons had dabbled in wooden lures long before the Slopenose came about in 1902. He also acknowledged that while his family was by no means the first to make wooden lures, they were the first to develop them as an industry:

> It may be of interest to you to know that I have in my possession a lure which my great-grandfather used on a lake near Dowagiac nearly 75 years ago. While my company does not claim to be the first to commercially produce the artificial wooden minnow, we are the first to commercially develop it and to institute the publicity and propaganda responsible for its subsequent acceptance as the most popular type of lure for American freshwater fishing.

Lincoln also characterized the relationship between Charles and his older, more adventuresome brother Will, who in those days still had a peripheral involvement with the company as a tester and evaluator of lures:

> While Charles Heddon is the active business head of James Heddon's Sons, it would not do to leave out Will Heddon, the other member of the sons. Mr. and Mrs. Will Heddon, who are located near Park Rapids, Minnesota, during the northern open season and in central Florida the other seven months of the year, do most of the experimental work and testing of Heddon products before they are placed on the market. One of their interesting points is that they have devoted the past 25 years exclusively to hunting and fishing, and with the camera, in the out-of-doors.

The Heddon factory, meanwhile, continued to grow and expand as James Heddon's Sons rapidly became one of the region's major employers. In 1922, the company reported a 50 percent increase in sales and orders and said there was a one-year backlog on orders for some of their most desirable products. Consequently, the building was again enlarged to add more warehouse and production space. The 18,000-square-foot addition was completed by mid-year.

That same year, the Heddons began preparations to add fly rod lures to their line. In 1923, those lures were introduced and became an instant hit. Factory records indicate they installed a 25-by-30-foot addition to their manufacturing area for their "cork and feather" lures destined to become hits with the American fly-fishing public. There were 155 employees at the factory that year.

The lures of the 1920s represent great change and innovation. There was the Vampire — later the Vamp — reintroduced under its new name in 1921. The slogan "Made by Heddon — and Well Made" appeared as well. New finishes included Pike Scale and the 210 Surface bait, a scaled-down version of the famous 200, made its inaugural debut.

48

By the 1920s, the Heddon factory had undergone multiple additions and added more and more employees to keep pace with a growing demand.

The Gamefisher appeared in 1923, along with the introduction of the classic Wilder-Dilg fly rod bait series. The first plastic lures appeared that year as well. The following year, 1924, saw the introduction of the Walton Feathertail, the Heddon-Stanley Weedless Pork Rind Lure, saltwater specials, and other lures. A newer slogan "Heddon Made — Well Made" also appeared.

Production continued to escalate. In his July 1924 interview published in *Sportsman's Digest*, Charles described his own favorite baits and added some details about how brisk the lure business had by this time become:

"I prefer either our Vamp or Game Fisher," Charles Heddon said. "I might add that we sold approximately 150,000 of the Game Fisher baits last year, its first season; our 1924 sales will considerably exceed the above number. Our total yearly output of artificial wooden minnows slightly exceeds half a million dollars, which may aid you in your gathering of statistics. Naturally, this does not obtain the proportions of some of our competitors as we have centralized on fewer items of production and cater only to that element of sportsmen who demand these."

Year after year, the new catalogs included a host of new baits, all of which caught fish. Many remained in the product line for decades, and others were short lived. In 1925 and 1926 alone, nearly a dozen new baits emerged, including the Baby Gamefisher (5400), Baby Vamp (7400), Heddon Stanley Ace (190) Musky Vamp Minnow (7600), small Torpedo (120), large Torpedo (130), and several saltwater specials (500,

600, 800, and 850).

Heddon also preyed upon smaller companies, often buying or acquiring patents of items that showed promise. In 1927, Heddon purchased the Outing company in nearby Elkhart, Indiana. Outing made a moderate line of camping and hunting equipment, including decoys, but also had a line of hollow bronze lures. Heddon manufactured the Outing tackle boxes for a few years but did not continue the Outing lures, which had been sold under the "Getum" name in the mid-1920s. Also that year, the famous Black Sucker had vanished from catalogs, and the popular Luny Frog baits appeared.

The following year, several new baits were introduced. They included the No. 160, No. 170, and No.

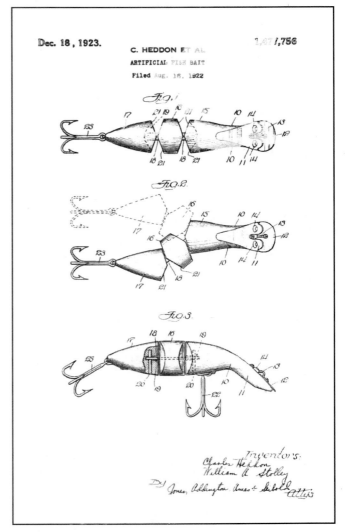

The segmented Gamefisher lure was one of many popular Heddon baits patented and produced in the 1920s.

370 Musky SOS lures; the Little Luny Frog, an array of baits in frog finish; the Jointed Vamp and the 6-inch No. 7550 Musky Vamp, which at first was known as the "Muskiteer Vamp," according to early box labels. Ice decoys disappeared that year.

By 1929, when the Great Depression began to unfold, there were still plenty of lures being made and sold. New arrivals included the No. 110 River Runt, the No. 80 Tiny Teaz, No. 1000 Triple Teazer, No. 4000 Meadow Mouse, and the stout, fat No. 300 Musky Surface bait. Heddon also began using plastics in 1929.

William Stolley was factory superintendent by this time. He had been close to the Heddon family for decades, having become acquainted with the late James Heddon as an aspiring beekeeper long before. A 1935 letter in possession of the National Heddon Museum quotes Stolley as saying the company had 210 employees with an annual income of more than $1 million.

The 1930s also saw the rapid expansion of plastic lures, and the Heddons were the first to see the true potential of the unusual new materials, some of which did not fare well when exposed to water and the atmosphere. The patented "spook" or "x-ray" finish became a Heddon hallmark that endured for decades and is still in use today.

An advertisement in the May 1935 edition of Sports Afield magazine extolled the attributes of these wonderful new lures: "Better than a bucket of LIVE minnows," writes Ivan A. Hoyer of Richland, Mo. "It's a natural go-getter for Bass, Pike, Pickerel, etc.; and also salt water game fish." The ad continues, explaining that there are two new "shore finishes" available that year: silver shore and green shore. The ad included a photo of outdoor author Robert Page Lincoln and his very powerful testimonial that the Spook River Runt is, indeed, a "dandy little lure."

The 1930s, which included the Great Depression, also saw the advent of other Heddon products that strayed briefly from the company's primary mission. In 1937, the factory in Dowagiac came out with a line of golf club shafts, part of a brief foray into other markets in the American recreation industry. In 1939, the company added ski poles — and even violin bows — to the company line.

Charles Heddon received a patent for a violin bow early in 1941. The patent papers noted that the bow featured an extruded tubing produced by Heddon. Fritz Chrysler, director of the Chicago Symphony and an accomplished violinist himself, endorsed the bow, saying Heddon's innovation made the product cheaper

and more accessible.

Although mildly profitable, these alternative products did little to dissuade the family from their first love: fishing tackle.

As president of Heddon, Charles rarely missed an opportunity to promote fishing as America's most wholesome of family pastimes. His interest in bringing children into the sport was both a marketing tool and a window into the morality of this remarkable man. His well-stocked library included excerpts from comments about fishing made by many famous people, and the following essay, printed and reprinted in many Heddon catalogs and publications, pretty much sums it up:

There are few anglers in penitentiaries. The "fishing bug" and the "crime bug" seldom reside in the same person. From George Washington to Franklin Roosevelt, many of our Presidents have been ardent fishermen.

For youth and adults, there is nothing more beneficial than to commune with Nature in her woods and on her waters. The refined, angling spirit cannot sin against fellow mortals, nor against society.

As ex-President Coolidge said: "There is something natural, homely, wholesome and unspoiled about the fisherman, which we should do well to cultivate."

Modern angling methods fire the imagination and challenge the skill. They also appeal to the sense of good sportsmanship. Fishing is now intensely pleasurable and engaging, since it has eliminated the prosaic, old-fashioned 'sit in the sun and wait' methods.

Col. Charles A. Lindbergh's father is quoted as having said: "The first time I really became acquainted with my son was when I took him on a fishing trip."

To Fathers and Mothers, my message suggests that you take your children to the quiet woods and mystical waters. It is Nature's best antidote for the innumerable besetting sins of modern society, and is so beautifully expressed by the late Dr. Henry Van Dyke in his book, Little Rivers...

"Only an idle little stream,
Whose amber waters softly gleam,
Where I may wade, through woodland shade,
And cast the fly, and loaf, and dream.
Only a trout or two, to dart,
From foaming pools, and try my art:
No more I'm wishing – old fashioned fishing,
And just a day on Nature's heart."

Even as Charles penned such eloquent essays and quoted his favorite prose from his cluttered office in a corner of the Heddon factory in the tiny, barely-known town of Dowagiac, events were unfolding elsewhere that would change the course of the world — and the recreation industry — forever. But Charles was not to be a part of it.

On November 11, 1941, a chilly Tuesday afternoon, Charles died suddenly at Epworth Hospital in nearby South Bend, Indiana. He was 65. According to the obituary that appeared the next day in the South Bend and Dowagiac newspapers, he had taken ill the previous evening while at the home of a friend and associate E. Bruce Laing.

According to newspaper accounts, Charles died less than 24 hours after leaving his desk at the Heddon factory. The cause of death was cerebral thrombosis, according to doctors, and funeral arrangements were quickly made to place one of Dowagiac's leading citizens to permanent rest.

Charles Heddon's close friend, writer, and author Bob Davis, fired off a telegram of condolence to the family, addressed especially to Charles's son John Heddon, whom he asked to place the letter in his late father's hand. "Farewell for the moment, Charley," wrote Davis. "You will see Uncle Jimmy when he comes to greet you on the Styx — the river between the living and the dead, where we anchor in the still water and fish together as in the unforgettable past."

A private funeral service was held at the family home at 303 Green Street at 2 p.m. that Friday. Only a few intimate friends, relatives, and close business associates were present. The family even asked that no flowers be sent. The *Dowagiac Daily News*, which Charles had founded many years before, carried a complete account of the funeral, with the notation that "No individual can be so vital a part of a community for half

BOB DAVIS
Noted Editor, Author and Sportsman
"Heddon Tackle is the product of fine ideals. This I know because of my intimate acquaintance with the Heddon organization for a third of a century."

Bob Davis, an accomplished angler and famous outdoor writer, frequently loaned his name to Heddon testimonials. Davis was a lifelong friend of the Heddon family.

a century and not leave a space that will be unfilled for many a year. It will be so with Charles Heddon."

An important chapter in America's angling history had come to an end. But another was soon to begin.

Charles Heddon enjoyed civilized sports such as golf and billiards.

Will Heddon, shown here in 1929 with grandson Welker Cochran, enjoyed fine touring cars. The family spent a great deal of time traveling between Florida and Michigan.

Dowagiac Creek, which formed the famous mill pond that lured the company founder to his destiny, remained a popular fishing mecca throughout the nineteenth century.

Good News for Fishermen who Golf, and who appreciate FINE Equipment

Leading Golfers Say:

"This Distinctive **HEDDON** Power Shoulder Makes a World of Difference!"

"THE HEART OF THE SHAFT" IS THE SHOULDER. AN ORIGINAL AND DISTINCTIVE HEDDON FEATURE.

Just try a Heddon-Shafted Club
The Shaft of Steel with the "Birdie" Feel

SEE HOW IT IMPROVES POWER, DISTANCE, AND CONTROL

To know how much your game can be improved by having a better shaft in your golf clubs, try a Heddon-Shafted Club. You'll be amazed how the exclusive "Double Whip" Power Shoulder increases shot control, power, and distance. Obtainable only in the Highest Quality Clubs produced by America's foremost makers.

We Draw and Temper Our Shafts and Rods!
Every Heddon Shaft is made in Dowagiac on the same Special Machines which produce Heddon "PAL" Steel Rods

JAMES HEDDON'S SONS • *Steel Golf Shaft Division, Dowagiac, Michigan*

The same shafts used to make Heddon's famous "Pal" rods also were useful for other products including golf clubs. Here is an early advertisement for the "Heddon-Shafted Club."

World War II and Beyond

Heddon produced wartime commodities such as ski poles and flexible radio antennas throughout World War II before returning to leisure products in the mid-1940s. The factory in Dowagiac was the nucleus of one of the nation's biggest tackle operations.

John Heddon, shown here with a pair of California billfish, took over the reins of the company during the opening months of World War II and was an active principal in Heddon until January 1, 1955, when he moved to California.

On December 7, 1941, barely four weeks after Charles Heddon's unforeseen death and funeral, an armada of Japanese planes and warships attacked Pearl Harbor. America was at war, and the nation set aside recreation and fishing to turn to more important matters.

The new president of Heddon was John Heddon, Charles's son, an only child much like his grandfather. Although John had spent much of his life working at his father's side and knew the business well, his first challenge as president was something entirely new: operating an industry in the midst of wartime. But he was ready.

Limited sales of already completed merchandise trickled on, but materials and supplies at the Heddon plant were converted to the manufacture of products to serve the war effort. One of the products made in Dowagiac was a fold-up box kite, used with emergency communications equipment for pilots shot down over enemy territory. Rod-making equipment was used to mass-produce ski poles and flexible radio antennas for military vehicles such as tanks and transports. Heddon, like thousands of other factories, diligently produced all it could in hopes the war would end. And eventually, it did.

During a ceremony on March 30, 1944, at Dowagiac High School, the Heddon employees and factory were honored as recipients of the "E" award for outstanding achievement in wartime production. Each employee received a lapel pin and the factory received a flag. "The production standard you are setting is inspiring and will serve as an example to all other Americans," wrote Undersecretary of War Robert Patterson in announcing the award to "the men and women of James Heddon's Sons." An extensive exhibit of the company's wartime contributions can be seen at the National Heddon Museum in Dowagiac.

The post-war years were productive and bountiful for the Heddon company, as the nation returned to leisure time after the hard years of war. The 1946, 1947, and 1948 catalogs featured only a limited line of tackle, but by 1949 and 1950, business was again booming, and the company offered a complete line of tackle with new items appearing each season. Other products, such as golf clubs, also were produced at the factory as the company sought to join the lucrative, post-war recreation market. Although the golf clubs were never a signature product of the company, they did gain some notoriety. For example, in 1949, Lloyd Mangrum won the Los Angeles Open using "Golf Craft" clubs made by Heddon, further popularizing the company's non-fishing products.

Fishing gear, however, remained the perennial priority. New for 1949 was the No. 2120 small size Crazy Crawler. The following year, the new "spook ray finish" was offered, and the "New for 1951" declaration in the next year's catalog included the "Pal Spook" solid glass baitcasting rod. Appearing in the catalog that year were the Flaptail Spook Jr., the Go-Deeper Crab, River Runtie Spook, Punkie Spook, and others destined to become favorites among anglers and later among collectors.

Also in 1951, John Heddon sold James Heddon's Sons to a new owner, the Murchison family of Texas, who also were the owners of the Dallas Cowboys football team. Clint and John Murchison, in addition to being businessmen hungry for new enterprises, already had made their wealth in oil.

Eight new lures were offered in 1952: the Tadpolly Spook, Tiny Runt, Tiny Torpedo, Tiny Lucky 13, Baby Lucky 13, Baby Dowagiac, Saint Spinner, and Widget. The following year saw the introduction of the Tiny Go Deeper Runt, Scissortail, Tiny Tad, and Spin Pal reels, in addition to the new "special sparkle" paint pattern.

That year, 1953, John Heddon resigned as president and was elected chairman of the board of James

This illustration from an old company catalog shows three generations of Heddon: James, Charles, and (center) John Heddon, who died in 1980 at the age of 80.

Heddon's Sons. J. Ward Hartke became the company's president, a title he held until 1962. John Heddon left the company's board on January 1, 1955, moving to Rancho Santa Fe, Calif., where he died in 1980 at the age of 80. His departure from the board was the end of the Heddon family's involvement in the company.

Just a few months after John Heddon terminated his involvement with the company his grandfather founded, W.T. Heddon passed away, on August 8, 1955. His wife Laura Heddon passed away five years later on October 26, 1960.

One of the most important non-family employees of Heddon is Trygve C. Lund, known as "Trig" by his friends and colleagues. Lund was an employee at the factory for a quarter of a century, serving eventually as vice president and factory superintendent.

He lives in the old Heddon family home on Green Street in Dowagiac, the house built by James Heddon. It is also the house where James Heddon himself passed away in December 1911.

"I bought this place from John when he left for California," Lund said during an interview in August 2000. "I've been here ever since. I've been lots of other places — even went to the Mustad Co. in Norway — and this house is the home to just come back to."

Lund worked closely with John Heddon for many years and helped smooth the transition from owner to owner that occurred during the company's later decades. Lund fondly remembers the 1950s as an era of change and innovation — and intense competition.

Trygve C. "Trig" Lund, whose many years as a Heddon superintendent, general manager and vice president gave him a wealth of knowledge about company history, discusses the lure-making industry during an August 2000 interview at his home in Dowagiac.

Trig Lund purchased his home in Greene Street from the Heddon family many years ago. Its basement is filled with mementos from the tackle industry. This is also the house where James Heddon died in 1911.

W.T. Heddon passed away on August 8, 1955. His wife Laura Heddon passed away five years later on October 26, 1960. This family photo, showing Laura with a snook caught off Little Gasparilla Island, was taken two years before her death.

"Anything that was new or good, that we didn't have, then we wanted it," he said. "We had 160 field testers. We had people you never even heard of as our field testers. They tried everything — I mean everything they could get their hands on and they reported back to us if it was something good or not."

Lund was a meticulous researcher and self-professed packrat who rarely discarded anything. And of course he was a fisherman as well. His first job after graduating from University of Minnesota in 1941 was with Kimberly-Clark, where he worked making ordnance materials for the war effort. He met the Heddons one day while discussing Carbo-Lite rings, which during non-wartime were fashioned into carbolox line guides used on fishing rods.

"Working with the Heddons was good," he said. "I really liked working for John Heddon and I loved the people at that place." But more than anything else, Lund was always fascinated by the lures and the new things that could be done to them to make them catch more fish.

"I'm an engineer," he said. "Sure, I'm interested in the production end of things but also the ideas that people had. It's wonderful to take something ordinary, change it just a little bit, and improve it 100 percent."

All the ideas and innovations that emerged in the 1940s and 1950s spawned a cold war of sorts here at home among tackle makers. Lund said security was always important on new ideas and products, especially those that were destined for introduction the following season.

Spying wasn't unheard of, even in Dowagiac. "I'd catch someone once in a while," Lund said. "Heddon was a well-liked company and very popular with the people of the area. If somebody came around doing some snooping, word would get back to us and we'd put a stop to it."

In his later years, Lund helped preserve the Heddon legacy after the closing of the factory and the discarding of decades of company history, records, and artifacts. As collecting gained interest, many a lure sleuth found his way to Lund's tackle-filled filing cabinets in the old Heddon family home in the 1970s and 1980s. "I guess you could say I saved a little bit of everything," he said. "And you wouldn't believe the lures that have been in this place over the years." Much of his archived material and tackle now resides safely in the National Heddon Museum.

Like the Heddons before him, Lund is a big believer in fishing as the great American pastime. Active as always in kids' fishing programs, Lund's philosophy is that everyone should have an opportunity to try their hand at angling. "If you get kids fishing and they start thinking like kids should, they don't get into all the crap that kids do nowadays."

Once the Heddons were no longer involved with the famous old company, it went through a series of ownership changes. After introducing successful baits like the Meadow Mouse Spooks, Stingarees, Sonics, and Sonars from 1956 to 1959, the company was sold in 1959 to Daisy Manufacturing Company. In 1962, Daisy President Cass Hough became president of Daisy-Heddon.

By the 1960s, the fishing tackle industry was varied and rapidly changing. Heddon's products had more and more competitors. A newspaper account published February 21, 1975, mentions layoffs of employees for two weeks, due to lack of orders. Later that year, in May and June, some employees were laid off for six more weeks.

The company was sold again in 1977, this time to Walter Kidde, a holding company of which Victor Comptometer was a principal. Some local investors who acquired the company in 1978 again returned control of the Heddon factory to Dowagiac, where Louis Wolfrane was president during this period.

By 1983, however, the company was up for sale once again. The buyer was EBSCO, a Birmingham, Alabama, company that owns the PRADCO company based in Fort Smith, Arkansas. EBSCO still owns the Heddon name today. The 1983 purchase was aided by an announcement six weeks earlier from the Michigan governor's office that a $700,000 loan had been arranged to help keep Heddon in Dowagiac. The governor's office also reported that year that Heddon still controlled 10 percent of the nation's "hard lure" market and was hoping to increase that share to more than 15 percent by 1986.

Despite the optimism and despite the economic aid from the governor, the official end of Heddon's long-standing existence in Dowagiac came in 1984, when the plant closed its doors for the last time.

The announcement was terse and sad. A letter dated July 5, 1984, and postmarked July 10, was delivered to Capitola "Cappy" Daron of Dowagiac. Daron was personnel manager and the highest ranking member of management remaining at the factory at the time. The writer was Clyde Gudemuth, the parent company's director of manufacturing. Here's what he had to say:

The Heddon factory building, covered in ivy, was vacant for many years until Don and Joan Lyons purchased the property in 1991 and opened the National Heddon Museum in 1995.

We have been unsuccessful in an attempt to develop an alternative activity for the Heddon facilities in Dowagiac. Unfortunately, the possibilities involved second parties and decisions have not been forthcoming. As a result of this failure, it is necessary to discontinue manufacturing operations at the Heddon plant on July 17, and all operations in your area on July 20. Your accrued vacation pay, through your last working day, will be mailed to you the following week. We are sorry that a complete closing of the facility at Dowagiac is necessary, but we are glad your pension plan is in effect and will be able to provide the benefits accrued by you during your service to the company and its predecessors.

Not long after the decision was made, the remaining stock was emptied, and the old brick factory lay dormant and closed. Daron returned on August 9, 1984, and locked the doors for the last time. The Dowagiac newspaper reported that company officials hoped the 100 laid-off workers could be retained in "possible future activities," but the general consensus was that lure manufacturing in Dowagiac had come to a permanent end.

Jeanne Hack, president of the local union that rep-

resented many factory employees, told the *Dowagiac Daily News* that more modern facilities at the Arkansas plant was one of the main reasons behind PRADCO's decision to consolidate operations in Fort Smith. The company that year reported sales of $10 million, with more than 250 employees in several divisions in its payroll.

Once closed, the factory remained dormant for many years. Today, however, the Heddon name is being kept alive by a new generation of civic-minded Dowagiacians. Don and Joan Lyons bought the aging factory in 1991 and opened the National Heddon Museum in 1995 after acquiring the company's archives from Trig Lund.

The museum, with a stunning public collection of angling artifacts and archival information, is housed in the old Heddon business office. "It's pretty much a labor of love," Joan Lyons said. "We both grew up fishing. Don, as a child, used to mow yards around town and one of the people he worked for was a Heddon sales rep who paid him in lures."

The rest of the brick factory building, which includes the old test tank in the basement where classic lures like the Zaragossa were first tried out in the 1920s, is devoted to the Lyons' manufacturing businesses. Don also has served as mayor of Dowagiac, a position that offers ample opportunities to attract attention to his town's world-famous name.

The Lyons, Lund, and others with an interest in preserving the nation's angling heritage also helped dedicate a new monument at the old mill pond east of town, now known as James Heddon Park. Although the original mill is long since gone and the road's configuration has been changed more than once, the mill pond is still there.

The monument, with a likeness of a classic blue-headed Slopenose lure, gives a brief history of James Heddon and the events that occurred there one summer afternoon long ago. Although the lure-making business no longer exists, the museum and the memorial at the mill pond will insure that the Heddon legacy in Dowagiac is preserved for future generations.

Today, there are still Heddons involved in fishing lures. Chuck Heddon, the grandson of W.T. Heddon, is an active and well-known collector and a veteran member of the National Fishing Lure Collectors Club and the Florida Antique Tackle Collectors. His collection includes some stunning experimental lures handed down from his grandfather. Chuck's willingness to share both his collecting knowledge and family history have greatly aided the honorable cause of preserving America's angling heritage.

The Heddon name also remains a valuable commodity from a commercial standpoint. "It's still very much a viable part of the basic nucleus of our brands," said Lanny West, senior director of marketing and international sales for PRADCO. "Anybody who shops at Wal-Mart, or at Bass Pro, still sees the Zara Spook, the Torpedo and a lot of the old lure names. We're even bringing back the Tadpolly."

West, in addition to being a PRADCO executive, also has a unique vantage point from which to reflect on Heddon history. He joined Daisy upon graduation from college in 1957 and was a member of the Daisy sales staff at the time Daisy acquired Heddon in 1959.

"I had been with Daisy a number of years prior to their acquisition of Heddon," he said. "At the time, I lived in Michigan, in Plymouth, and I guess I spent a week every month in Dowagiac. And I loved going there, and seeing all the people at the factory."

In all, West's association with the Heddon name spans more than four decades, a life for which he is grateful. "There were so many wonderful people associated with this industry, and I know the halls of the old factory in Dowagiac very well. Today, there are probably no more than four or five us left."

Heddon lures, meanwhile, are in ample supply — not only for the angling market but for collectors of contemporary items as well.

The parent company licenses occasional products manufactured with the Heddon name, such as T-shirts, commemorative lures made for the National Fishing Lure Collectors Club and a few other items. But the lures are still the most important seller, especially in overseas markets, according to West.

"Heddon has been selling in Japan, for instance, since the '50s and '60s," he said. "You talk about keeping a brand alive? It's phenomenal. Remember the Big Bud lure? We've produced thousands of them, in all sorts of colors other than with Budweiser on it. People even fish with them over there, but it's become a collectors' issue in Japan as much as the fishing."

Heddon lures also are popular in other countries, including along the Normandy coast, where Super Zara Spooks are one of the hottest sellers for sea bass. "That's a famous lure from way back, and it still is today," West said. "There has probably been more ink, more stories, more articles, on the Zara Spook than any other lures in the fishing tackle industry. It's that famous 'walk-the-dog' action."

The Heddon legacy, therefore, is still unfolding. The company's lures, under various names and trademarks, continue to catch fish anywhere there are bass lurking beneath the water. Collectors from as far away as Great Britain and Japan recognize and appreciate the famous Heddon lures. And as we close this chapter, we can say with relative certainty that collectors and anglers yet to be born will come to know and appreciate the legacy of an aging beekeeper from Dowagiac who lived and died so long ago.

As president, John Heddon presided over many company functions. He is shown in this undated photo in the back row, sixth from the right. Note the large "leaping bass" banner in the background.

By the 1940s, the old mill pond where James Heddon first cast his home-made baits had changed significantly from the earlier years. Today, the mill no longer stands.

Heddon company employees pose for a photo during a fishing outing. There was no better way to promote morale and fellowship, according to John Heddon, than to fish together.

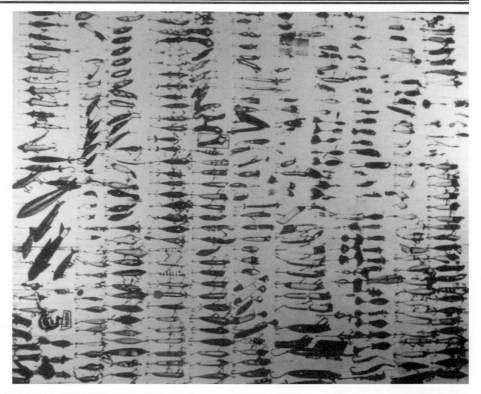

The factory lure collection in Dowagiac
was displayed on a large wallboard. The
collection once included lures from many
manufacturers. In 1977, lure collector
and author Clyde Harbin helped the
company sort out and re-arrange the
board to include only Heddon products.
Look closely and you will see early
Heddon hand-carved frogs, decoys, and
many other treasures. Many of these
early baits are now in storage, in the
possession of EBSCO.

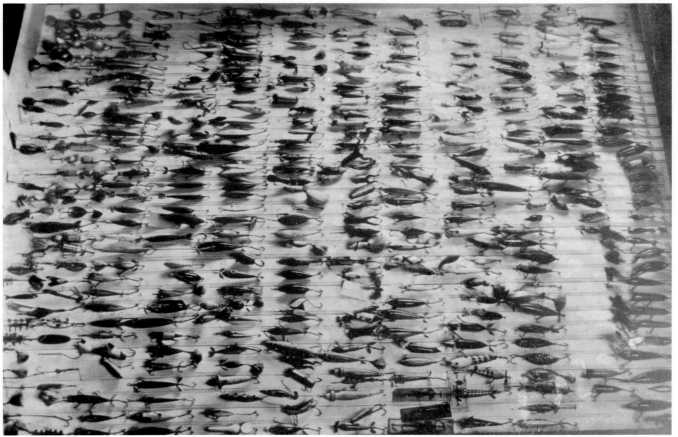

Heddon General Manager Trig Lund (left) looks over the company's collection of lures with Heddon Research Director Earl Miller. This 1960s photo appears in the company's 1965 catalog.

Meet the Heddon Gang
Fishermen All!

(1) Lyell Wooster, Vice-President

(2) H. E. Schmedlen, N.E. States

(3) Homer Circle, Ass't Sales & Adv. Mgr.

(4) "Trig" Lund, Factory Sup't.

(5) Bill Moore, S.W. States.

(6) Tom Denmark, Florida

(7) Leo Petronave, Pacific Coast States

(8) Charles Brockman, Ohio, Ind. and Ill.

(9) Frank Carter, S.E. States

(10) "Speed" Swift, Mid-Central States

(11) Ralph Beam, Canada

(12) Lou S. Caine, Vice-President

(13) Bob Crowder, Rocky Mt. States

(14) Bill Diers, Alaska

(15) John Heddon, President

(16) Jack Riehl, North Central States

Working for Heddon in the 1940s and 1950s must have been a rewarding career. Take a look at all the smiling faces! Some famous names are in this line-up of company employees.

The basement of the old factory building includes the famous "lure test tank" where the Zaragossa and other classics were tried out in the 1920s. Co-author Bill Roberts dangled a Slopenose above the tank during a visit to the building.

James Heddon Park now occupies a corner of the old mill pond east of town where the company founder first cast his wooden lures. This monument includes a well-sculpted likeness of the early Dowagiac Slopenose lure. People like Don and Joan Lyons, owners of the National Heddon Museum, have worked diligently to insure that the Heddon legacy is never forgotten.

Chuck Heddon, grandson of Will Heddon, is an active collector who enjoys sharing his family's legacy. Heddon, a Florida resident, is shown here accepting an award for his lure display during a Florida Antique Tackle Collectors convention. Chuck's father, Jim Heddon, worked at the Heddon Factory for three years in the early 1930s.

The Heddon family's lure collection includes some rare prototypes that Chuck Heddon inherited from his grandfather, Will Heddon. Shown here are an experimental gar type lure; a Kinney Bird lure painted at the Heddon factory; a forerunner to the Walton Feathertail; and a collar bait similar to the Slopenose and 200 Surface lures.

Few things are as inspiring as a shiny Heddon lure from this famous company's early years of production. The finely turned bodies often had a dozen separate coats of primer, lacquer, paint, and varnish. The final product rivaled fine jewelry and was surpassed only by Mother Nature herself.

The first commercially produced Heddon lures emerged in 1902, and the product line expanded rapidly. By the 1920s, a glimpse into the tackle box of any serious fishermen, anywhere in the country, certainly would include an assortment of lures that owe their origins to the factory in Dowagiac.

This chapter traces the evolution of Heddon lures

from the very beginning, and includes values and prices. You will also find examples of the endless variations of certain baits and hardware — further testament to the efforts by this company to constantly improve upon their own creations.

It is important to understand that value depends on several factors: age, condition, color, rarity, and demand. The prices we will offer are subjective and can vary widely, especially where condition is concerned. A flawless mint specimen often will command 10 times the price of an identical lure that is well used with chips, age lines, and varnish loss. Boxes also greatly enhance the value of a lure.

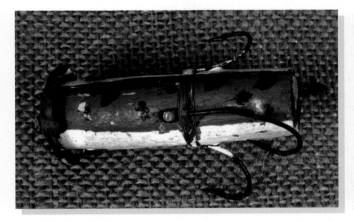

This frog is the earliest frog known among all the Heddon frogs, circa 1897. It is identical to the one that Will Heddon described in a 1927 interview as being Jim Heddon's first lure: "One day my father whittled out a 'stick' on which he put gang hooks and on the front of the bait a bottle top which caused a spray." This bait is authenticated as having come from the Heddon Company archives and being the oldest one in existence. This bait is too rare to value.

Here is another of James Heddon's hand-carved frogs, circa 1897. Found in an apple barn in upstate New York in 1988, this is the only Heddon Frog, not from the Heddon archives, that has been tested and documented to be correct. This frog was given to an acquaintance of Jim Heddon sometime before the turn of the century. The friend had an apple orchard and was also active in the beekeeping business. This lure also is too rare to value.

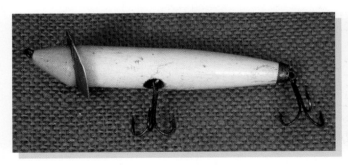

The Dowagiac Perfect Surface Casting Bait, circa 1902, is the first lure produced commercially by Heddon. Known to collectors as the "Slopenose," these lures were sold with rimless cups sunk into the hook sockets. The finish on these early lures is very granular and almost chalky in texture. By the end of the 1902 season, these paint finishes were replaced with the typical white enamel. Perhaps this is why very few have survived. Only four of the rimless two hook baits are known to exist in collections today. This lure is too rare to value.

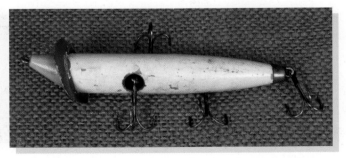

The Dowagiac No. 2, nicknamed by collectors the "four-hook Slopenose," is one of the earliest ever found. The first such baits were sold with "rimless cups" sunk into the hook sockets. Whenever one of these baits appears, remember that it's probably a lure produced within the first 30 to 40 days of Heddon's production. Only three examples of this lure are known today, making it impossible to value.

The Dowagiac Underwater, circa 1902, was listed in the first catalog as having a hanging weight that aids materially in the casting and sinking of the bait, as well as keeping it from revolving and twisting the line. The Heddons felt this external weight was superior to one that was inserted in the body of the bait because it could be adjusted to prevent the lure from revolving. This explains so many changes in a matter of only a few months. This particular bait displayed here is the very earliest of the Dowagiac Underwaters for 1902, probably produced in the first 60 days of production. Note the floppy type prop in lieu of the long sweeping one on this early bait. Only three of these Underwaters are known to exist in collections today, making this bait impossible to value.

The Dowagiac Underwater, circa 1902, is the second version with the external belly-weight. It most likely was produced in the summer of 1902. Note the long, sweeping propeller and the brass nose and tail cap. The bait and correct picture box displayed here are extremely rare. There are fewer than a dozen baits known and probably half that many boxes. Value range: $2,500.00+ for the lure; significantly more if the box is included.

The Dowagiac Underwater, circa 1902, was the first of Heddon's many lures designed to sink beneath the surface. The first Underwater featured the hanging belly-weight that is absent on all of the versions that followed. This particular bait was the last of three different versions of the Underwater in 1902, with its production occurring only in the fall of that year. The bait, 3⅝", is longer and skinnier that the first two versions of Underwaters in 1902. Value range: $2,500.00+ for the lure; significantly more with the box.

This photo shows the rapid succession of the rare Dowagiac Underwater lures. All of the hanging belly-weight versions likely were produced in the spring, summer, and early fall of 1902. The three examples shown here exhibit three specific stages of development, each with significant improvements over their predecessors in hardware, size or paint. At one time, collectors believed those variations represented different years. We now know the changes occurred in a matter of months. Value: $2,500.00+ each.

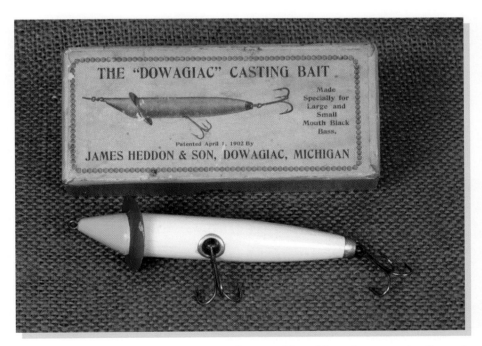

The Dowagiac Perfect Surface Casting Bait, or Slopenose, followed the rimless cup version discussed earlier. This lure has rimmed, gold-washed cups, and a painted red collar. Value range: $750.00 to $850.00 for the lure. With the box, $2,500.00+.

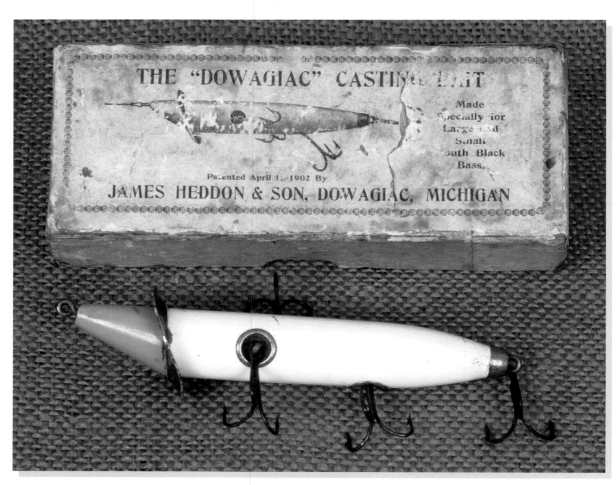

The Dowagiac No. 2 or four-hook Slopenose is rarer than the two-hook version. Like the example on the bottom of page 67, it followed the rimless cup baits and is sometimes found in this early white picture box. Dating to around 1902, its value range is $850.00 to $1,000.00. With the box, $2,500.00+.

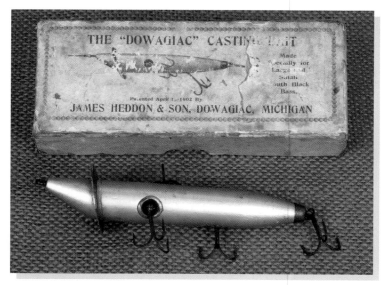

This rare aluminum finished version of the Dowagiac No. 2 is more desirable due to its unusual color. Value range: $1,000.00 to $1,200.00. With the box, $2,500.00+.

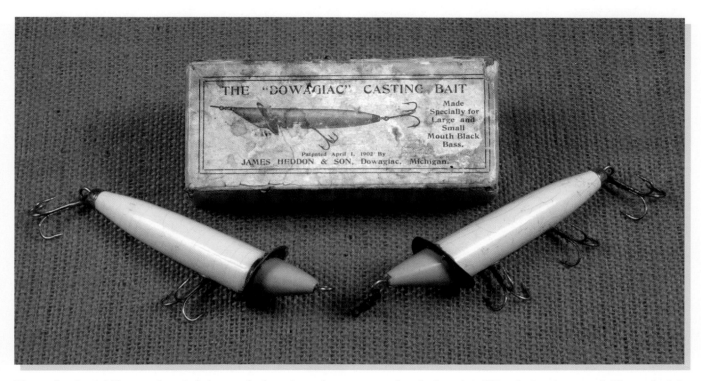

These yellow-headed Slopenose lures include a two-hook version and an even rarer three-hook version. This color is quite unusual. The two-hook is one of four known, while the three-hook model is, at this time, unique. The nickel hardware, which replaced the gold-washed cups, dates these lures to around 1906. Value range: $2,500.00+ without the box.

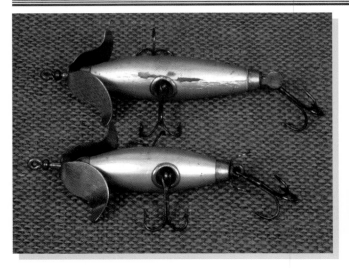

These two Dowagiac Underwater lures date to the 1903 season which brought the aluminum finish to supplement the basic white. Aluminum finish baits were made in two sizes. Unlike the white lures, which were dipped, the aluminum finished baits were most likely hand-painted. Value range: $1,000.00 to $1,200.00.

These circa 1903 Dowagiac Underwater lures have two internal belly-weights that replaced the external weights. Another feature was the fixed tailpiece or rudder added to counteract line twist. The lure was offered in two lengths, 2" and 3". Value range: $1,000.00 to $1,200.00.

This circa 1903 underwater minnow has remained shrouded in mystery over the years. Collectors refer to this uncatalogued bait as "the missing link" that preceded the 100 Underwater introduced in 1904. It has the larger 3" Dowagiac Underwater body with the "Killer style" props and was the last bait to use the brass nose cap. It is impossible to value.

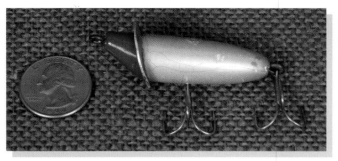

This circa 1906 Slopenose bait is in aluminum finish with red painted collar. Value range: $1,000.00. With box, $2,500.00+.

This 2" fly rod-sized version of the Slopenose lure came from the Heddon factory archives and was not produced commercially. Finished in aluminum with red head, it likely dates to the pre-1905 era and is too rare to value.

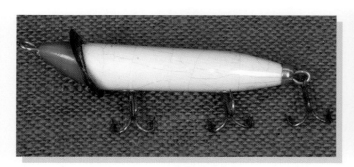

The three-hook Slopenose is an unusual variation dating to around 1906. It has nickel plated cups and tail cap. Value range: $1,000.00.

This 1904 version of the Dowagiac No. 100 Underwater is one of the earliest, with milky glass eyes, unusual red dots, brass cup hardware and three belly-weights. Value range: $1,000.00.

This is another circa 1904 version of the Dowagiac No. 100, with the early green crackleback finish, three belly-weights and sweeping gills — but without the red dots in the example discussed previously. Value range: $750.00 to $850.00.

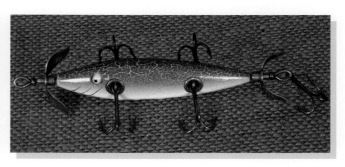

This circa 1904 Dowagiac Minnow No. 150 is in crackleback finish, with three belly-weights and sweeping gill marks. Value range: $1,500.00+.

This circa 1904 Heddon Dowagiac No. 100 Underwater has three belly-weights and brass cups. Finished in aluminum, its value range is $1,200.00 to $1,500.00.

This 1905 version of the Heddon Dowagiac No. 150 is finished in an unusual wide crackleback paint pattern and has a blunt head and tail, preceding the "high-forehead" models of the same era. Value range: $1,500.00+.

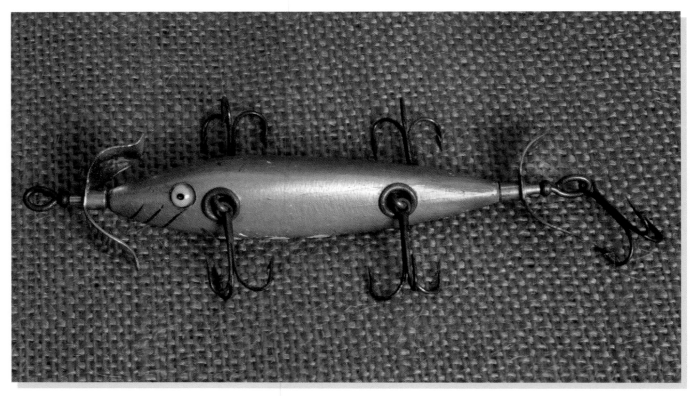

This circa 1904 Dowagiac Minnow No. 150 was Heddon's first commercially produced, minnow-shaped body. It is found with three belly-weights and shallow, cone-shaped brass cups. Although usually found in crackleback finish, this minnow is finished in aluminum, a very rare color for this bait. Value range: $2,500.00+.

This early Heddon No. 300 Surface Minnow has unusual red blush chin markings instead of the usual hand-painted gills. Shown here with the correct, circa 1905 box, its value range is $2,500.00+.

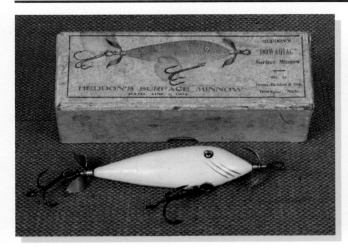

This Heddon No. 300 Surface lure is the high-forehead example with sweeping gills, circa 1905. This beautiful picture box was the first style made for these lures and likely was in production less than a year. Value range: $800.00 to $1,000.00 for the lure. With box, $2,500.00+.

This early aluminum finish No. 300 Surface lure is circa 1905, with the shaped head and black, sweeping gill marks all the way up to its glass eyes. Value range: $1,000.00+.

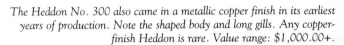

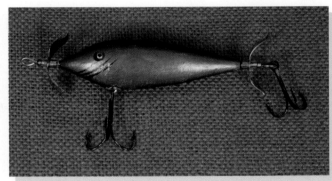

The Heddon No. 300 also came in a metallic copper finish in its earliest years of production. Note the shaped body and long gills. Any copper-finish Heddon is rare. Value range: $1,000.00+.

This circa 1908 example of the No. 300 Surface Minnow has an unusual four-hook configuration that is rarely found. Note the early rainbow finish with the hooks mounted toward the rear of the lure. Value range: $750.00 to $850.00.

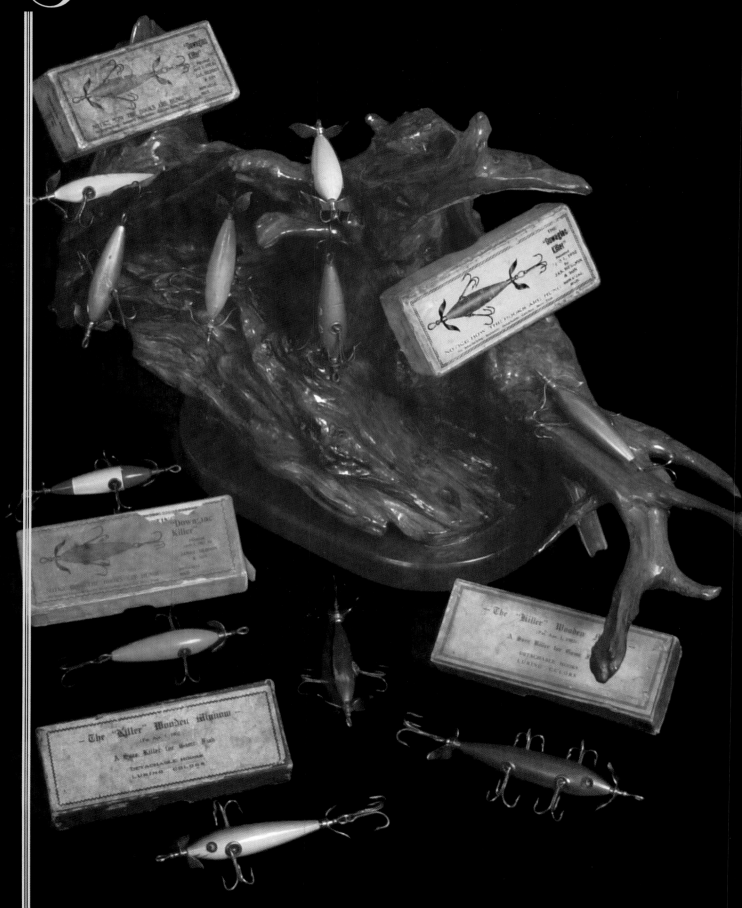

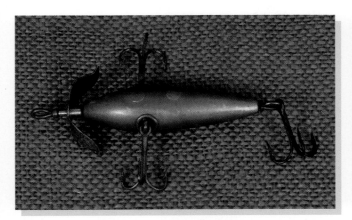

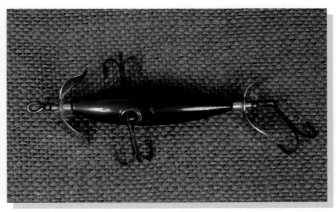

The demand for a cheap but substantial artificial lure that would be as effective as the premium baits brought about the Dowagiac Killer in 1905. This No. 400 two belly-weight, round-bodied lure without eyes, and with one unmarked propeller, is shown in an uncatalogued gold finish. Value range: $500.00+.

This unusual dark-copper, almost maroon metallic-finished No. 450 Killer has three belly-weights and unmarked props fore and aft. Only a few baits in this color have turned up. Value range: $600.00 to $800.00.

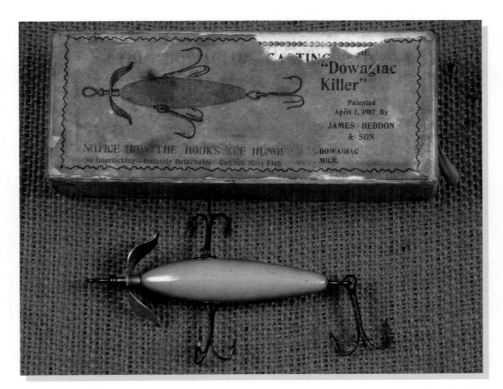

This super tough circa 1905 No. 400 Killer, in solid yellow, is a three belly-weight model and is displayed with its correctly marked box. This particular box, which is probably the earliest known, has a wavy line border and is labeled over a four-hook Dowagiac Expert box. Value range: $500.00+. With box, $2,500.00+.

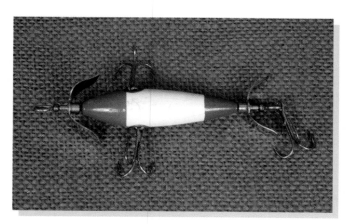

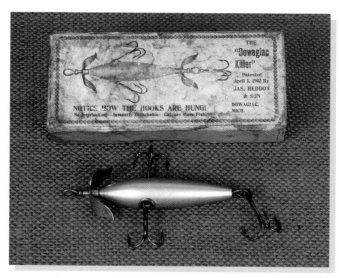

This is a three belly-weight No. 450 Killer in the traditional red/white/red finish. Most lures in this finish have one belly-weight. Value range: $500.00 to $700.00.

This circa 1905 Dowagiac Killer No. 400 has three belly-weights and is shown in aluminum finish. It is accompanied by its original No. 450 box. Note the oak leaf border. Value range: $500.00 to $700.00. With box, $2,500.00+.

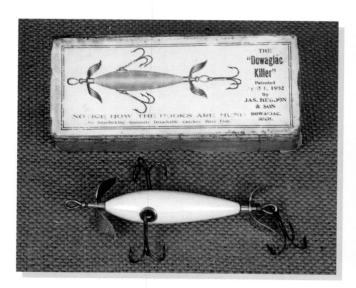

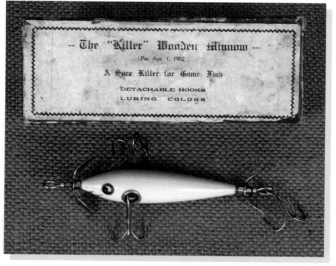

This Dowagiac No. 450 Killer is in all respects the same as the "No. 400 Killer," but has unmarked propellers both at front and rear. The white, two belly-weight bait has brass hardware and is shown with a double border Killer box. Value range: $300.00 to $350.00. With box, $2,000.00+.

The Killer Wooden Minnow, dating 1906 – 1907, is a rare, three-hook, round-bodied lure shown in slate finish. It is displayed with its correct, super rare, maroon box. The wavy line border box shows an April 1, 1902 Patent, but makes no mention of Heddon. Once thought to have been made in Chetek, Wisconsin, the bait was most likely made in the Heddon Dowagiac plant and sold to wholesalers like E.K. Tryon Co. and VL&A to re-sell under their own labels. Value range: $300. With box, $2,000.00+.

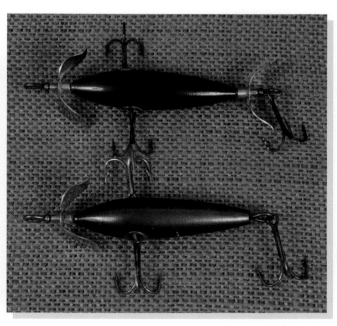

This five-hook Killer Wooden Minnow has a round body and aluminum finish and likely dates to the 1908 – 1910 era. The straight line, double border box shows an April 1, 1902 Patent date on the box top. Value range: $350.00. With box, $2,000.00+.

This pair of Killers, a No. 400 and No. 450, are both in the rare copper finish. Circa 1905. Value range: $400.00 to $500.00 each.

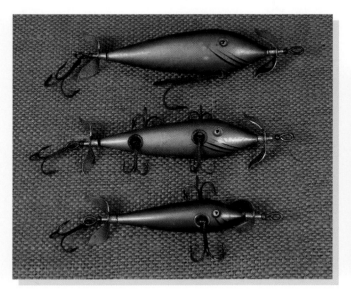

This trio of early Heddons in copper finish all date to around 1905. Note the long, sweeping gill marks and brass hardware. All are high-forehead Heddons. Value range: $1,000.00+ each.

This 1905, two belly-weight Dowagiac No. 150 has milky eyes and the rare "blush red" chin that preceded hand-painted gillmarks. Later No. 150s from the 1920s on returned to the blush chin, but this was the first. Value range: $500.00 to $600.00.

Circa 1905, this Dowagiac No. 150 minnow has the extra-long sweeping gills and high forehead, making it one of the earliest. Value range: $750.00 to $850.00.

This green crackleback No. 100 Underwater is in a "Second" box that likely was an effort by the company to market their slightly marred lures. Dating to spring 1905, this is the only known example of this rare box, which is far too unique to value.

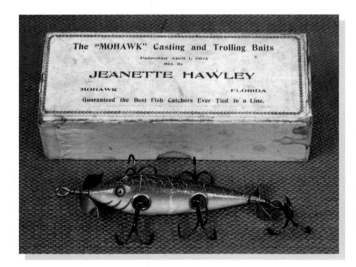

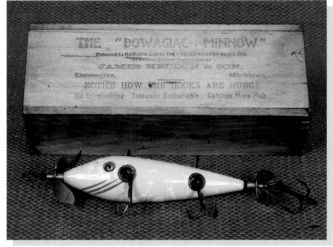

The Jeanette Hawley Mohawk Casting and Trolling Bait dates to 1905. Will and Laura Heddon made limited numbers of the high quality lures in their Florida home. The lures came packaged in the unique Hawley box, of which only two are known. Jeanette Hawley was Laura Heddon's pen-name. This bait was made from the same five-hook body as the Heddon high-forehead No. 150 style minnow. Its rarity makes it impossible to value.

The early Dowagiac No. 150 Underwater minnows had brass cups and the high-forehead body. Finished in solid white, its value range is: $500.00 to $700.00. With correct slide-top box, $2,000.00+.

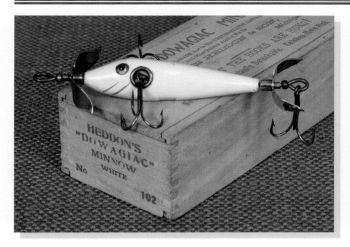

This solid white Dowagiac No.100 Underwater, circa 1905, has two belly-weights and is in its correct slide-top wooden box. Value range with box: $1,500.00+.

This early rainbow, high-forehead No. 150 Underwater is in its correct box, circa 1905. Value range with box: $1,500.00+.

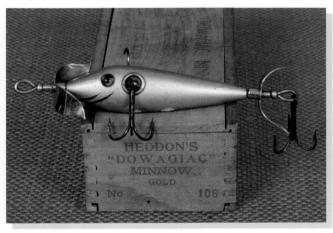

Dating to 1905, this gold Underwater No. 100 Dowagiac has brass hardware and sweeping gills. Value range with correct wooden box: $1,500.00+.

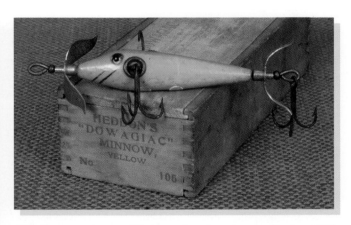

All yellow was an unusual Heddon color, shown here on this circa 1905 Dowagiac No. 100 minnow. Value range with correct wooden box: $1,500.00+.

Early Underwater Minnows also came in solid red, as evidenced by this 1905 model in its correct wooden box. Value range: $1,500.00+.

The No. 175 Heavy Casting Minnow used the body of the 150 but had three large hooks instead. Note the larger cup hook hangers and correct wooden box. Dating to 1906, its value range is $200.00 to $300.00. With box, $1,000.00+.

 79

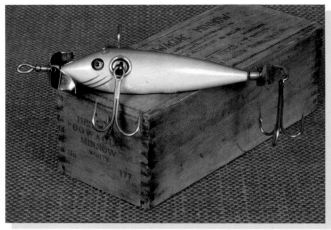

This unusual No. 175 Heavy Casting Minnow is much shorter than most and has lower placed gill marks. It is a unique variation and too rare to value.

The No. 175 Heavy Casting Minnow also was made in a beautiful slate finish, shown here in the correct circa 1907 wooden box. Value range: $200.00 to $300.00. With box, $1,000.00+.

This circa 1906 model Dowagiac No. 100 minnow has two belly-weights and is shown in a striking blended red finish. The bait is displayed with its correct box, which has a Canada patent on the lid and is marked on the end #104. Value range with wooden box: $750.00 to $850.00.

This Dowagiac No. 100 underwater dates to 1906, has two belly-weights, and is finished in early perch. Note the vertical bars in the paint finish. Later non-scale perch patterns had diagonal bars. Value range: $200.00 to $300.00.

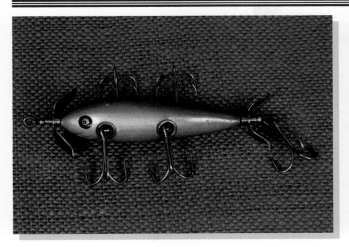

This 1906-vintage No. 150 Underwater is in aluminum finish and has the blunt nose and two belly-weights. Value range: $300.00 to $400.00.

This No. 100 Dowagiac in aluminum dates to 1907 and has one belly-weight. Value range: $300.00 to $400.00.

This 1906 Dowagiac No. 100 has two belly-weights and is finished in early rainbow. With correct wooden box, value range: $500.00 to $650.00.

The Dowagiac No. 150 Underwater was frequently sold in rainbow. Note the typical rainbow pattern here that remained in the catalog for many years. This cup-rigged model with one belly-weight has a value range of $100.00 to $150.00. With correct wooden box, $500.00+.

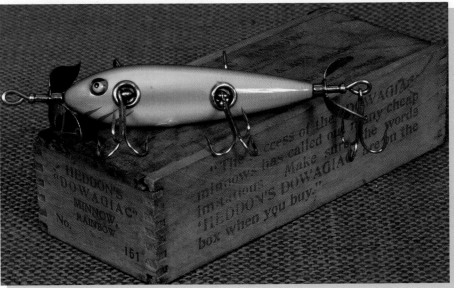

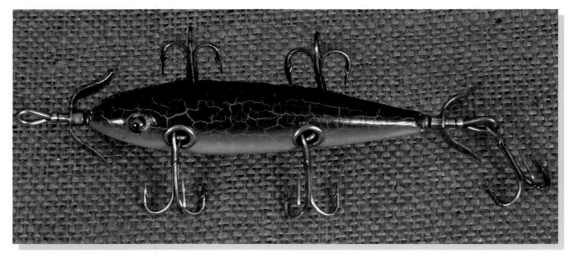

This stunning Dowagiac No. 150 is finished in brown sienna with an orange belly. Dating to around 1910, this unusual colored lure with one belly-weight has a value range of $200.00 to $300.00.

This rare Dowagiac No. 150 is finished in green crackleback with a solid red belly. Note the extraordinary combination of rare color and pristine condition. Its value range, due to these factors, is $800.00 to $900.00.

This unusual fat-bodied Dowagiac No. 150 is finished in Sienna Rainbow, a very rare color. Due to its condition and unusual color, value range: $800.00 to $900.00.

The No. 50 Artistic Minnow, introduced in 1907, was a tiny lure that came with its own casting weight or buoy. These lures can be found with one, two or three belly-weights. Value range: $100.00 to $300.00. With early box, $700.00+.

The Dowagiac No. 20 was a baby underwater minnow similar to the 100 series lure but utilizing the body style of the Artistic Minnow. No. 20s can be found in boxes for Artistic Minnows, such as this green crackleback specimen. Value range: $150.00 to $200.00. With box, $600.00+.

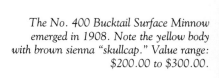

The No. 400 Bucktail Surface Minnow emerged in 1908. Note the yellow body with brown sienna "skullcap." Value range: $200.00 to $300.00.

Rainbow is the hardest color in which to find the No. 400 Bucktail Surface Minnow which was sold only for two years. Value range: $250.00 to $350.00.

The No. 400 Bucktail Surface Minnow also came in a white finish with blue crackleback skull cap. The white introductory box is exceptionally scarce, possibly made only one year. Value range: $250.00 to $350.00. With box, $1,200.00+.

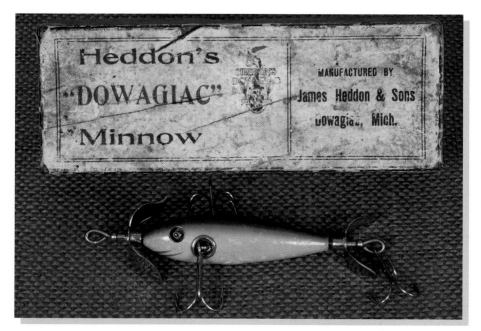

This is the 1910 model of the Dowagiac No. 100 Minnow, finished in early rainbow. Note the unusual box with the center-bass logo, which appeared only in the 1909 and 1910 catalogs. Value range: $100.00 to $125.00. With box, $500.00+.

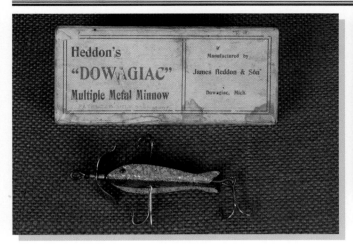

The No. 500 Multiple Metal Minnow was a finely made lure first offered in 1908. Normally found in nickel or gold finishes, this example is gold with gold glitter. Value range: $150.00 to $300.00. With box, $1,200.00+.

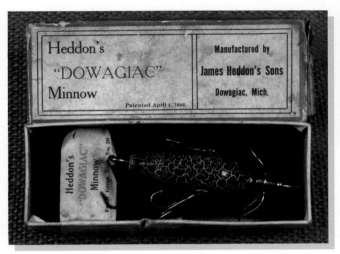

The Dowagiac No. 20 also is found in its own tiny maroon box similar to the Artistic Minnow box. This green crackleback example has a value range of $150.00 to $200.00. With box, $500.00+.

This circa 1909 No. 700 musky minnow is straight out of the Heddon archives. This magnificent lure is painted in solid red finish, which was not a catalogued color for 1909. The bait was never fitted with its five extra large and extra strong treble hooks. The bait still has paint in all the holes where the cups would be fitted and is as new as the day it rolled off the assembly line. Its origins make it too rare to value.

This Dowagiac No. 20 is in the rare aluminum finish. Value range: $300.00 to $400.00.

The Dowagiac Muskollonge Minnow No. 700 five-hooker is one of Heddon's largest and finest baits, with most having four or five belly-weights. Collectors refer to this version as the "sway belly model." The minnow shown here is in the fancy green back, white belly color, and is the same length as the three hook No. 700s at 4¾", not including hardware. Value range: $1,000.00.

According to the 1909 catalog, this No. 700 minnow was designed specially for catching Muskollonge and is entirely too heavy for bait-casting. Its weight, 3 ounces, and general construction are designed to hold and attract the "big ones," and the bait should properly be used for trolling. The minnow was offered in three colors, shown here in rainbow. Value range: $1,000.00.

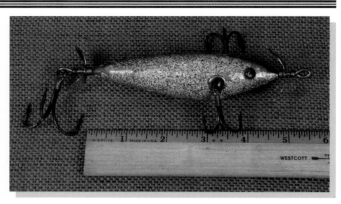

This later, fat-bodied No. 700 musky minnow has three hooks, blush red chin splash and is accompanied by its beautiful, large, white box. Value range: $1,000.00. With box, $1,500.00+.

The No. 700 musky minnow rarely came in saltwater white with glitter. Value range: $1,000.00.

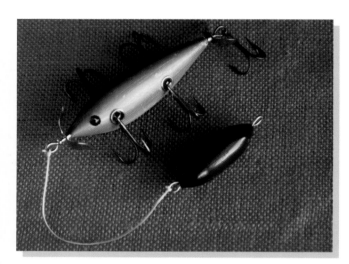

The No. 700 musky minnows also can be found in the elongated, leaping bass boxes also used to sell musky-sized Vamp lures. Value range: $1,000.00. With box, $1,300.00+.

As if the weight of the No. 700 musky minnows wasn't enough, Heddon offered a huge, musky-sized casting weight to further aid the use of these monster lures. Value range for the lure: $1,000.00. With the weight, $1,500.00.

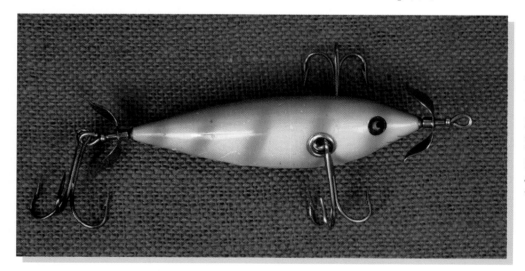

The best description for this No. 700 musky minnow would be "Wow" — straight out of the Heddon archives, and in a wild, uncatalogued and unheard-of color. The color is best described as a yellow body with a peach-colored back and rose-colored ribs. It is too unique to value.

THIS IS IT

Heddon's
Swimming
Minnow

It Swims!
It Swims! It Swims!
It Swims!

The No. 900 Swimming Minnow typically had a tail treble and a double hook mounted with a pin in its belly. Dating to 1909, this bait has a value range of $300.00 to $400.00. With box, $1,000.00 to $1,400.00.

The Heddon No. 900 Swimming Minnow is seldom found rigged with three trebles, as this model obviously has been. Value range: $300.00 to $500.00.

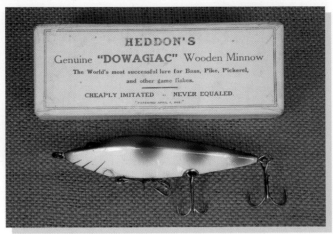

This No. 900 Swimming Minnow dates to around 1911, as evidenced by the white pasteboard box of that period. Note the extra belly hook between the pin and rear hook. Value range: $300.00 to $400.00. With box, $1,000.00+.

The No. 800 Swimming Minnow was introduced in 1910 and was a baby counterpart to the 900. Note the special box in which it was sold. Value range: $400.00 to $500.00. With box, $1,200.00.

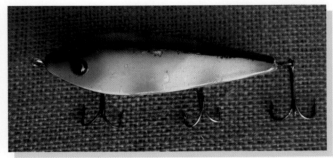

This is an uncatalogued No. 850 Swimming Minnow, a hybrid between the 800 and 900 models that are also rigged with treble hooks. Value range: $450.00 to $550.00.

Swimming Minnows occasionally are found in the downward leaping boxes introduced in 1912. The No. 900 minnows were last catalogued in 1913. Value range: $400.00. With box, $500.00.

This No. 850 Swimming Minnow two-hook model is packaged in the rare "Pine Tree" box sold only in 1912 and correctly marked for this lure. Value range: $400.00 to $500.00. With box, $1,000.00.

The No. 11 Light Casting Minnow is the yellow-spotted version of the No. 10, which is white spotted. This 1912 lure was found in a circa 1907 No. 50 Artistic Minnow box, illustrating the company's practice of later re-labeling unused boxes. Value range: $150.00 to $200.00. With box, $400.00.

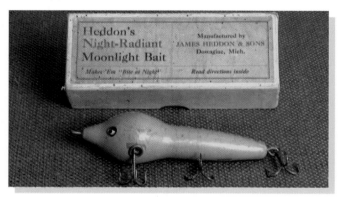

Heddon's Night-Radiant Moonlight Bait, No. 1000, is an extremely rare, bulbous surface bait that was never catalogued by Heddon. This circa 1910 example is new in the box with papers that describe the lure as the strongest, self-radiant, self-glowing lure ever produced. Probably a dozen of these baits are known to exist; however only a couple of boxes with papers have ever been found. Value range: $2,500.00+.

Rainbow-colored Dowagiac No. 150 lures are among the most common baits to be found in the short-lived "pine tree" box used in 1911. The lure has cup rigs and marked props. Value range: $150.00 to $200.00. With box, $450.00 to $500.00.

Casting weights made from the wood bodies used for No. 850 Swimming Minnows also were fashioned into casting weights for tournament competition and practice. Note the beautiful, early Heddon fish decal. Value range: $300.00 to $400.00.

The wonderful No. 1000 Night-Radiant Moonlight Bait was never catalogued when it was made in 1910, but it was shown only once on the back cover of the Heddon 1965 catalog. The bait displayed here is straight out of the Heddon Factory archives and is the very bait shown on that 1965 catalog.

This slate-finish No. 300 Surface lure is in its correct pine tree box. The lure is a fat-body model with marked props and cup hook rigs. Value range: $300.00 to $350.00. With box, $500.00 to $650.00.

This all-red Dowagiac No. 100 is in a correct pine tree box, circa 1911. Value range: $250.00 to $300.00. With box, $450.00.

This fat-bodied, slightly sway-bellied Dowagiac No. 100 in rainbow finish is circa 1911, the last year this plain white pasteboard box was used. Value range: $125.00 to $200.00. With box, $350.00 to $500.00.

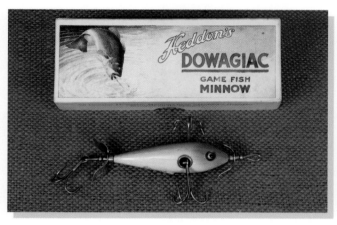

This slate-bodied, red-eyed Dowagiac No. 100 is from 1912, packaged in the first downward leaping bass box with the plain white border. Later boxes had blue or red borders. Value range: $125.00 to $150.00. With box, $300.00.

The paint finish on this fine old Dowagiac No. 150 is green crackleback with red belly. The box is the earliest, white-border downward leaping bass version. Value: $200.00 to $250.00. With box, $400.00.

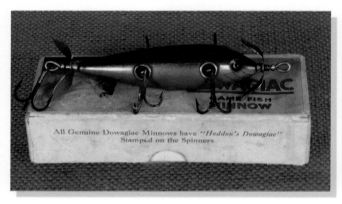

This aluminum-colored Dowagiac No. 150 has a crackleback finish over its back, an unusual and rare color. Value $200.00 to $250.00. With box, $350.00.

The pasteboard box for this slate-colored No. 175 Heavy Casting Minnow is correctly marked No. 177. This lure dates to 1911. Value: $300.00 to $350.00. With box, $500.00.

This is a sienna fire Dowagiac No. 100, circa 1911. Value: $200.00 to $250.00. With box, $400.00.

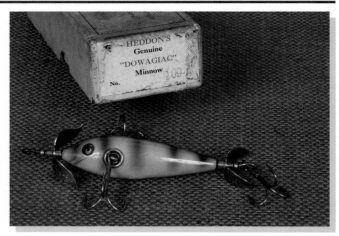

This Dowagiac No. 100 is in early perch finish with vertical bars. The box number, 109-A, is correct. Value: $150.00 to $200.00. With box, $450.00.

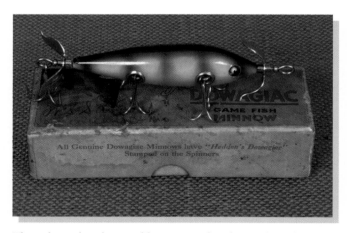

The early perch with vertical bars was made only into the early teens. This Dowagiac No. 150 is in a white-bordered downleaping bass box. Value: $200.00 to $250.00. With box, $400.00.

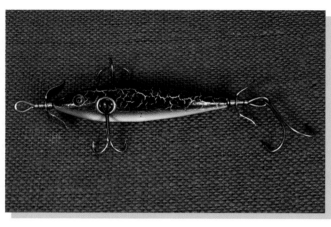

This unusual slim-bodied Dowagiac No. 150 was made with only three hooks instead of five. Value range: $250.00 to $300.00.

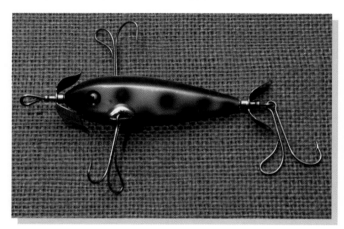

The Dummy Double, No. 1500, was introduced in 1913 and featured the unique double hooks. Note the bulging "football" hardware on this example. Value range: $350.00 to $450.00.

This No. 20 Dowagiac is outfitted with unusual, smaller-than-usual sized Dummy Double hooks. It likely was an experimental or custom ordered bait, making it too rare to value.

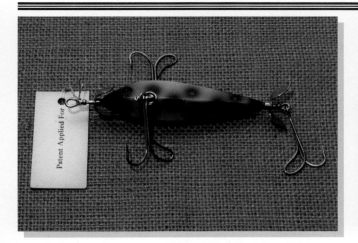

This No. 1500 Dummy Double has the more typical "L-rig" hardware. Note the "patent applied for" tag on this lure from the Heddon factory archives. Value range: $300.00 to $350.00.

The No. 1500 Dummy Double can be found in colors including slate, rainbow, blended red, and the classic green crackleback. The example shown here is in frog spot. Value range: $300.00 to $400.00.

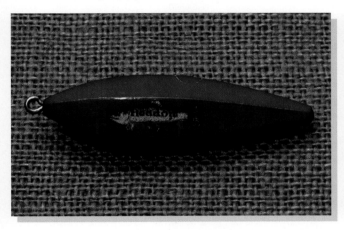

This casting weight was made from a No. 1500 Dummy Double lure body and has the distinct Heddon fish decal. Value range: $300.00 to $400.00.

The Dowagiac Minnow No. 1400, often referred to as the "Single Hook Minnow," is sometimes considered to be the "Holy Grail" of Heddon lures. This bait was designed to comply with the law in states where multiple hooks were not allowed. The flat belly minnow was equipped with two spinners and a single hook fastened with a special "staple rig" preventing the hook from striking the body. Value range: $600.00 to $800.00.

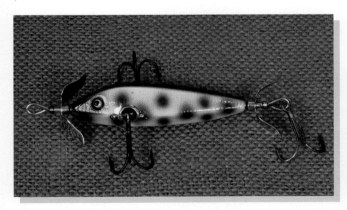

This lure is a six-sided Dowagiac No. 1400 with a flattened belly but didn't get hardware put on it until around 1916. In lieu of the special "single hook" hardware used in 1913, this bait was rigged with L-rig hardware like a five-sided series #0 minnow. This is the only one known with this unusual hardware and cannot be valued.

This six-sided, flat-bellied paint stick is straight out of the Heddon archives and is a No. 1400 Single Hook Minnow body. This is the only one known and would be impossible to value.

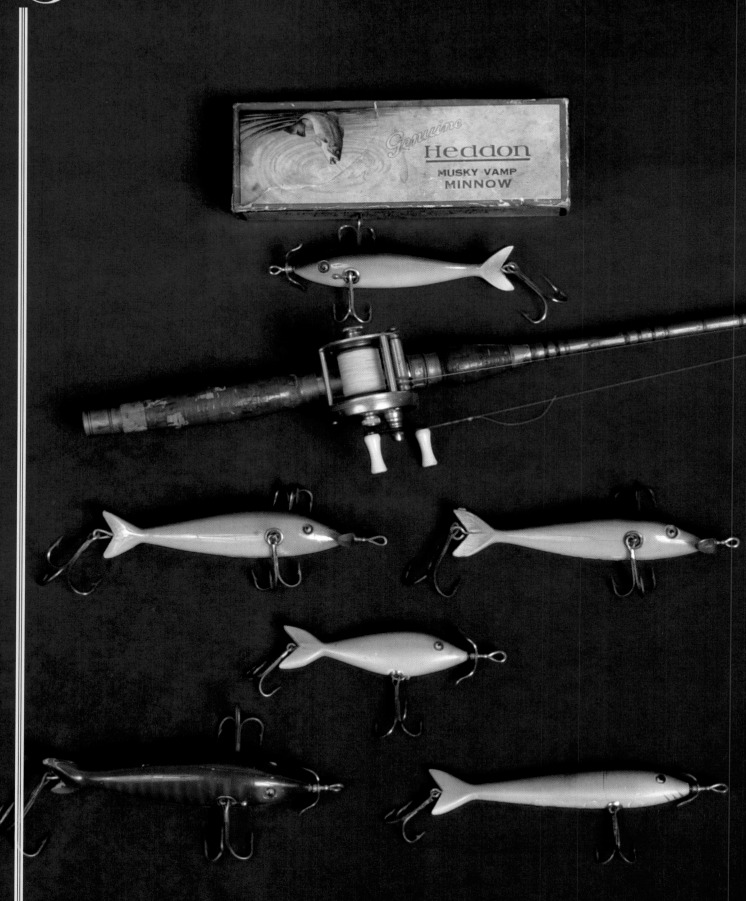

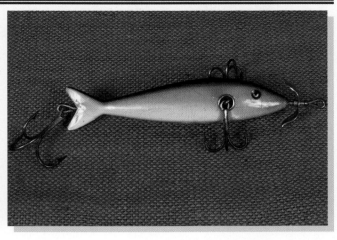

The Heddon Black Sucker is a wonderful carved-tail musky bait and one of the most desirable in luredom. This new-in-box No. 1300 is in the traditional black sucker finish. Note the pinkish hue on the sides. Value range: $900.00 to $1,000.00. With box, $1,400.00.

This No. 1300 Black Sucker is in Sucker finish, not Black Sucker. Note the absence of the pink highlights on the sides of this lure, which is the earliest of these unique baits. Value range: $900.00 to $1,000.00.

Only a couple of these extremely rare, thin-bodied versions of the Black Sucker are known to exist. This is thought to be the very first Black Sucker. The bait comes with two cup-rigged trebles and is shown in sucker finish with a light green back. It is too rare to value.

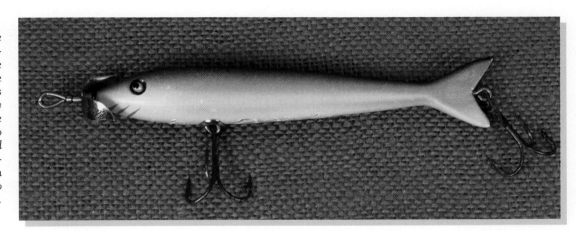

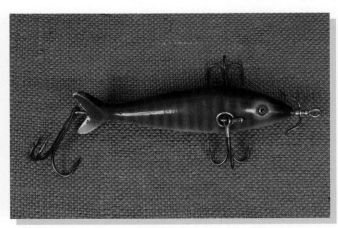

This is a Baby Black Sucker. The body of this bait is thin like the earlier "thin Black Sucker," but has L-rig hardware. The bait was probably made in 1916 along with the introduction of the L-rig fasteners but was never carried in the line. This bait is shown in sucker finish with a black back. It is too rare to value.

This No. 1300 Black Sucker is in Heddon's beautiful Natural Scale pattern. Its unique color makes it too rare to value.

This circa 1913 ice decoy was Heddon's first production model. It has metal bat-like wings, a single line tie, and a natural wood tail. The tail on this decoy is curved, but some have been found to be straight. This minnow only came in two catalogued colors: fancy back with white belly, and perch. Value range: $1,200.00+.

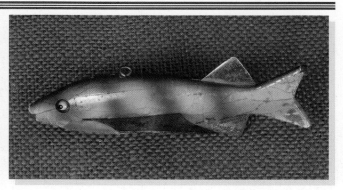

The 1913 catalog says that this ice decoy minnow is designed for swimming or gliding automatically when raised or lowered in the water on the end of a line. Take note of the bat-like wings, the single line tie on the top of the minnow, and the natural tail formation. This decoy is painted in natural perch finish and has a straight tail in lieu of the usual curved tail. Value range: $1,000.00+.

This rare, all-yellow ice decoy minnow has the early bat wings and carved tail. It is a factory prototype from the factory archives and has five belly-weights. It is too unique to value.

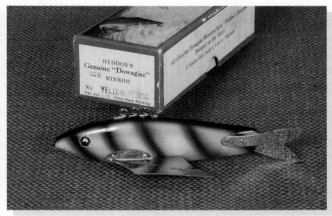

This is the later bat-wing, metal-tailed decoy that followed the wood-tail models. Note the intricate pigtail line tie on the top and the correctly marked and numbered box. Value range: $500.00 to $600.00. With box, $1,000.00+.

The later ice No. 400 Ice Decoys had "four-point" nickel wings, glass eyes, and multiple line ties. The wings, by the way, are the same pieces of metal used on the No. 1600 Deep Diving Wiggler lures. Value range: $400.00 to $500.00. With box, $800.00+.

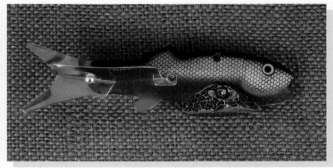

This circa 1930 Ice Spook fish decoy was never catalogued and is made of a plastic material called Heddylin, like pyralin. It has metal fins and an external weight on the bottom of the minnow, which is usually painted in crackleback finish. This decoy is painted in a shiner scale finish. Value range: $300.00 to $350.00.

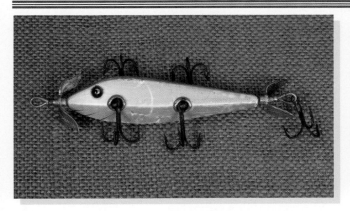

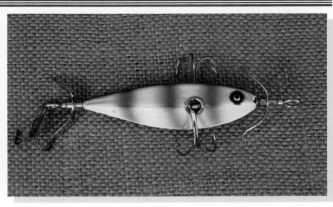

The Dowagiac Minnow No. 0 was described in the 1912 catalog as being 5-sided with hooks mounted on the distending sharp line running the entire length of the bait, thus holding the hooks well out of the way from the body. This bait is shown in a non-catalogued aluminum finish and is longer than the standard 3½". Value range. $200.00 to $250.00.

This series No. 0 Dowagiac is shown with cup-rig hardware. The most unusual thing about this lure is that it has a "sway-belly," sometimes seen in much larger baits. The early perch finish was not a catalogued color and is extremely tough to find. Value range: $300.00 to $350.00.

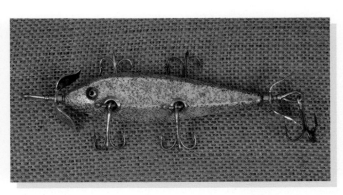

This is a very rare circa 1912 No. 00 minnow and is from the Heddon Factory archives. The body at 2⅞" is shorter than any other No. 0 or No. 00 minnow. Then to top it off, it's a five-hooker. The minnow is beautifully finished with a white body and small red and green spots and is too unique to value.

This No. 00 Dowagiac is in saltwater white with glitter finish – an unusual color for this lure. Value range: $300.00 to $350.00.

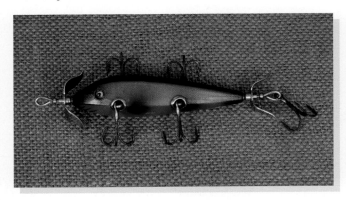

The five-hook Dowagiac No. 00 baits are often found in red with black spots, one of three catalogued colors for this early lure. Value range: $150.00 to $200.00.

This series No. 0 minnow is shown with L-rig hardware. The paint finish on this lure is shiner scale, a new color for 1922, and was not a catalogued color for this bait. Another interesting feature of is the front prop, which is marked "A & I." This would indicate that the lure was sold through Abbey & Imbrie in New York. Value range: $200.00 to $250.00.

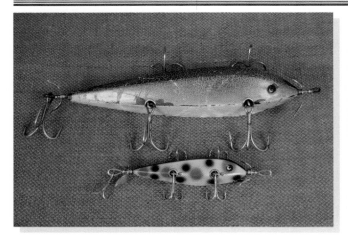

This is one large Heddon minnow, measuring 8¾" and dating to 1912. Even larger in length and girth than the famed "747" Heddon minnow, it has seven belly-weights and is often called the "Big O." This model is one of only two known to have survived. Value range: $2,500.00+.

This is a typical Heddon No. 0 three-hook underwater lure in the traditional carnival spot or "strawberry" finish. Value range: $125.00 to $200.00. With box, $300.00.

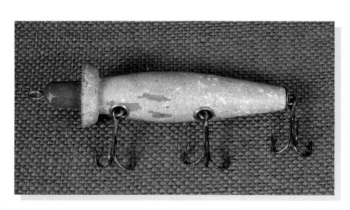

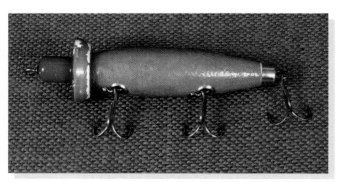

Heddon marketed a No. RH 1001 "peckerhead" type bait around 1910. This is the earliest version with cup rigs and luminous paint. Value range: $350.00 to $400.00.

This 1916 version of the No. RH 1001 bait has L-rig hardware and a metal tailcap, leaving no doubt as to its origins in Dowagiac. Value range: $350.00 to $400.00.

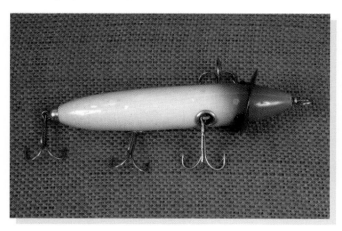

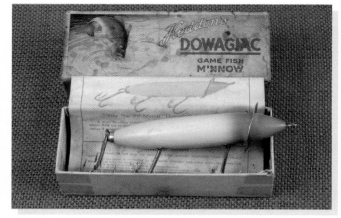

This is a rare four-hook version of the No. 200 Surface lure. Value range: $300.00 to $350.00.

This early version of the No. 200 Surface lure is the successor of the Slopenose bait, which is still pictured in the enclosed flyer. The white border leaping bass box is circa 1912. Value range, with box, $250.00 to $350.00.

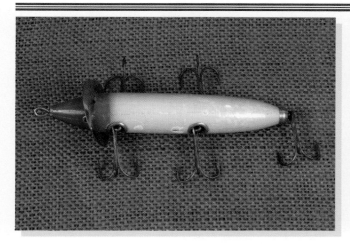

This is a five-hook version of the No. 200 Surface lure, circa 1912. Value range: $400.00 to $500.00.

The No. 200 Surface lure also can be found with two hooks, as this unusual blue scale specimen shows. Value range: $100.00 to $150.00.

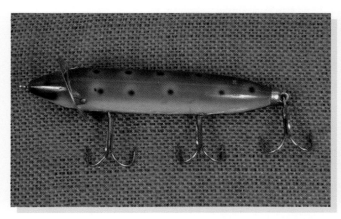

This early frogspot No. 200 Surface lure has tiny spots and the black "moustache" paint on its nose. Value range: $100.00 to $150.00.

This later version of the No. 200 Surface lure is in mouse flock, complete with black glass eyes and the cloth whiskers. Value range, with box: $100.00 to $150.00.

The No. 200 Surface is occasionally found in solid black. Value range, with box: $100.00 to $150.00.

This No. 200 Surface is in beautiful Natural Scale finish and has glass eyes and two-piece hardware. Value range: $150.00 to $200.00.

This is an extremely rare uncatalogued Dowagiac Surface No. 200 Special bait, circa 1915, and to date only three are known to exist. Two are featured here in this book, and the third was a gift from Laura Heddon to her grandson Chuck Heddon. Note the absence of the normal #200 series collar on this L-rig surface bait. The attractive bait is shown here in imitation frog finish and has marked propellers both in front and back. The bait comes packaged in a rare, correctly marked, downward leaping bass extended box. It is too rare to value.

This is the other #200 special bait in this collection. This one is painted in a solid white finish and also comes packaged in a rare, correctly marked, downward leaping bass box. Like the example above, it is too rare to value.

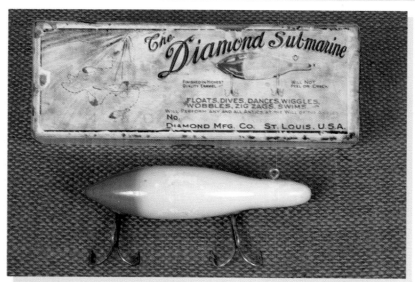

The early Diamond Submarine or "Bottle-Nosed Tadpolly," as it is referred to by collectors, pre-dates the Heddon Tadpolly introduced in 1918. This unusual lure is definitely made by Heddon, but the relationship with the Diamond Manufacturing Co. of St. Louis is unclear. What is known is that Diamond discontinued selling the baits before Heddon's Tadpolly was marketed. Value range: $200.00 to $300.00. With box, $500.00.

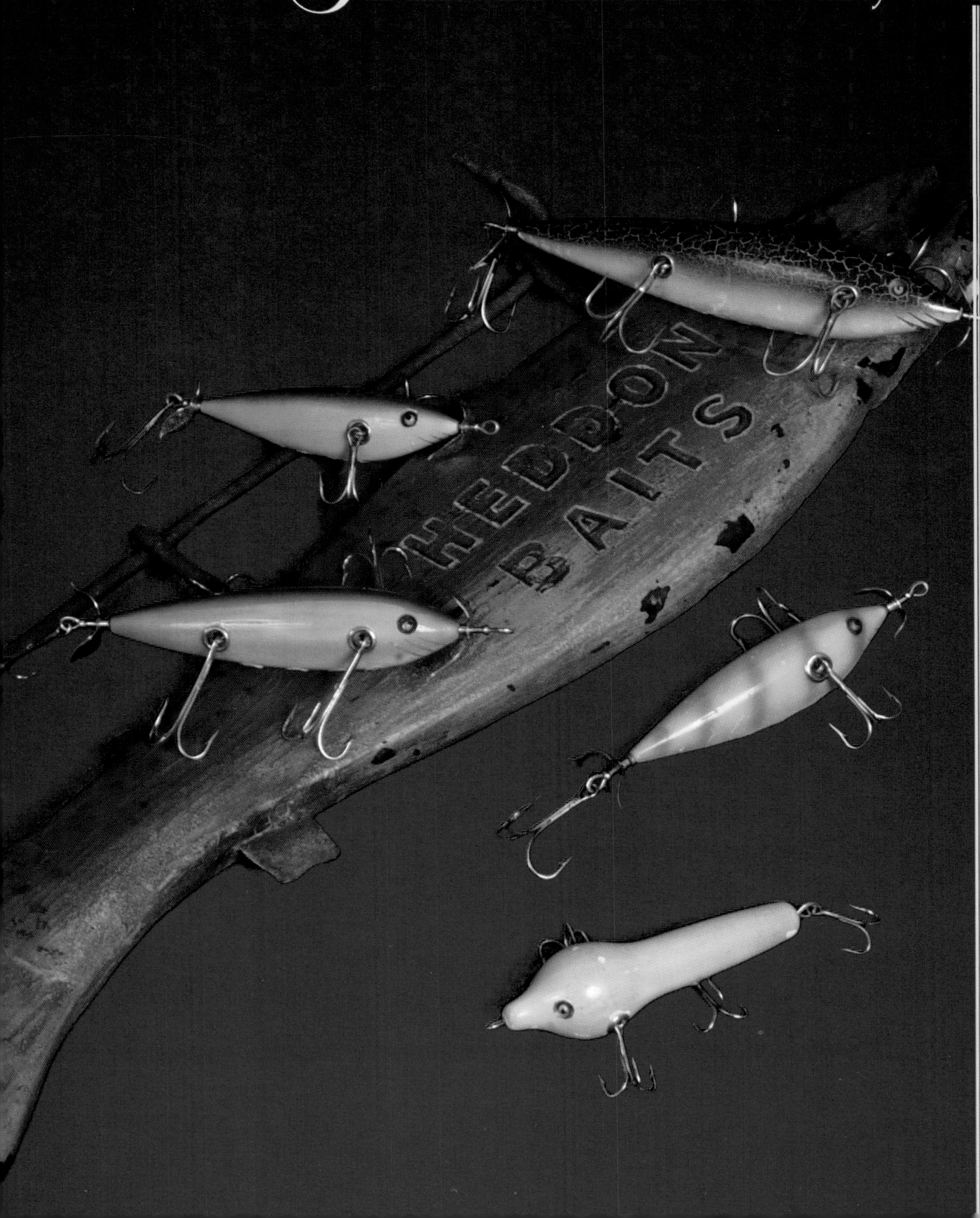
HEDDON
BAITS

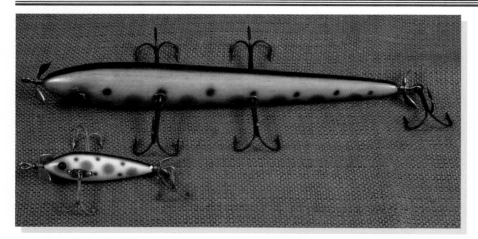

This lure measures 10" — without the hardware! It is a Musky Surface Minnow and one of two known to exist. Both trace their origins to the Heddon factory. This is the longest of all Heddon lures, but it was never produced commercially. It is too rare to value.

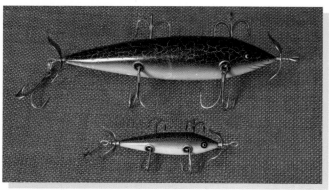

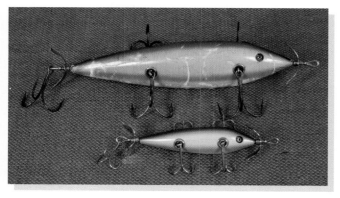

This 1910 bait, the No. 7000 "Mascallonge" minnow, was made in Dowagiac and sold through Von Lengerke & Antoine (VL&A) in Chicago. The only known reference was in the No. 55 VL&A Catalog, which described the minnow as being made by hand and with the finest enamel. The length of the body is 8", and it weighs a whopping nine ounces. The minnow was sold in two variations, No. 7000 white body, fancy green back; and No. 7001 rainbow, green back, red sides blending to white. Over the years collectors have lovingly nicknamed this bait the "747" after the jumbo jet of the same name. Value range: $2,000.00+.

This is another Dowagiac VL&A model "Mascallonge" minnow, No. 7001. It appears only in one catalog by the famous sporting goods outfitter. Rainbow is one of two colors used on the lure. Value range: $2,000.00+.

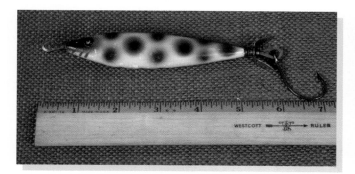

The Coast Minnow, a shaped-body beauty from 1913, has five belly-weights and hand-painted gills. They were made with a special, high-strength hook and marketed for fish that bite from the rear. Value range: $300.00 to $350.00.

This is a front-propeller model of the Coast minnow in a beautiful spotted finish. Front prop models are rare. Value range: $300.00 to $400.00.

Coast Minnow lures were made in four sizes. The examples here, all in rainbow, are No. 4, 5½"; No. 1, 4½"; No. 2, 3½" and No. 3, 2½". Note the difference in the hardware on the two smaller examples here, one of which has a rear prop and a leader. The other has a front and rear prop and no leader. Value range $300.00 to $400.00.

This is the first model Coast Minnow in green crackleback. Note the twisted wire line-tie and the semi-floppy propeller. It's possibly a transition bait from North Coast Minnow, thought to have been the impetus for Heddon's lure. Value range: $300.00 to $400.00.

This pair of front-prop Coast Minnow lures illustrate the flat line-tie and long rear hook. Note the wonderful crackleback finish on the top lure. The other has a green back with gold specks. Front prop models are later, made around 1922, but harder to find. Value $300.00 to $400.00.

The No. 1700 Near Surface Wiggler dates to the early teens. This bar perch model has the pigtail line-tie and is new in the box. Value range: $150.00 to $200.00. With box, $300.00.

This unusual No. 1700 is finished in red scale and has the distinct inchworm line tie. Value range: $200.00 to $300.00. With box, $400.00.

Blue scale is one of Heddon's prettiest finishes. Note the black around the eyes that is absent from a similar color — green scale. This No. 1700 Near Surface Wiggler is new in the box. Value range: $200.00 to $300.00. With box, $400.00.

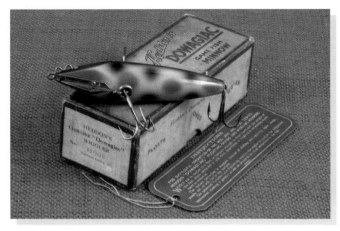

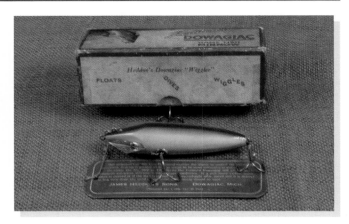

This No. 1600 Deep Diving Wiggler also dates to the early teens. This is a side-hooked model in the correct, unusual tall box with the red cardboard instruction tag. Value: $200.00 to $300.00. With box, $400.00.

Here is a rainbow No. 1600 Deep Diving Wiggler, also in the tall box. Note the side hooks and red cardboard tag. Value range: $200.00 to $300.00. With box, $400.00.

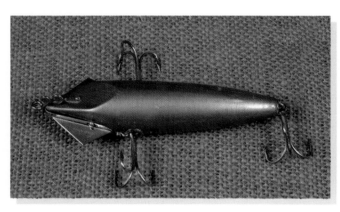

This rare aluminum finished No. 1600 has side hooks. Value range: $350.00 to $400.00.

This belly-hooked No. 1600 is in beautiful frog spot finish and has the earliest style separate diving planes. Later models had a one-piece plane. Value range: $150.00 to $200.00.

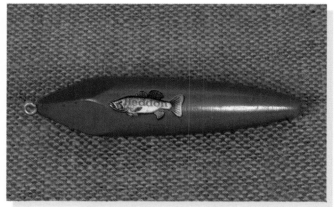

This No. 1600 is in brilliant frog scale finish, almost resembling a snake's skin. Value range $200.00 to $250.00.

This rare Heddon casting practice weight was made from the wooden body of the No. 1600. Value range: $250.00 to $300.00.

This is an unusual, thin-bodied No. 1700 Near Surface Wiggler in green scale finish. Value range: $150.00 to $200.00.

The No. 1900 Baby Crab Wiggler dates to 1916 and was often accompanied by a color flyer and red cardboard hang tag. Value range: $40.00 to $75.00. With box, $150.00.

The No. 1800 Crab Wiggler, a bit larger than the 1900, dates to 1915. Note the "U" collar on this lure, making it an early one. Value range: $40.00 to $75.00. With box, $150.00.

This Crab Wiggler is in Natural Crab finish. Its "U" collar dates it as one of the earliest. Value range, $40.00 to $50.00.

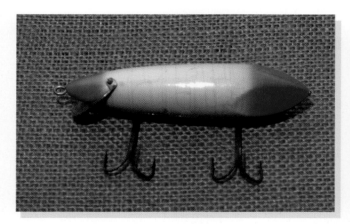

This unusual Crab Wiggler utilizes the body for another lure, the No. 1600 Deep Diving Wiggler. This circa 1930 lure was sold during the Depression and has a marked "U" collar and very tiny, 1/8" cup hardware that matches the tail inserts on the 1600 and 1700 lures. Value range: $100.00 to $150.00.

This unusual Crab Wiggler has side mounted hooks and utilizes the body of a fat No. 140 Flipper. Heddon lures turn up in many variations. Value range: $100.00 to $125.00.

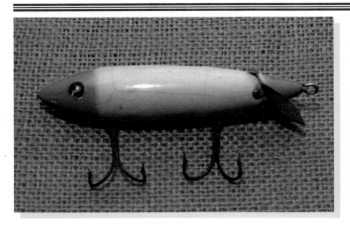

This Crab Wiggler utilizes the body of another lure, the No. 140 Flipper. It is likely this was another Depression era lure during which the factory used parts and bodies from discontinued lures. The cups are ⅛" wide. Value range: $100.00 to $125.00.

This No. 1900 Crab Wiggler in rainbow still has the original pork-rind attachment on its rear hook. Value: $40.00 to $75.00.

This is the No. 1950 Midget Crab Wiggler, the smallest of several versions of this plump, attractive lure. Value range: $40.00 to $75.00.

This No. 1800 Crab Wiggler is in Red Scale finish, one of Heddon's most desirable. Value range: $125.00 to $175.00.

This circa 1936 lure is the No. 9900 Crab Spook made of pyralin. Note the bead eyes. These lures came in many unusual and attractive finishes. Value: $20.00 to $40.00.

This later model No. 9900 Crab Spook has the added feature of a spinner on the nose. Value: $20.00 to $30.00.

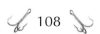

The No. 7000 Dowagiac Deep-O-Diver is the smallest of the Crab Wiggler type lures and emerged in 1919 in this rare white introductory box. Value: $40.00 to $65.00. With box, $200.00.

This No. 3000 Spindiver is in rainbow finish, in its correctly numbered Heddon box. The lure was designed to float when not in motion and to dive beneath the water when retrieved. Value: $250.00 to $350.00. With box, $450.00.

Green crackleback was one of the many colors for the No. 3000 Spindiver. This example is new in the box. Value range: $300.00 to $500.00. With box, $500.00+.

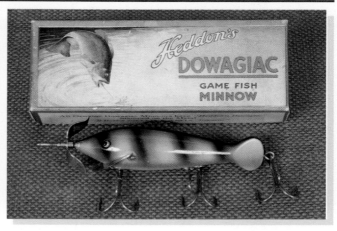

The No. 3000 Spindiver, circa 1918, is one of Heddon's handsome plugs. Note the carved wooden tail and distinct diving lip. This example, in its own box, is in bar perch finish. Value: $250.00 to $350.00. With box: $450.00.

This No. 3000 Spindiver is in brilliant goldfish scale, one of Heddon's most elusive colors. It must have been quite a sight to the fish! Value range: $350.00 to $400.00. With box, $500.00+.

The No. 2000 Wiggle-King was introduced in 1918 and came packaged in this unusual introductory box. Wiggle-King lures had cup rigging and a distinct, two-faced cut on the mouth. Some Wiggle-King boxes made no mention of Heddon. Value range: $40.00 to $75.00. With box, $250.00 to $300.00.

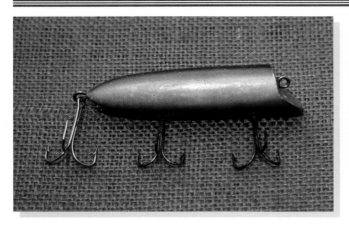

The No. 2000 Wiggle-King lures are most often found in rainbow, seen here, red and white, or frog spot. Value range: $40.00 to $75.00.

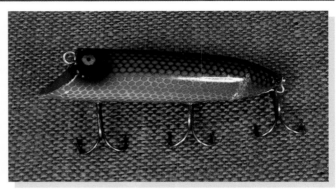

The long-lived No. 2500 Lucky 13 first appeared in 1920. This rare early version resembled the Wiggle-King and is found in red scale, a color introduced in 1919. Note that this lure has cup rigs and painted eyes. Later Lucky 13s had neither painted nor glass eyes until much later in the production years when painted eyes were used on most baits. This unique lure is too rare to value.

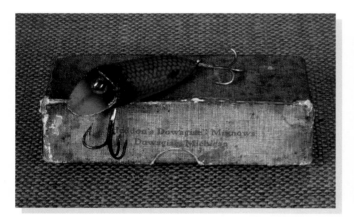

This is the No. 2400 Lucky 13 Junior introduced in 1919. The first version came in this greenish box similar to the introductory carton for the Wiggle-King but without writing on top. Value range: $40.00 to $50.00. With box, $150.00 to $200.00.

The No. 2500 Lucky 13 can be found in many colors, hardware configurations, and with or without glass eyes. This popular lure is one of Heddon's most common, as many were made. Value range depends on color and condition, $10.00 to $75.00.

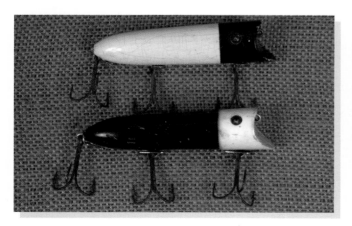

The No. 2500 Lucky 13 lures are among several of Heddon's baits that can be found in a black and white or white and black color pattern. Value range: $25.00 to $50.00.

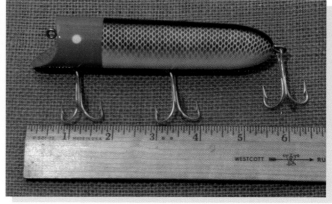

This is a musky-sized Lucky 13 with late 1940s surface hardware. Value range: $100.00 to $150.00.

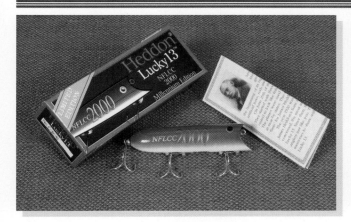

The National Fishing Lure Collectors Club marketed this commemorative Lucky 13 during its year 2000 national convention in Little Rock, Ark. Value range: $20.00 to $25.00.

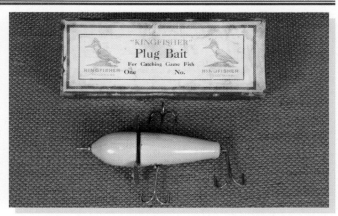

The Kingfisher Plug Bait from the early teen years is a Heddon product sold by the Edward K. Tryon Corp. of Philadelphia. Plug baits are similar to the Ans Decker bait of New Jersey and the Pflueger Globe, both made during the same era. Value range: $150.00 to $200.00. With box, $400.00.

This No. 20 Baby Dowagiac Minnow was sold under the Kingfisher label by the Edward K. Tryon Co. in the early teens. Value range: $125.00 to $150.00. With box, $175.00 to $200.00.

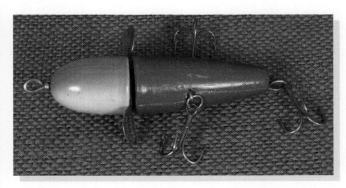

Although most Heddon-made Plug Baits had cup rig hardware, this example has staple rig hardware. Value range: $150.00 to $200.00.

This Heddon-made Plug Bait is in traditional rainbow pattern with cup rigs. Value range: $125.00 to $150.00.

Kingfisher underwater minnow boxes most often contain Pflueger products. However, the company carried Heddon minnows prior to marketing the Pflueger "Neverfail" lures. This is a Heddon-made No. 100 Dowagiac sold by the Tryon Co. under their label around 1910. Value range: $100.00 to $125.00. With box, $175.00 to $200.00.

This slide-top wooden box marketed by Tryon contains a pre-1910 rainbow Heddon underwater minnow. Value range: $100.00 to $125.00. With box, $250.00 to $300.00.

The popular No. 300 Surface bait came in many colors and hook configurations. This rainbow example has four hooks, with the side-trebles mounted to the rear. This bait dates to around 1910. Value: $300.00 to $400.00.

This No. 300 Surface bait in green crackleback, circa 1920, has a slightly fatter body than usual. Note that the side trebles are mounted at the rear. Value range: $300.00 to $400.00. With box, $800.00.

Another of the Heddon "trade minnows" is this No. 150 Dowagiac sold by the Diamond Manufacturing Co. of St. Louis, Mo. Value range: $100.00 to $125.00. With box, $250.00 to $300.00.

This No. 300 Surface bait is a four-hook model in L-rig from around 1916. Note the unusual line tie, most often found on Heddon's Coast Minnow lures. Value $250.00 to $300.00.

This four-hook No. 300 Surface bait has L-rig hardware and the extra hooks are mounted to the front. Value range: $250.00 to $350.00.

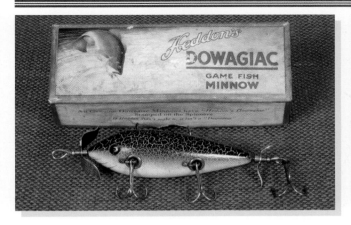

This No. 300 Surface bait has five trebles and is rigged much like a Dowagiac 150. Note the fat body and correctly marked box. Five-hook 300s are very rare. Value range: $700.00 to $900.00. With box, $1,200.00.

This rare seven-hook No. 300 Surface bait is in pike scale, an unusual color for this lure. This bait has the most treble hooks of any Heddon lure. Value range: $300.00 to $400.00.

This No. 300 Surface bait in blue and white finish is unusual due to its color, normally found on the 200 Surface lures. Value $500.00 to $600.00. With correct box, $750.00 to $900.00.

This is the Victory Rainbow finish offered by Heddon at the end of World War I. This No. 300 Surface bait has hand-painted gills and a beautiful blended paint finish. Value $600.00 to $700.00.

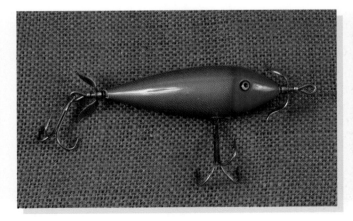

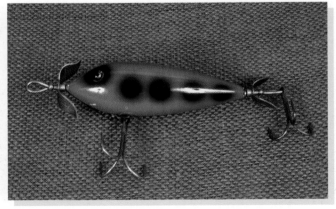

This gold No. 300 Surface bait also has a blended red head. Few Heddon lures are found in this color. Value $600.00 to $700.00.

Another rare-color No. 300 Surface lure is this example, painted orange with black spots. Value range: $500.00 to $600.00.

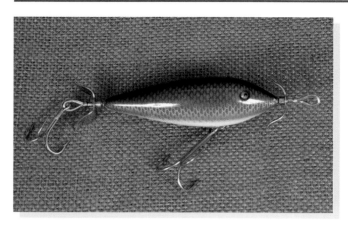

Red scale is a favorite among collectors. This No. 300 Surface bait has a value range of $400.00 to $500.00.

This three-hook Yellow Shore finish No. 300 Surface bait is from around 1937. Shore finishes most often are found on plastic lures. Value range: $250.00 to $300.00.

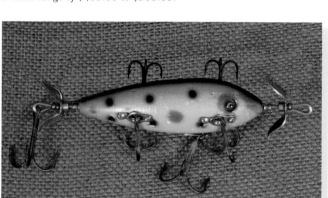

This unusual No. 300 Surface bait has a spotted yellow paint pattern similar to those found on Creek Chub products. It has six hooks and toilet seat hardware. Value range: $250.00 to $350.00.

This is the No. 350 Musky Surfusser, a large, heavy bait made for musky and other large fish. Dating to the 1930s, it is almost always found with heavy-duty toilet seat hardware. Value $200.00 to $300.00.

This is a seldom-seen Heddon No. 250 Dowagiac, an underwater lure similar to the No. 150 but with a belly and tail treble instead of four side-mounted hooks and a tail treble. Dating to the mid-1920s, its value range is $250.00 to $350.00.

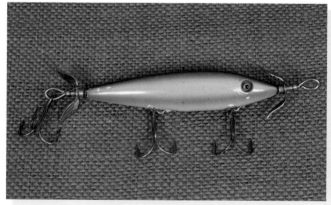

This Heddon No. 250 has L-rig hardware, two belly trebles, and a tail hook and two belly-weights. Value range: $350.00 to $450.00.

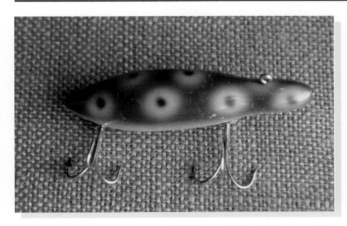

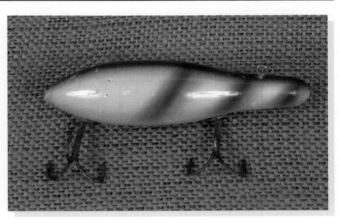

The Diamond Submarine bait, or "bottle-nosed Tadpolly," was marketed by the Diamond Manufacturing Co. of St. Louis, but is obviously a Heddon-made product. Value range: $200.00 to $300.00.

This Diamond Submarine bait is in one of Heddon's most distinct paint finishes: bar perch. Value range: $200.00 to $300.00.

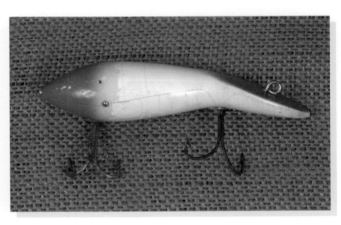

This factory prototype of the popular Tadpolly lure has a No. 3000 Spindiver diving lip. Its uniqueness makes it impossible to value.

This slant-faced Tadpolly prototype has a strong resemblance to the J.K. Rush Tango lures made in New York in the late teens, the period from which this factory item was made. It is too rare to value.

The No. 5000 Tadpolly was first offered in 1918 and came in its special introductory box. It is the first model with the heart-shaped diving lip and the "high-hump" line tie. Value range: $50.00 to $75.00. With box, $200.00 to $250.00.

The larger, No. 6000 Tadpolly also was first offered in 1918. It has the heart-shaped lip but a standard line-tie. Value range: $35.00 to $65.00. With box, $175.00 to $250.00.

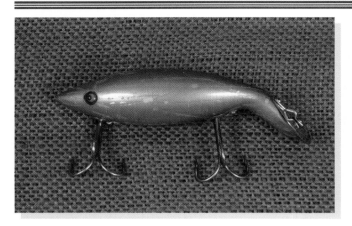

This No. 6000 Tadpolly is in aluminum finish, a rare Heddon color. Value: $75.00 to $150.00.

The No. 70 Heddon-Stanley Weedless Pork Rind lure featured a pyralin body, glass eyes and a prop marked Stanley for the inventor. Dating to 1924, its value range is $15.00 to $30.00. With box, $50.00 to $75.00.

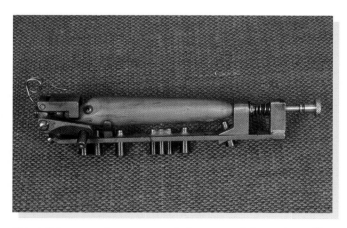

This drill jig was used to stamp out the L-rig screw holes on the Heddon 7500 Vamp lure.

This one-of-a-kind No. 5000 Tadpolly closely resembles the Deep-O-Diver lure produced a few years later. The spotted finish is an apparent expreimental color tried out at the factory. The box has an offset thumbnail cutout that is centered on most similar boxes. It is too unusual to value.

This wooden lure blank was a gift to co-author Bill Roberts from Heddon historian Clyde Harbin. It was found in Minneola, Fla., where Will and Laura Heddon carved and painted the Dowagiac-made blanks into lures.

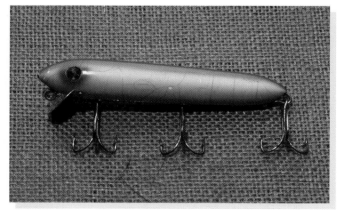

This round-nosed No. 7500 Vamp is in rainbow finish. Dating to the late teens, it is somewhat of a mystery among collectors. Its rounded face resembles the No. 110 River Runt. Value range: $150.00 to $200.00.

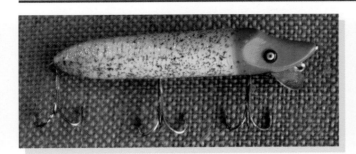

The No. 7500 Vamp is one of Heddon's most enduring and most common lures. Introduced in 1920 as the Vampire, it became the Vamp a year later. This example is in redhead/flitter color pattern. Value range: $40.00 to $50.00.

The No. 7400 Baby Vamp was introduced in 1925. This color is frogspot. Value range: $40.00 to $50.00.

Frog Scale is a pattern found on Vamp lures. The red head/frog scale finish on the top lure is the rarer of the three. Value range: $40.00 to $100.00.

This No. 7500 Vamp is in Luny Frog finish, markedly different from the traditional frog spot finish. Value range: $50.00 to $75.00.

This No. 7500 Vamp in blue scale finish has a value range of $75.00 to $100.00.

This no-lipped No. 7400 Baby Vamp is unusual in that it has no diving lip. The paint finish is called Allen Stripey. Designed for saltwater use and dating to the 1930s. Value range: $50.00 to $75.00.

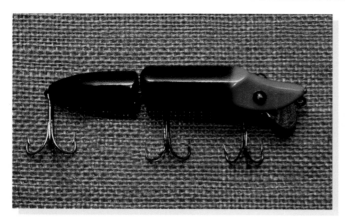

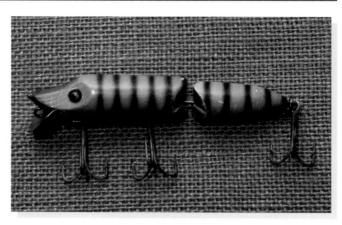

The No. 7300 Jointed Vamp was first offered in 1927. This example has a hard-to-find black paint finish with red head. Value range: $40.00 to $75.00.

This No. 7300 Jointed Vamp is in Heddon's unusual "bumblebee" finish found only on a few lures and flyrod baits. Value range: $50.00 to $100.00.

The six-inch No. 7550 Musky Vamp is large and well made. This example is in Natural Scale finish. Value range: $200.00 to $250.00.

The No. 7550 Musky Vamps came in extended boxes that utilized the regular label from standard sized lure boxes. Frog spot is a rare color for this bait. Value range: $250.00 to $300.00. With box, $400.00.

The eight-inch No. 7600 Musky Vamp is one of Heddon's largest lures. Dating to 1925, they came packaged in their own special white box at first. Value range: $300.00 to $400.00. With white box, $650.00 to $800.00.

White with red around the eyes is a popular finish on this 8" lure. Value range for the No. 7600 Musky Vamp in the correct white box: $650.00 to $800.00.

The No. 7600 Musky Vamp also can be found in an extra-large leaping bass box, as evidenced by the red head/salt flitter finished example. Value range: $300.00 to $400.00. With leaping bass box, $500.00 to $700.00.

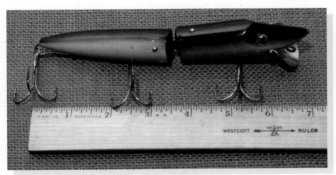

The Jointed Musky Vamp, No. 7350, dates to around 1933. This color finish is black sucker, and the eyes are zinc instead of the usual glass. The hardware is heavy-duty as found on most musky baits. Value range: $100.00 to $150.00.

This is the Harden's Whiz bait, made by Heddon for Walter Harden. The circa 1930 lure has the body of a Baby Vamp and two props but no diving lip. It can also be found with three trebles. Value range: $250.00 to $300.00.

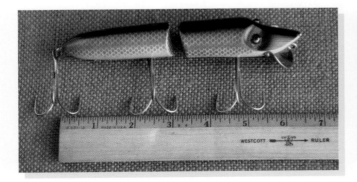

This unusual Jointed Musky Vamp utilizes the body of the 8" Musky Vamp but has been shortened. It is too unusual to value.

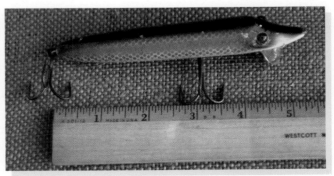

Another strange variation between the No. 7500 Vamp and the 6" Musky Vamp is this 5½" bait with a very slender body. Again, too unusual to value.

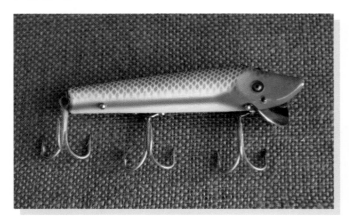

This is the No. 7540 Great Vamp introduced in the late 1930s for musky and salmon fishing. Note the pin near the tail to secure the hook mount. This 5" lure has glass eyes and a value range of $125.00 to $150.00.

The No. 9500 Vamp Spook and No. 9730 Jointed Vamp Spook were the later versions of the popular Vamp line. Both are made of plastic and can be found in many colors. Value range: $10.00 to $15.00.

The No. 210 Surface lure was the smaller successor to Heddon's popular 200 Surface lure. This example is yellow with black spots, a pattern similar to strawberry. Value range: $75.00 to $150.00. Common colors are worth much less.

The No. 210 Surface also is found in bumblebee finish. Value range: $75.00 to $150.00.

Later No. 210 Surface lures had glass eyes, as seen on this black and white example dating to the 1930s. Value range: $40.00 to $60.00.

The No. 40 Walton Feathertail lure, circa early 1920s, was a weighted casting plug. This new-in-box example has the much rarer Stanley Weedless attachment not found on all lures. Value range: $75.00 to $100.00. With weedless attachment and box, $150.00 to $200.00.

This is the standard No. 40 Walton Feathertail lure with a propeller on the front. Value range: $50.00 to $75.00.

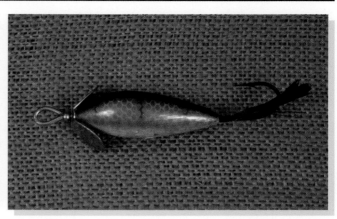

This is an early version of the No. 40 Walton Feathertail that has a marked Stanley prop and no eyes. Value range: $100.00 to $150.00.

The Kinney Bird lure was patented on September 20, 1927, by Herbert A. Kinney and painted by Heddon for Old Hickory Rod and Tackle Co. of Tampa, Fla. This lure is painted in redwing blackbird finish. Value range: $750.00+.

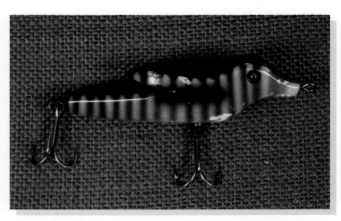

This Kinney Bird lure is painted in Natural Bar finish, a variation devised by Heddon. Value range: $750.00+.

Some Kinney Bird lures were hand-painted by Kinney himself and had a folksy, primitive look compared to the airbrushed Heddon models. All Kinney Bird lures have wonderful appeal. Value range: $750.00+.

The No. 5500 Gamefisher was introduced in 1923. The three-section lure remained a popular fish catcher. This example is in yellow with gold spots, a very rare Heddon finish. Value range: $75.00 to $100.00.

This frog scale No. 5500 Gamefisher lure is in its correct early box. Only a few have been found in this color. Value range: $75.00 to $100.00. With box, $150.00.

The No. 5500 Gamefisher is occasionally found with glass eyes which matches the original patent drawing. Most Gamefishers have a marked headplate, but this one is unmarked. This lure has no scales or paint in the joints and utilizes screws to attach the segments instead of pins found on most Gamefishers. Value range: $300.00 to $400.00.

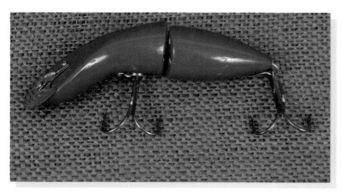

The No. 5400 Baby Gamefisher appeared in 1925 and had two pieces instead of three. It was designed to wobble as it went through the water. Rare in solid red color. Value range: $40.00 to $60.00.

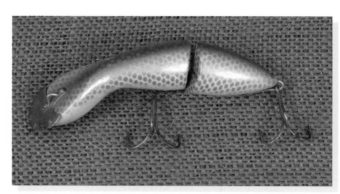

This No. 5400 Baby Gamefisher is in a lighter-than-usual blue scale finish. Value range: $75.00 to $100.00.

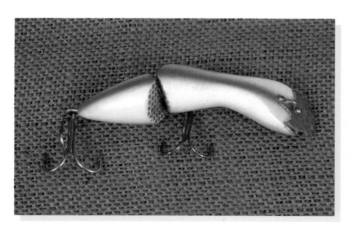

With a red stripe down its back and white sides, this No. 5400 Baby Gamefisher is in another unusual, unnamed color finish. Value range: $75.00 to $100.00.

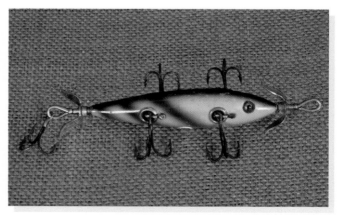

By the 1920s, Heddon was making Dowagiac No. 150 minnows in unusual colors. This one is natural crab, usually found on the Crab Wiggler lures. Value range: $200.00 to $250.00.

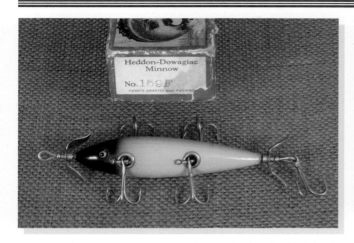

This Dowagiac No. 150 minnow is yellow with a blended black head. Value range: $300.00 to $450.00. With box: $500.00.

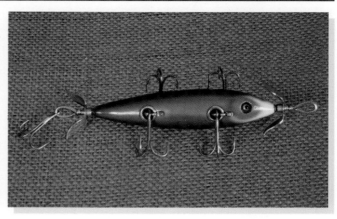

Gold metallic paint, red eye shadow, and an ivory white painted nose make this Dowagiac No. 150 minnow from the 1920s a very unusual creature. Value range: $300.00 to $400.00.

Later Dowagiac No. 150 minnows had toilet seat hardware. This frogscale pattern lure is new in its correct box. Value range: $200.00 to $300.00. With box, $350.00.

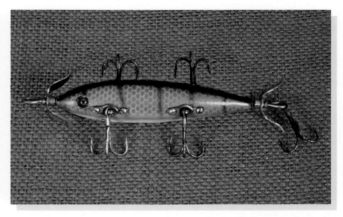

This is one of the few Dowagiac No. 150 minnows to be found in pike scale finish. It has toilet seat hardware and marked props. Value range: $200.00 to $300.00.

This early L-rig Dowagiac No. 100 is in green crackleback with red head. In addition to its unusual color, it has its own legacy: it came from the tackle box of Spanky McFarland, the child actor immortalized in the "Little Rascals" and "Our Gang" comedies. It is impossible to value.

This strawberry spot Dowagiac No. 100 has two-piece hardware which dates it to the 1930s. Value range: $150.00 to $200.00.

The No. 6500 Zaragossa emerged in 1920 and was billed as "The Florida Wonder." It was the forerunner of the famous Zara Spook. The minnow shown is finished in brilliant gold fish scale and comes with the correct red border, downward leaping bass box. Note that the word "Genuine" appears on the box top, circa 1924. Value: $125.00 to $150.00. With box, $200.00.

This perch scale Zaragossa type bait is a Harden's Star version of this famous lure. Note the WH (Walter Harden) prefix on the box endflap. This lure has glass eyes and two-piece hardware. Value range: $300.00 to $350.00. With box, $450.00.

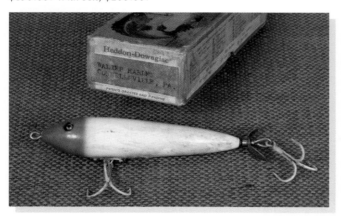

This red and white Harden's Star Zaragossa is an earlier model, illustrated by Harden's own brown label pasted over the end flap on the Heddon box. Harden, of Connellsville, Pennsylvania, used the modified baits for his own particular style of bass fishing in Florida. Value range: $300.00 to $350.00; with box, $400.00.

This green scale No. 6500 Zaragossa has a River Runt lip, an unusual feature. The x-ray in the photo shows there are belly-weights on either side of the forward belly hook to give the bait proper floating balance in the water. This could be a prototype or special order lure. It is too rare to value.

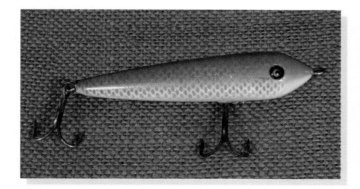

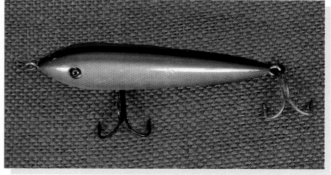

This is the early "blunt-nose" No. 6500 Zaragossa, and the color is goldfish scale. Value range: $150.00 to $200.00.

This glass-eye No. 6500 Zaragossa is in rainbow scale, circa 1920s. Value range: $150.00 to $200.00.

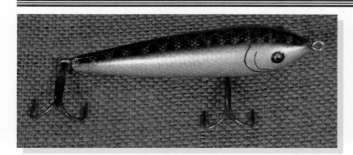

This is one of very few silver herring finish No. 6500 Zaragossa lures that have been found. Value range: $300.00 to $350.00.

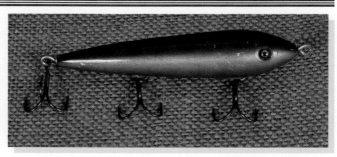

This No. 6500 Zaragossa is gold with a bronze back, a color not mentioned in Heddon catalogs. Value range: $300.00 to $350.00.

This glass eyed lure is redhead and bullfrog finish. It has two-piece hardware, making it one of the later No. 6500 Zaragossas from the 1930s. Value range: $250.00 to $300.00.

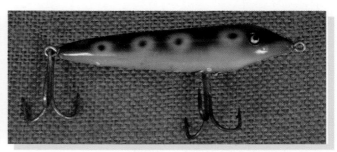

This very early No. 6500 Zaragossa in frogspot finish is the rare "no-chin" model. Apparently the factory testers at one time thought the chinless feature enhanced the action, but it was soon abandoned in favor of the more common rounded-chin versions. Value range: $250.00 to $300.00.

The No. 6500 Zaragossa outlasted many Heddon lures and was made from the 1920s into the 1950s. This lineup illustrates some of the variations and colors to be found on earlier versions.

This No. 6500 Zaragossa has extra long hooks and a broad smile. Collectors refer to this hand-painted chin model as the "Smiley Face" Zaragossa. Value range: $200.00 to $300.00.

The popularity of the No. 6500 Zaragossa led to the marketing of this No. 6400 Zaragossa Junior in Japan. Value range: $100.00 to $150.00. With box, $175.00.

The No. 9250 Zara Spook, made of plastic, was the successor to the wooden Zaragossa. Many Zara Spooks remain on active fishing duty today. They were introduced in 1939. Value range for older models: $10.00 to $20.00.

These metal paint masks were used at the Heddon factory during the manufacture and painting of the famous bass lures.

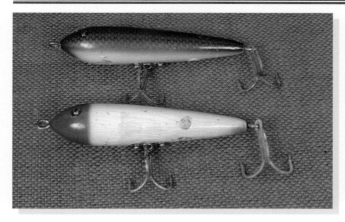

The success of the No. 6500 Zaragossa led to the creation of a handful of Musky Zaragossa lures. These big baits were never produced commercially. The examples shown are from the Heddon factory archives board and are too rare to value.

This Musky Zaragossa from the factory archives board has props fore and aft. The diving lip is from the 8" Heddon Musky Vamp, the only hardware that would fit this big lure, whose head is more than an inch in diameter. It is too rare to value.

The No. 8500 Basser was introduced in 1920. Early models, like this new-in-box specimen in rare yellow with gold spots, had glass eyes and L-rig hardware. Value range: $100.00 to $125.00; with box, $150.00.

This No. 8500 Basser in Shiner Scale is new in the box and was found in the sample room of a rival company — Pflueger — which always acquired and tested baits from their competitors. Value range: $100.00 to $125.00.

This blue-headed No. 8500 Basser is one of the more unusual colors that can be found. Value range: $100.00 to $125.00.

This blue scale No. 8500 Basser is new in the correct box. Value range: $100.00 to $125.00.

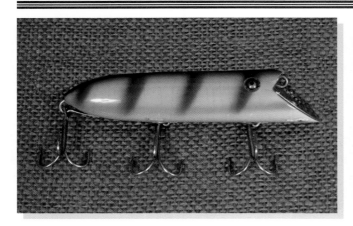

This No. 8500 Basser is in bar perch, a favorite color among collectors. Value range: $75.00 to $100.00.

This No. 8500 Basser is in redhead with frog scale finish. Value range: $75.00 to $100.00.

The No. 8500 Basser is sometimes found with two hooks instead of three, an early green scale example. Value range: $50.00 to $75.00.

This extra large No. 8500 Basser is called the "Daddy Basser," and it is labeled as such on the diving lip plate. This perch scale example is the only one known in that color. Value range: $200.00 to $300.00.

This No. 8500 Daddy Basser is in green crackleback finish. Dating to around 1920, it has a value range of $150.00 to $250.00.

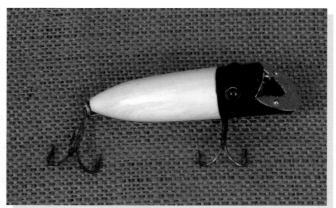

The No. 8400 Plunking Basser has two hooks and glass eyes. It is shorter than the standard Basser. Value range: $50.00 to $75.00.

Here is a No. 8400 Plunking Basser beside the larger standard No. 8500 Basser. Note that No. 8400 Plunking Bassers have only two treble hooks.

This is the No. 8520 Deluxe Salmon Basser in Allen Stripey finish. Note the pull-away wire hook hanger that was made for large, toothy fish. The hooks were held tightly to the body until a fish struck. Value range: $50.00 to $75.00.

The single-hook Deluxe Salmon Basser, No. 8510, featured a large, strong hook mounted onto a wire belly clip. This 1930s lure has a value range of $50.00 to $75.00. With box, $100.00.

The No. 8540 King Basser is 4½" long and features pull-away string hardware on the belly. These lures were mainly used to troll for salmon. Value range: $40.00 to $75.00.

The No. 8560 King Basser was 6" long and more than 1" in diameter. It was a trolling bait for big salmon. Value range: $50.00 to $75.00. With box, $100.00.

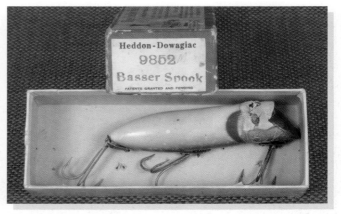

The No. 9850 Basser Spook was an early plastic lure, many of which have decomposed due to the instabilities of early plastics. It also came in a No. 9840 Basser Spook Junior, a two-hook model. Value range: $20.00 to $40.00. With box, $50.00.

This No. 9850 Basser Spook is in Heddon's "Fish Flesh" box introduced in 1932 for their new plastic lures. Value range: $20.00 to $40.00. With box, $75.00.

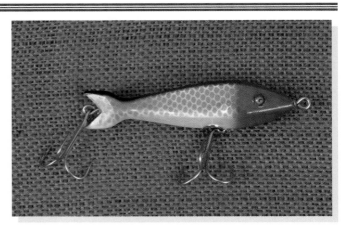

This is the No. 600 "Big Joe" saltwater special lure, circa 1924. Value range: $50.00 to $75.00.

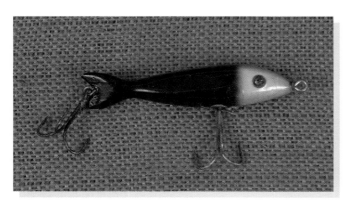

This No. 600 "Big Joe" is black with a blended white head. Value range: $50.00 to $75.00.

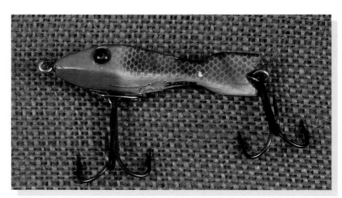

This is the No. 500 "Little Joe" bait with a beautiful carved wooden tail. The color, red head and perch scale, is unusual for this lure. Note the two-piece hardware, dating this bait into the 1930s. Value range $50.00 to $75.00.

This No. 500 "Little Joe" is finished in pearl paint with a hint of red around the eyes. Value range: $50.00 to $75.00.

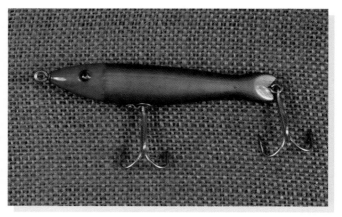

This is the No. 800 "Big Mary" saltwater special finished in gold with a red head. Value range: $75.00 to $100.00.

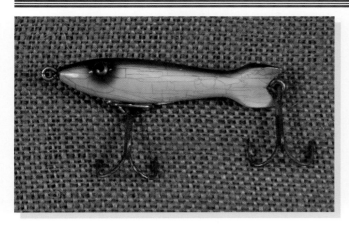

The No. 850 "Little Mary" saltwater special is slightly smaller. This example has two-piece hardware and glass eyes. Value range: $50.00 to $75.00.

Here is a No. 850 Little Mary in blue pearl x-ray finish, dating this lure to the 1930s. Value range: $100.00 to $125.00.

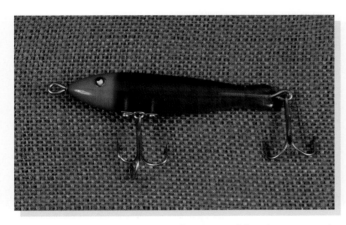

The Sea Spook No. 9800 was a pyralin version of the saltwater special, circa 1930s. Value range: $75.00 to $100.00.

Here are two Florida Special lures — a No. 10-B on top and a No. 10-S at bottom. Note the nose propeller, hexagonal shape, and hand-painted gills, circa 1921. Value range: $125.00 to $175.00.

This is the No. 580 "Wee Willie" saltwater special, an uncatalogued bait. This one is in blue pearl x-ray finish. Value range: $50.00 to $100.00.

Measuring barely over 2", the No. 580 "Wee Willie" came loaded with two large belly-weights. This black with white head example also has an orange stripe down its back. Value range: $50.00 to $100.00.

The No. 580 "Wee Willie" also came in a salt flash with yellow head finish, circa 1925. Value range: $75.00 to $100.00.

This fat-bodied No. 140 Flipper is packaged in a special order box labeled 1809D Special, perhaps because the extra large lure was made from a Crab Wiggler (No. 1800) body. Value range: $150.00 to $250.00. With box, $300.00.

This rainbow No. 140 Flipper, circa 1927 – 1928, has a value range of $75.00 to $100.00.

This stunning red head frog scale No. 140 Flipper is from the 1920s. Value range: $100.00 to $150.00.

This Depression-era bait is a Heddon Stanley Style No. 100 Dowagiac. The round body is believed to be from a Baby Vamp. The extra large, 5⁄16″ cups are for Musky Vamp lures, and the props are marked Stanley. Dating to around 1929, it has a value range of $70.00 to $150.00.

The No. 5100 Tadpolly, known to collectors as the "Tadpolly Runt," dates to around 1938. It is rarer than other Tadpolly lures and has a value range of $100.00 to $150.00.

The No. 5100 Tadpolly also can be found in black with white head. Value range: $100.00 to $150.00.

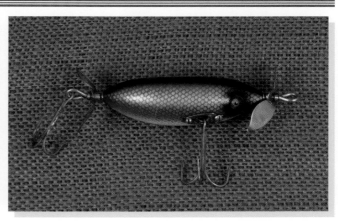

The No. 140 SOS Wounded Minnow is the smallest version of this common lure, circa 1928. The color is called dace. Value range: $30.00 to $50.00.

The No. 160 SOS dates to the 1920s and was made to "Swim On Side," hence the name. Value range: $30.00 to $50.00. With box, $75.00 to $100.00.

The No. 170 SOS is the largest of the standard bass sizes for this lure. This color is redhead/pickerel finish. Value range: $100.00 to $150.00.

This rare No. 370 Musky SOS in its original, early white-bordered box. The paint finish on this huge lure is black sucker. Value range: $250.00 to $300.00. With box, $450.00+.

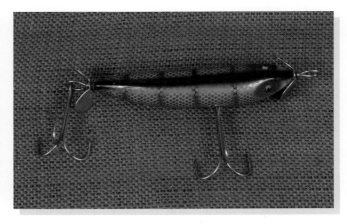

Here is another No. 370 Musky SOS in pike scale. Value range: $250.00 to $300.00.

The No. 130 Torpedo and its smaller counterpart, the No. 120 Torpedo, date to 1925 and have a value range of $50.00 to $150.00. These examples are in Heddon's "saltwater" color, referred to in catalogs as white with flitter.

This No. 130 Torpedo is in a unique finish: black with red nose and tail. This uncatalogued lure dates to the mid 1920s. Value range: $100.00 to $300.00.

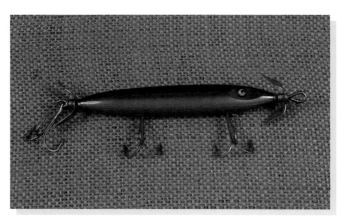

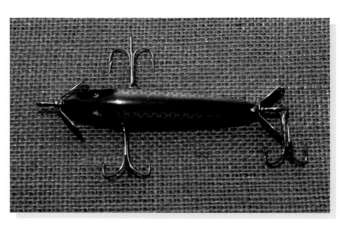

This No. 130 Torpedo is in eel finish, a color not often found. Value range: $100.00 to $300.00.

This No. 120 Torpedo has side hooks and marked Stanley props. The color is Shiner Scale. Value range: $75.00 to $100.00.

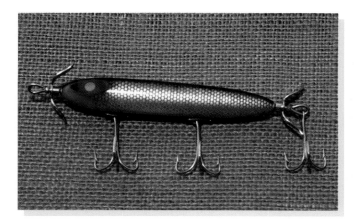

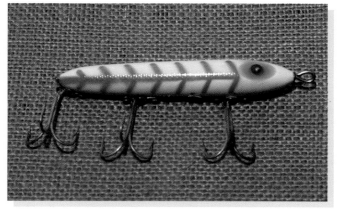

This No. 130 Torpedo in dace finish came from the factory archives and was never drilled for eyes, which are simply painted on. It is too unique to value.

This is the No. 30 Saltwater Torpedo, a later version, circa 1947. It has glass eyes but no propellers. Value range: $40.00 to $70.00.

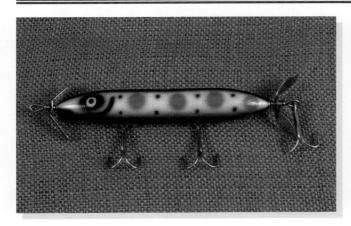

This is the No. 9170 Musky Surface Spook, a very long, plastic lure related to the Torpedo baits. Value range: $200.00 to $300.00.

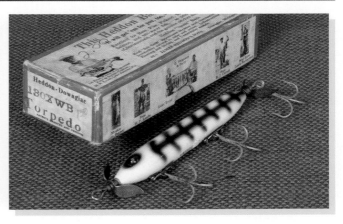

This No. 130 Torpedo is painted in a shore finish more reminiscent of the saltwater torpedoes and the plastic baits of the era. The XBW on the box stands for black and white shore. Value range: $50.00 to $75.00. With box, $100.00.

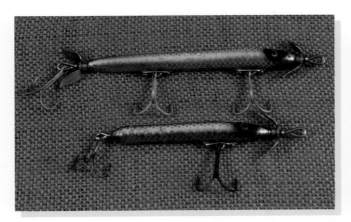

This is a No. 9130 Torpedo Spook accompanied by its uncatalogued smaller brother, the Baby Torpedo Spook. Both baits are early plastic versions. Each has glass eyes and two-piece hardware. Value range: $50.00 to $100.00.

The No. 220 Weedless Wizard was introduced in 1928. Later that year, its name was changed to the Weedless Widow, which remained in the Heddon line many years. This paint finish is Luny Frog. Value range: $25.00 to $50.00.

This No. 220 is in yellow shore finish with a red eye mask. Value range $25.00 to $50.00.

This redhead/shiner scale No. 220 Weedless Wizard has an unusual "mask" around its painted eyes. Value range: $25.00 to $50.00.

This silver shore No. 220 has a value range of $25.00 to $50.00.

The No. 70 Drewco lure was a wooden pier bait, circa 1934, used for saltwater fishing. This example is white with yellow head. Value range: $50.00 to $75.00.

The No. 8300 Zig-Wag lure was new in 1928 and was accompanied by a special cardboard hang tag. This example is in Heddon's Luny Frog finish, which was new that year. Value range: $50.00 to $75.00; with box, $100.00.

The No. 8300 Zig-Wag is in wonderful green crackleback with a red head. Note the black eye shadow on this three-hook version. Value range: $50.00 to $75.00.

The No. 8300 Zig-Wag is painted black with a red head. Value range: $50.00 to $75.00.

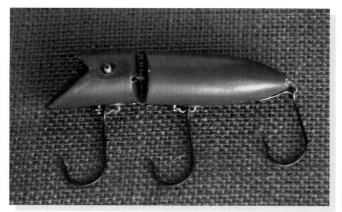

This rare all-red Zig-Wag is from the Heddon factory archives collection. Notice the single hooks. Value range: $50.00 to $75.00.

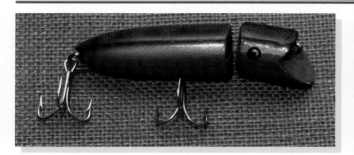

The No. 8300 Zig-Wag also was made in a two-hook configuration, seen here on a lure finished in silver herring. Value range: $50.00 to $75.00.

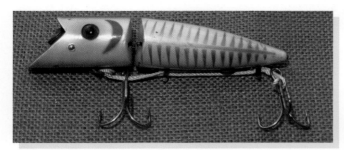

The No. 8360 King Zig-Wag was popular for salmon. Measuring almoost 6", the lure has a value range of $50.00 to $75.00.

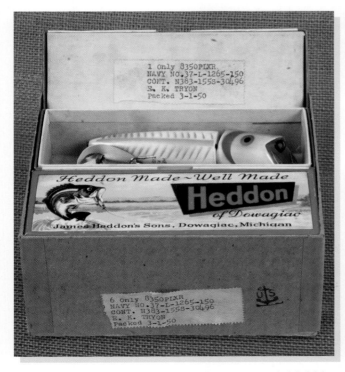

The No. 8350 King Zig-Wag was sold by the Tryon Co. of Philadelphia to the U.S. Navy for use in survival kits in the 1950s. This is a six-pack of specially packaged baits for the Navy. Value range: $75.00 to $100.00 each, including the box.

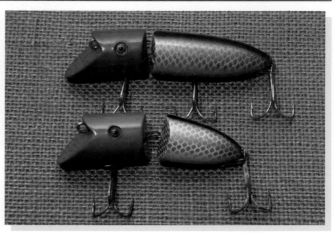

The No. 8340 Zig-Wag Junior was a slightly smaller version of the popular bait. The two lures are seen side-by-side for comparison. Both are in redhead/shiner scale finish. Value range: $50.00 to $75.00.

This No. 8350 King Zig-Wag is slightly smaller than the No. 8360 and also was used for salmon and other large fish. The color is yellow scale. Value range: $50.00 to $75.00.

The No. 3500 Luny Frog, new in 1927, was made of pyralin, a ceramic-like material. The color also was called Luny Frog. This is a Heddon Classic. Value range: $50.00 to $75.00.

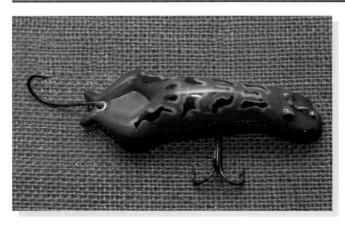

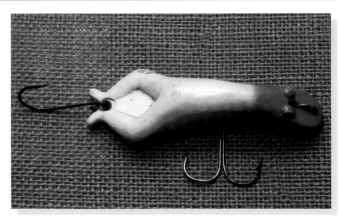

A closed-leg version of the No. 3500 Luny Frog also was made. Note the enclosed webbing between the rear legs, apparently to add strength. Value range: $50.00 to $75.00.

The red and white No. 3500 Luny Frog is rare due to its color. Value range: $150.00 to $200.00.

The No. 3400 Baby Luny Frog was a smaller version of its classic brother. Value range: $50.00 to $75.00; with box, $100.00 to $125.00.

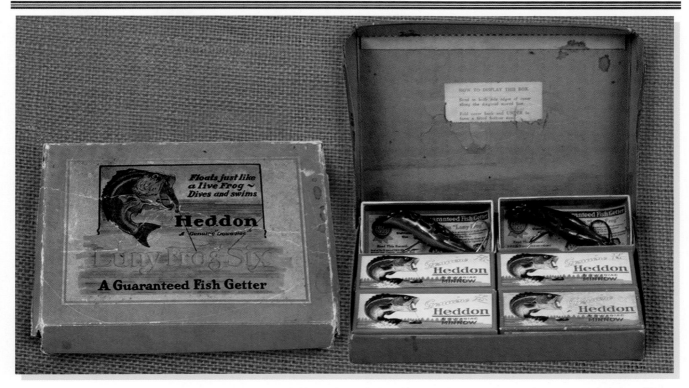

The Luny Frog came packaged in special "six-pack" cartons holding individually boxed lures. Value range for complete carton with six boxed lures: $1,000.00+.

The No. 3200 Spoon-Y Frog was new in 1927 and was a frog-shaped metal bait available in many finishes, including red and white. Value range: $25.00 to $50.00.

No. 3200 Spoon-Y Frog lures also were offered in a special presentation box holding six lures. Value range for entire package, with lures: $500.00+.

The No. 1000 Triple Teazer featured three metal minnows swimming together, along with a weedless attachment and dressed tail hook. New in 1929, it has a value range of $25.00 to $50.00; with box, $75.00.

This is the rare gold finish version of the No. 1000 Triple Teazer. Note the gold-plated fish and the matching gold tail hackle. Value range: $25.00 to $50.00.

The No. 9000 Shrimpy Spook is a wonderful pyralin saltwater lure introduced in 1930. Note the tiny bead eyes and lifelike whiskers which are often missing from these lures. This lure has toilet seat hardware. Value range: $50.00 to $75.00.

The No. 110 River Runt and its many variations and successors are among Heddon's most popular and long-lived lures. This early wooden model, dating to 1929, is pearl with red eyes. Value range: $50.00 to $75.00.

This all-red No. 110 River Runt has two-piece hardware, dating it to the 1930s. Value range: $50.00 to $75.00.

The No. L-10 Laguna Runt was similar to the No. 110 River Runt but made without a diving lip. This lure dates to the 1930s. Value range: $25.00 to $50.00.

This all-white No. L-10 Laguna Runt has black eyes with a red dot in the center. These eyes normally are found on Heddon's mouse flock lures, such as the Flaptail and Crazy Crawler. Value range: $50.00 to $75.00.

This is a later No. 610 Sea Runt with painted eyes and surface rig hardware. It is from the 1940s. Value range: $25.00 to $50.00.

The Heddon No. 610 Sea Runt has a belly-weight to make it sink. This glass-eyed version dates to the 1930s and is pearl with pink spots. Value range: $50.00 to $75.00.

The No. 4000 Meadow Mouse was new in 1929. Earliest models such as the one shown here have L-rig hardware and a narrow, marked diving lip. Value range: $25.00 to $50.00.

These No. 4000 series Meadow Mouse lures are both in black and white finish. Note the reversed diving lip on the lower lure, making it an uncatalogued color version of the "Munk Mouse" discussed below. Value range: $25.00 to $50.00.

The F-42 "Munk Mouse" version of the Meadow Mouse, circa 1941, was made to look like a chipmunk. Note the reversed diving lip in the chin. Value range: $50.00 to $75.00.

Here is another variation of the Munk Mouse. Note the reversed Crab Wiggler lip. Value range $50.00 to $75.00.

This very scarce No. 260 Surface Minny bait was only catalogued for 1934 and 1935 and has only been found in two-piece hardware. It came in four different colors. Value range: $100.00 to $150.00; with box, $200.00.

The 1934 Heddon catalog says that this No. 260 Surface Minny top-water floating spinner bait "kicks up a lively fuss." The bait shown here is finished in beautiful red and white. Value range: $100.00 to $150.00.

The No. 2160 Sam Spoon is from the 1930s and was extra heavy for large fish. Offered with a treble or single hook, the example shown here is in Allen Stripey finish and has a value range of $50.00 to $75.00, with the box.

The No. 2160 Sam Spoon also came in a red and white enamel painted finish. Value range: $25.00 to $50.00.

The No. 490 Spoon-Y Fish was new in 1930 and came in three sizes. The example shown here is painted in shiner scale. Value range: $25.00 to $50.00.

The No. 6600 Darting Zara was new in 1933. The oldest models have L-rig hardware and glass eyes, such as this strawberry spot version. Value range: $100.00 to $150.00.

This spotted No. 6600 Darting Zara has a paint job similar to the Creek Chub Darter and a body strikingly similar to the competitor's lure as well. This L-rig version has a small tack in the notch of the mouth and is marked "Second." Value range: $100.00 to $150.00.

The No. 195 Yowser is a metal bait dating to 1935. It is hard to find. Value range: $75.00 to $100.00; with box, $125.00.

The No. 195 Yowser was made in several colors and styles. These lures resemble Al Foss products of the same era. Value range: $75.00 to $100.00.

The No. 520 Shark Mouth Minnow dates to 1935 and is aptly named. Made of heavily painted metal. Value range: $75.00 to $100.00; with box, $125.00.

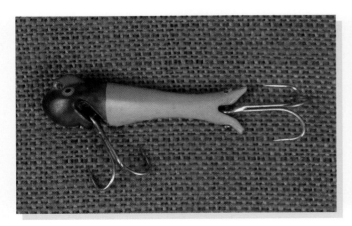

The Shark Mouth Minnow No. 520 also was made in yellow with red head. Because the bodies are painted metal, finding them in perfect condition is a challenge. Value range: $75.00 to $100.00.

This No. 520 Shark Mouth Minnow is in strawberry finish. Value range: $75.00 to $100.00.

This is the No. 510 Metal Minn lure. The all-metal version of the Saltwater Special has painted eyes and two-piece hardware. It dates to 1934. Value range: $75.00 to $100.00.

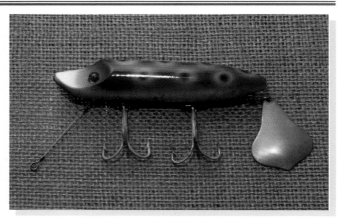

The No. 7000 Flaptail dates to 1935. Most have two-piece hardware, glass eyes, and a wire line leader attachment. This is a frogspot version. Value range: $50.00 to $75.00.

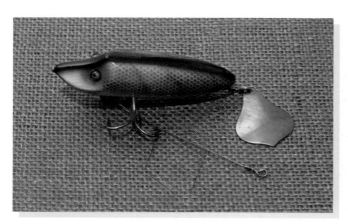

The No. 7110 Flaptail Junior came out in 1935. This version in perch scale has glass eyes and only one treble hook. Value range: $50.00 to $75.00.

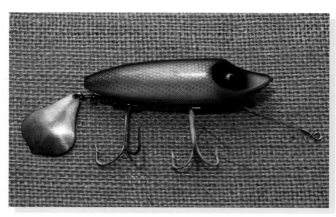

This No. 7110 Flaptail Junior has two treble hooks. The color is dace. Value range: $50.00 to $75.00.

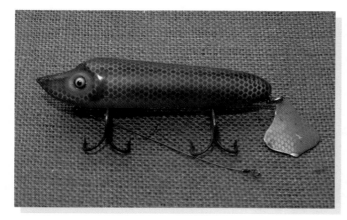

This No. 7050 Flaptail Musky is unusual, with a copper scale finish and a scale finish flapper at the tail. This is likely a special order bait and cannot be valued.

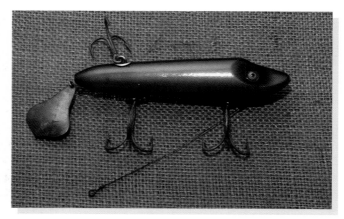

This is a No. 7050 Flaptail Musky with a factory-added treble at the top of the tail. The purpose of this feature is uncertain. The rarely-seen color is copper sheen. Value range: $75.00 to $150.00.

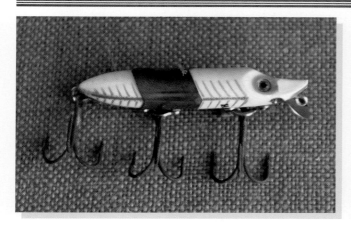

This KF 9750 King-Fish Vamp Spook is in white shore finish with the typical reflector band. Value range: $25.00 to $50.00.

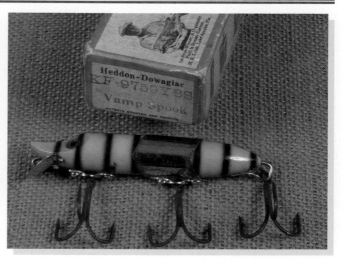

This is a No. KF 9750 King-Fish Vamp Spook dating to 1934. The bumblebee color is rare. The saltwater bait has a reflector jacket encircling the middle of the bait to "center the strike." Value range: $50.00 to $75.00; with box, $100.00.

The No. 9750 Vamp Spook, first offered in 1934, is the plastic successor to the popular wooden Vamp lures. This example in dace finish has a value of $25.00 to $50.00; with box, $75.00.

This No. 9750 Vamp Spook has a plastic diving lip. Value range: $25.00 to $50.00.

This No. 9750 Vamp Spook in pike scale is in its original "Fish Flesh" box with the foil insert on the bottom. Value range: $25.00 to $50.00; with box, $75.00.

The No. 9730 Jointed Vamp Spook came in many colors, including plain white. Value range: $25.00 to $50.00.

The No. 280 Stanley Queen lure appeared in 1927. This example is painted in shiner scale finish, but they are often found in nickel or gold plated. Value range: $25.00 to $35.00; with box, $50.00.

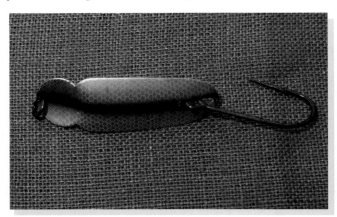

The No. 390 Stanley Silver King is the largest of the Stanley spoon baits. This one is in shiner scale finish and has a value range of $25.00 to $50.00.

The No. 730 Punkinseed is a wooden bait from the 1940s. Earliest models have the line tie in the chin or the mouth. Later models have the line tie only in the notch of the mouth. Punkinseeds also are commonly found in plastic as well. This lure is in shad finish. Value range for older models: $75.00 to $125.00.

The Stanley lures came in several sizes and some unusual paint finishes. They were advertised as "the only solid metal bodied bait with a full wooden minnow action." Various sizes included the No. 190 Ace (left); the No. 280 Queen (other lures in this photo), and the largest, the No. 390 Stanley Silver King. Value range: $25.00 to $35.00.

The No. 740 Punkinseed dates to 1940. The earliest models are wooden, have the line tie in the chin, and are fitted with two-piece hardware. This lure is in red and white shore minnow finish. Value range: $75.00 to $125.00.

The No. 7510 Giant River Runt was a big salmon bait introduced in 1938. Note the large "teddy bear" glass eyes. The color is Allen Stripey. Value range: $150.00 to $200.00.

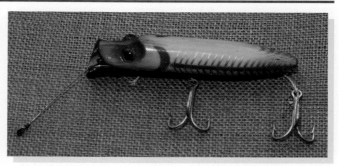

The diving lip on this unusual green No. 8850 Salmon River Runt is listed as "special" in the catalog and resembles a shoehorn. The huge fat lure is 5" long. Value range: $50.00 to $75.00.

The fat, 5" No. 8850 Salmon River Runt is a wooden bait with "teddy bear" glass eyes and belly-rigged string hardware. It has a Vamp-type lip and a yellow scale finish. Value range: $50.00 to $75.00.

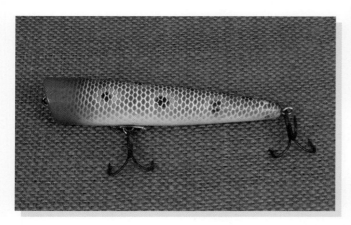

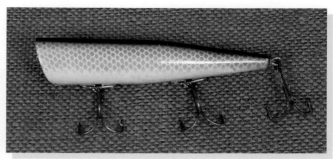

This uncatalogued giant Chugger-type bait is in shiner scale and has two-piece hardware from the 1930s. This example has three trebles instead of two. Value range: $200.00 to $300.00.

This uncatalogued, giant wooden Chugger type lure is finished in red-head and frog scale paint. It is from the two-piece hardware era, dating it to the 1930s. It remains somewhat of a mystery to collectors and has a value range of $200.00 to $300.00.

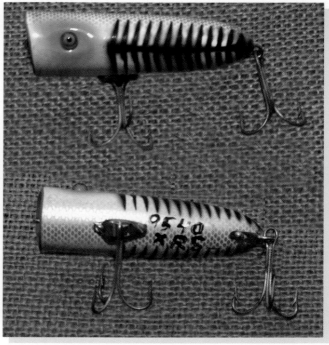

This is the first No. 9540 Chugger, a wooden lure with two-piece hardware. It dates to 1938 and has two-piece hardware. Value range: $75.00 to $100.00.

This wooden factory prototype for the No. 9540 Chugger has two-piece hardware and glass eyes. It is too rare to value.

The No. 9540 Chugger was reissued with other Heddon classics in the 1960s. Although most of the reissued lures are common, the nail-on glass-eyed Chugger sold with the others is rather hard to find. Value range: $25.00 to $50.00.

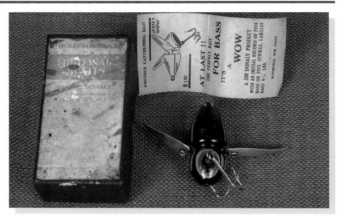

Heddon's Crazy Crawler lures were inspired by Jim Donaly's "Wow" lures from New Jersey. Donaly received a patent for his bait in 1928. He died in 1935 and his wife and daughter ran his factory briefly before the operation was sold to Heddon.

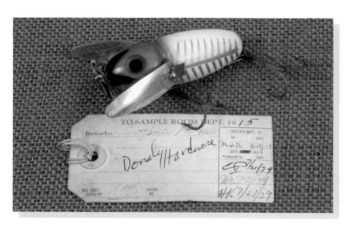

This early Heddon Crazy Crawler from the Pflueger factory sample room has a tag dated 1939, which notes that the lure has Donaly hardware. Value range: $25.00 to $50.00.

The No. 2100 Crazy Crawler, advertised as new in 1940, is found with two-piece or surface rig hook hangers and was made for many years, beginning in the late 1930s. These two early examples are in black shore finish and have the unusual white eyes. Value range: $50.00 to $75.00.

This is the bug-eyed variation of the No. 2100 Crazy Crawler. Value range: $25.00 to $50.00.

This No. 2120 small-sized Crazy Crawler has the cone-shaped tail found on some models. Value range: $25.00 to $50.00.

This No. 2120 Crazy Crawler in black shore finish has the "mask" on its head and is in the correctly marked box. Value range: $50.00 to $75.00.

These three Crazy Crawler lures include the 2120, the 2100, and the 2150 Crazy Crawlers, all in Chipmunk and in original correct boxes. Value range: $125.00 to $150.00; with box, $200.00+.

This No. 2150 Musky Crazy Crawler is in red and white finish and has the Donaly hardware attaching the wings. Value range: $75.00 to $125.00.

This No. 2150 Musky Crazy Crawler has standard Heddon hardware attaching the wings. The unusual redhead and silver scale/silver shore finish is uncatalogued. Value range: $100.00 to $150.00.

The No. 310 Tiny Spook is from the late '50s and early '60s. Value range: $5.00 to $10.00.

The No. 9250-1 RESEARCH Zara Spook is a plastic lure from the 1950s. Note the unusual colors. These are great lures to collect and to fish with. Value range: $20.00 to $50.00.

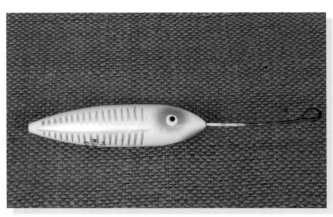

The No. 9149L Wounded Spook is a circa 1939 plastic lure with two-piece hardware in the older Brush box. Value range: $25.00 to $50.00.

This paint stick for a Wounded Spook lure was used at the Heddon factory in Dowagiac.

The No. 440 series Saint Spinner is from the 1952 and has a value range of $10.00 to $20.00 in the box. Note the strawberry paint finish.

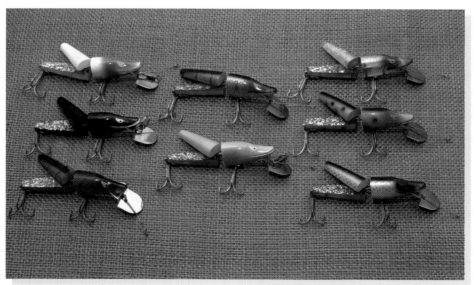

The No. 9830 Heddon Scissortail lures were introduced in 1953 and are popular among collectors of Heddon plastic. The solid plastic lures came in at least eight wonderful colors. Value range: $15.00 to $35.00.

These later plastic lures include the No. 9000 Tadpolly Spook, Tiny Tad, Clatter Tad, and Magnum Tadpolly. These common lures are from the 1950s and many are still being fished with. Value range: $5.00 to $20.00.

These are Tadpolly Spook salesman's samples, complete with factory numbers on the belly, in some unusual colors.
They have never been outfitted with hooks.

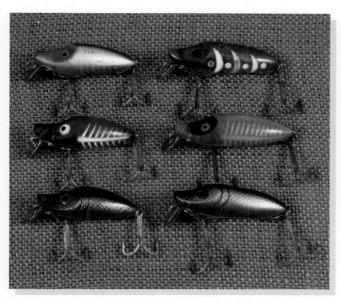

These plastic No. 9110 River Runt Spooks are from the 1950s and come in a variety of interesting colors. Value range: $5.00 to $20.00 each.

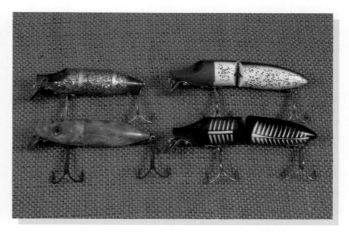

This frame includes a pair of River Runt Spook Floaters, No. 9400; and a pair Jointed River Runt Floaters, No. 9430. Value range: $5 to $20.00 apiece.

This frame includes two No. D-9110 Go-Deeper River Runt lures with long diving lips; and a pair of No. D-9330 Jointed Deep Diving River Runt Spook Sinkers. These plastic lures are from the 1950s. Value range: $5.00 to $20.00.

Here we have a wooden No. B110 Midget Digit (center left, black with white head) and two plastic No. 9020 Midget Digits; and a trio of D-9010 Midget Go-Deeper River Runt Spooks. Value range: $5.00 to $25.00 each.

These four lures are circa 1950s No-Snag River Runt Spook lures, No. N9110, in various colors. Note the weedless attachment on the note. Value range: $10.00 to $20.00 each.

The top and bottom lures are No. 9330 Jointed River Runt Spook Sinkers; and three of the four baits in the center are various examples of the No. 340 Tiny Runt. The white shore lure on the right is a No. D-350 Tiny Go-Deeper Runt. All are from the 1950s and have a value range of $5.00 to $20.00 each.

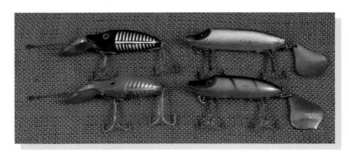

On the left are two scoop-lipped D9110 Go-Deeper River Runt Spook lures; to the right are a pair of No. 9700 Flaptail Spook Junior lures. Value range: $10.00 to $25.00 each.

These are circa 1930s pyralin No. 9100 Super Dowagiac Spook lures with glass eyes. Value range: $25.00 to $50.00 each.

This assortment of Vamp Spook lures includes a pair of earliest No. 9500 glass-eyed versions with the plastic diving lip (top left and right); and a jointed (No. 9730) and two non-jointed (No. 9750) versions of the plastic Vamp Spook. Value range: $25.00 to $50.00 for the glass-eye models; $10.00 to $15.00 for the others.

Here are three No. 9540 Chugger Spook lures and one No. 9520 Chugger Spook Junior from the 1950s. They have a value range of $10.00 to $15.00 each.

This circa 1950s salesman's sample board includes a No. 350 Tiny Runt; No. 360 Tiny Torpedo; No. 370 Tiny Lucky 13; D350 Go-Deeper Tiny Runt; No. 390 Tiny Tadpolly Spook; No. 9000 Tadpolly Spook; and No. 9540 Chugger Spook. Value range: $5.00 to $20.00 each.

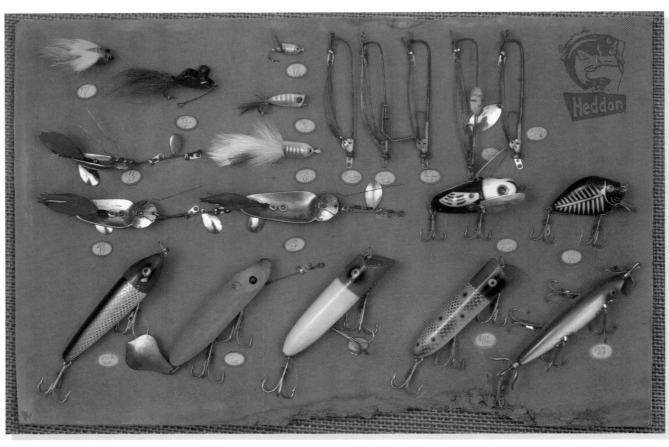

Here's another 1950s salesman's sample board. The contents include a No. 975 Bass Bug Spook; a No. 85 Popeye Frog; a No. 910 trout-sized Wilder-Dilg Spook; a No. 940 Popper Spook; and a No. 930 Wilder-Dilg Spook; five versions of the Heddon Stanley Weedless Hook; a No. 280 nickel Queen Stanley; a No. 190 nickel Ace Stanley; a No. 290 gold Queen Stanley; a No. 2120 Crazy Crawler; a No. 730 Punkinseed; a No. 6500 Zaragossa; a No. 7000 Flaptail Mouse; a No. 2500 Lucky 13; another No. 2500 Lucky 13; and a No. 150 Dowagiac Underwater Minnow.

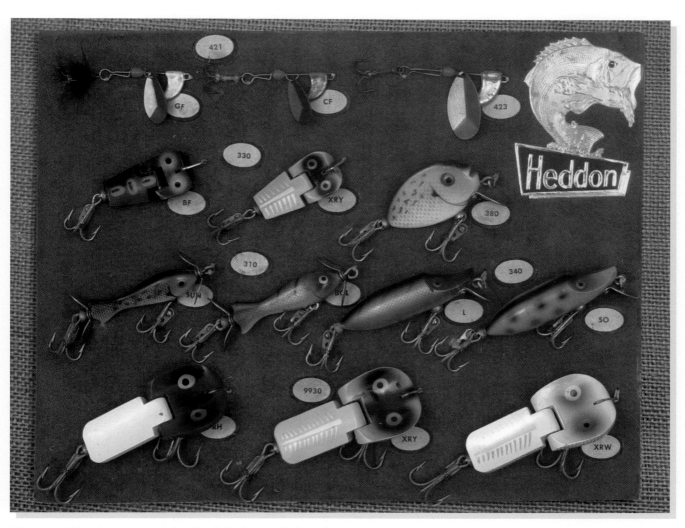

This circa 1950s salesman's sample board includes three marked Gamby spinners; two No. 330 Tiny Stingaree lures; a No. 380 Tiny Punkinseed Spook; two No. 310 fish-shaped Tiny Spooks; two No. 340 Tiny Floating Runt Spooks; and three large-sized No. 9930 Stingaree lures.

Another salesman's sample board from the 1950s includes a No. 9020 Midget Digit; No. 9010 Midget River Runt Spook Sinker; No. 9110 River Runt Spook Sinker; No. 9400 Floating River Runt Spook; No. 110 River Runt; No. D9010 Midget Go-Deeper River Runt; No. D9110 Go-Deeper Standard River Runt; No. 9330 Jointed Sinking River Runt Spook; No. 9430 Floating Jointed River Runt Spook; No. 9140 Wounded Spook; No. 9540 Chugger Spook; No. 210 Super Surface; No. 9100 Dowagiac Spook; No. 7500 Vamp; No. 9750 Vamp Spook; No. 7300 Jointed Vamp; No. 9260 Zara Spook; and No. 130 Torpedo.

Heddon Color Codes

Code	Color	Code	Color
0	Black sucker	2LUM	White luminous body; red eyes and tail
0	Fancy green back; white belly	2M	White body; red gills
0	White	2RET	White body; red eyes and tail
0	White body; green and red spots	2RH	White body; red head
0	White body; red head and tail	8RH	White body; gold speckled; red head
0	White body; red, green, and black spots	9A	Yellow perch
0	Green crackleback	9B	Green frog
0LUM	Luminous	9BB	Meadow frog (brown)
1	Rainbow	9BF	Bull frog
1	Yellow body; green and red spots	9BK	Brook trout
1	Yellow body; red, green, and black spots	9BP	Blue pearl
2	Fancy sienna yellow	9BW	Black and white
2	White	9BWH	Black body; white head
2	White body; red eyes; slate back	9C	Imitation crab
2	White body; red top	9COP	Copper sheen
2	White; red head	9D	Green scale
2	White; red eyes and tail	9DRH	Green scale; red head
3	Aluminum	9E	White body; greenish black spots
3	Fancy green back; white belly	9F	Yellow body; black head
4	All red	9G	Black body; orange tail
4	Blended red	9G	Solid black
4	Bright red body; dark green back	9GC	Green crab
5	Fancy green back; white belly	9GRHT	Black body; red head and tail
5	Yellow	9GW	Glow-worm (luminous)
5	Yellow; red and green spots	9GWH	Black; white head
6	Gold	9H	Red scale
6	Rainbow	9J	Frog scale
7	Fancy sienna	9JRH	Frog scale; red head
7	White body; slate colored back	9K	Gold fish scale
8	White body; gold flitter	9L	Yellow perch scale
9	White body; silver flitter	9LC	Luminous crab
_____	Black, crackled back; white belly	9LD	Light green scale
_____	Plain green back; white belly	9LUM	Luminous
_____	Red body; black spots	9M	Pike scale
_____	Yellow body; brown and red spots	9M	Pike scale; green and yellow tail
_____	Yellow body; fancy mottled back	9MRH	Pike scale; red head
_____	Yellow body; green and black spots	9N	Red dace scale
02XS	White and red shore minnow	9NC	Natural crab
0S	White; red and green spots	9P	Shiner scale

Code	Color
9P	Shiner scale; gray tail
9PAS	Allen stripey
9PBH	Blue herring
9PG	Golden shiner
9PL	Pearl
9PLB	Blue pearl
9PLXB	Blue pearl shore minnow
9PLXR	Blue pearl x-ray shore minnow
9PRH	Shiner scale body; red head
9PRH	Shiner scale; red head
9PSRH	Spotted; red head
9R	Mullet scale
9R	Natural scale
9RB	Rainbow
9RH	White body; silver specks; red head
9RH	White; red head
9RHH	Silver flitter; red head
9RRH	Natural scale; red head
9SD	Shad
9SH	Silver herring
9SPRH	Spotted body; red head
9SS	Silver scale
9T	Dark green back; gold speckled
9V	Orange; black spots
9W	Solid white
9X	Blue scale
9XBW	Black and white shore minnow
9XGF	Greenfish shore minnow
9XRG	Green shore minnow
9XRS	Silver shore minnow
9XRW	Red and white shore minnow
9XRY	Yellow shore minnow
9XS	White and red shore minnow
9XS	White shore minnow
9XSK	Goldfish shore minnow
9Y	Solid yellow
9YBS	Yellow body; black stripes
9YF	Yellow body; flitter
9YRH	Yellow; red head
9YS	Yellow scale
9YXB	Yellow body; black bone
9Z	Purple back scale
B	Black
B	Brass
BB	Black
BF	Bull frog
BF	Copper without weed guard

Code	Color
BFW	Copper with weed guard
BGL	Bluegill
BH	White body; blue head
BM	Brown mouse
BR	Brown
BR	Brown body; wings and hackle
BSD	Blue shad
BW	Black and white
BWH	Black; white head
BY	Black and yellow
BYG	Yellow; gold plated minnows
CD	White; black spots
CF	Copper finish
CM	Chipmunk striped
CP	Copper plated
CR	Blue, yellow, red transparent
CRA	Crappie
DG	Dark green body and wings; black hackle
DG	Dark green body; green hackle
E-9110GB	Green and black water-wave everlasting
E-9110RW	Red and white water-wave everlasting
E-9110YB	Yellow and black water-wave everlasting
F	Nickel plate without weed guard
FR	Red ibis
GCB	Green crackle back
GC	Green crab
GF	Gold finish
GF	Green frog
GFB	Goldfish with black
GFR	Goldfish with red
GM	Gray mouse
GP	Gold plate
GR	All gray
GR	Gray body; wings and hackle
GW	Glow-worm (luminous)
GWR	Gold scale; red gills
L	Yellow perch scale
LC	Luminous crab
LUM	Luminous with red head
MG	Gold scale musky
N	Natural
NC	Natural crab
NP	Nickel plate
NPWR	Nickel plated; white and red
NS	Natural shrimp; transparent
P	Shiner scale
PCH	Perch

Code	Color	Code	Color
PRH	Shiner scale; red head	WB	White and black
R	Red body and wings; yellow hackle	WBC	Black and white crackleback
RB	Rainbow	WF	Nickel plate with weed guard
RH	White body; red head	WH	White head
ROB	Rock bass	WH	Walter Harden
S	Spotted	WR	White and red
S	Transparent; red and green spots	WR	White body and wings; red hackle
S	White; spotted body	XBW	Black and white shore minnow
SO	Orange body; red and black spots	XRS	Silver shore minnow
SD	Shad	XRW	Red and white shore minnow
SF	Silver flitter	XRY	Yellow shore minnow
SFB	Silverfish with black	XS	Red and white shore minnow
SFR	Silverfish with red	XWB	White and black shore minnow
SG	Silver and gray	Y	All yellow
SHA	Shad	YB	Yellow and black
SP	Sparkle	YF	Yellow frog
SRB	Silver; red and black spots	YRH	Yellow; red head
SS	Silver flitter	WILBOURNE'S SPECIAL	
SSD	Silver shad		Blended orange back; yellow body
SUN	Sunfish		

0	Dowagiac Minnow
00	Dowagiac Minnow
2	Dowagiac Minnow (4-hook slopenose)
L-10	Laguna River Runt
10B	Florida Special
10S	Florida Special
10	Light Casting Minnow
11	Light Casting Minnow
20	Dowagiac Minnow
30	Salt Water Torpedo
40	Westchester Bug Flyrod Bait
50	Artistic Minnow
50	Bass Bug – Bass Size
B50	Baby Bass Bug – Trout Size
70	Stanley Weedless Pork-rind Minnow
70	Drewco
74	Fuzzi-bug Trout Size
75	Fuzzi-bug Bass Size
80	Tiny Teaz Flyrod Bait
85	Pop-eye-frog Flyrod Bait
90	Bubbling Bug Flyrod Bait
100	Dowagiac Minnow
110	River Runt
110	Original River Runt Spook Sinking Model
B-110	Midgit Digit River Runt Sinking Model
120	Torpedo
130	Torpedo
140	Flipper
140	S.O.S. Wounded Minnow
150	Dowagiac Minnow
160	S.O.S. Wounded Minnow
170	S.O.S. Wounded Minnow
175	Dowagiac Heavy Casting Minnow
190	Heddon Stanley Ace
B190	Heddon Stanley Ace Bullet
195	Yowser Spinner Bait
200	Dowagiac Surface Lure
210	Super Surface Bait
220	Weedless Wizard or Weedless Widow
J220	Weedless Widow Junior
250	Dowagiac Minnow
260	Surface Minny
280	Heddon Stanley Queen
290	Heddon Stanley King
296	Musky King Stanley
300	Surface Minnow
300	Musky Surfsser
300	Widget Flyrod Bait
300	Top Sonic
310	Tiny Spook
320	Tiny Crazy Crawler
330	Tiny Stingaree
325	Ultra Sonic
335	Tiny Chugger Surface
340	Tiny Runt Floating
350	Tiny Runt Sinking
D350	Go-deeper Tiny Runt
350	Musky Surface
360	Tiny Torpedo
365	Baby Zara-spook
370	Tiny Lucky-13
370	Muskie S.O.S. Minnow
380	Tiny Punkinseed
382	Punkin Spin
385	Sonic Spook
390	Silver King Stanley Metal Bait
390	Tiny Tad
395	Fire Tail Sonic
400	Dowagiac Killer
400	Decoy Ice Minnow
400	Fidget
401	Fidget Flasher

402	Fidget Feather		710	Flap-tail Bug
402	Bucktail Surface Minnow		720	Flap-tail Bug
411	Spinfin		730	Punkinseed Sinking Model
412	Spinfin		740	Punkinseed Floater and Diver
413	Spinfin		750	River-runtie
420	Whis-purr Spinner		790	Spoonyfish Spoon
421	Gamby Spinner		800	Swimming Minnow
423	Gamby Spinner		800	Salt Water Special – Big Mary
425	Whis-purr Spinner		850	Swimming Minnow
431	Sonar		850	Salt Water Special – Little Mary
433	Sonar		900	Swimming Dowagiac Minnow
435	Sonar		910	Wilder-Dilg Bass Size
440	Saint Spinner		920	Wilder-Dilg Spook Bass Size
450	Dowagiac Killer		930	Wilder-Dilg Trout Size
451	Wag Spinning Lure		930	Wilder-Dilg Spook Trout Size
460	Hep Spinner		940	Popper Spook Flyrod Bait
461	Hep Spinner		950	River-runtie Spook Flyrod Bait
462	Hep Spinner		960	Bug-a-bee Spook Flyrod Bait
463	Hep Spinner		974	Bass-bug Spook Trout Size
464	Hep Spinner		975	Bass-bug Spook Bass Size
470	Fin-jig		980	Punkinseed Spook Flyrod
490	Spoonyfish Spoon		980	Punkie Spook
500	Multiple Metal Minnow		1000	Night-radiant Moonlight Bait
500	Salt Water Special		1000	Triple Teazer
510	Metal-minn		1001	Heddon "Woodpecker" Type Bait
520	Shark-mouth Minn		1010	Tiger
550	Float-hi Bug Flyrod Bait		1020	Tiger
580	Wee Willie		1030	Tiger
590	Spoonyfish Spoon		1130	NPWR "Slick-trick" Casting Spoon
600	Salt Water Special		1190	Devil Ace
610	Sea Runt		1280	Devil Queen
610	Coast Minnow No. 3		1290	Devil King
620	Coast Minnow No. 2		1291	Devil King
630	Coast Minnow No. 1		1300	Black Sucker Minnow
640	Coast Minnow No. 4		1400	Single Hook Minnow
700	Dowagiac Musky Minnow		1500	Dummy Double

1600	Deep Diving Wiggler	7050	Giant Flap-tail
1700	Near Surface Wiggler	7110	Flap-tail Junior
1800	Crab Wiggler	7300	Jointed Vamp
1900	Baby Crab Wiggler	7350	Giant Jointed Vamp
D1900	Go-deeper Crab	7400	Baby Vamp
1950	Midget Crab Wiggler	7500	Vamp
2000	Wiggle King	7510	Giant River Runt
2100	Crazy Crawler	7540	Great Vamp
2120	Crazy Crawler	7550	Musky Vamp
2150	Crazy Crawler Musky	7600	Musky Vamp
2160	Sam Spoon	7725	Cousin 1 Spook
2200	Slant Head Lucky-13	8050	Crackleback Spook
2400	Lucky-13 Junior	8300	Zig-wag
2500	Lucky-13	8340	Zig-wag Junior
W2500	Wood Lucky-13 Re-issue bait	8350	King Zig-wag
3000	Spin-diver	8360	King Zig-wag
3200	Spoon-y Frog Metal Bait	8400	Plunking Basser
3400	Little Luny Frog	8500	Basser, Head-on Basser, Daddy Basser (Musky)
3500	Luny Frog	8510	Deluxe (Salmon) Basser (Single Hook)
4000	Meadow Mouse	8520	Deluxe (Salmon) Basser (Two Trebles)
F4000	Meadow Mouse (Fur Finish)	8540	King Basser
F4200	Munk-mouse (Fur Finish)	8550	King Basser
5000	Tad-polly	8560	King Basser
5100	Tad-polly Runt	8850	Salmon River Runt
5400	Baby Game Fisher	9000	Shrimpy-spook
5500	Game Fisher	9000	Tadpolly Spook
6000	Tad-polly	9010	Midget River Runt Spook Sinking Model
6500	Zaragossa and Musky Zaragossa	9020	Midgit Digit River Runt Spook
6600	Darting-zara	9100	Dowagiac Spook
7000	Flap-tail	9110	River Runt Spook Sinking Model
7000	Deep-o-diver	D-9010	Midget Go-deeper River Runt Spook
7000/7001	Dowagiac VL&A Mascallonge Minnow	D-9110	Go-deeper Standard River Runt Spook
7025	Prowler Spook	N-9110	No-snag River Runt Spook
7040	Husky Flap-tail	9120	Crazy Crawler Spook
7050	Prowler Spook	9130	Torpedo Spook Sinker
7050	Flap-tail Muskie	9140	Wounded Spook

9160	Wounded Spook		9500	Floating Vamp Spook (Pyralin)
9170	Musky Surface Spook		9520	Baby Chugger Spook
9200	Darting Zara-spook		9540	Chugger Spook
9200	Dying Quiver Spook		9600	Salt Spook (Pyralin)
9205	Dying Flutter		9630	Punkinseed Spook Sinking Model
9210	Darting Zara-spook		9700	Floating Flap-tail Spook Junior
9210	Darting Zara-spook With Tail Spinner		9730	Jointed Vamp Spook
9240	Zara-spook Junior		9750	Vamp Spook
9250	Zara-spook (2 hooks)		KF9750	King-fish Model Vamp Spook
9260	Zara-spook (3 hooks)		9800	Sea Spook
9330	Big Hedd Spook		9800	Meadow Mouse Spook
9330	Jointed Sinking River Runt Spook		9810	Salmon Basser Spook
9345	Deep 6		9830	Scissortail Spook
9385	Super Sonic		9840	Basser Spook Junior
9400	Floating River Runt Spook		9850	Basser Spook
S-9400	Silver Salmon Runt Spook		9900	Crab Spook
9430	Floating Jointed River Runt Spook		9930	Stingaree
D-9430	Jointed Go-deeper River Runt Spook		9930	Cobra

Heddon often used vivid illustrations to market the company's finely made fly rod baits, which also helped sell Heddon lines, flyreels and fly rods.

FAMOUS FLY ROD LURES

"Wilder Dilg Spook" ®
"Bass Bug Spook" ®
"Popper Spook" ®
"Flaptail Bug"
"Pop Eye Frog" ®

Heddon Fly Rod Lures

Heddon fly rod lures, like Heddon baits, are lures "that will catch fish." The "Wilder Dilg" lures, were designed by B. F. Wilder and Will Dilg, two world-famous anglers of a past generation — and are dear to hearts of oldtimers. Other famous anglers co-operated in designing more recent models, with the result that those illustrated on the following pages represent "America's Choice" in fly rod lures.

The adage that good things can emerge from small packages certainly holds true when it comes to Heddon's wonderful fly rod lures. From a specially built section of the brick factory in Dowagiac came some of the most beautiful wooden, cork and — in later years, plastic — fly rod baits to be found anywhere.

According to company history published in the last version of the James Heddon's Sons "Indoctrination Booklet" given to new employees and sales representatives, Heddon was one of the earliest and most important producers of fly rod lures, having begun production in 1922.

"Among the best-known were the Wilder-Dilg fly lures perfected by B.F. Wilder, of New York, and Will H. Dilg and christened after twelve of the country's foremost anglers. Included were such well known personages as Irvin Cobb, Zane Grey and Gifford Pinchot. Following World War II, the market for these lures was practically demoralized by the influx of extremely low-priced imports from Japan. They were dropped from the Heddon line in 1954."

The following pages will help recognize, date, and value the fly rod lures made by Heddon. Values given are for examples in excellent or near-excellent condition, including the hair and feathers.

This very rare fly rod Vamp is a factory prototype. Its uniqueness makes it impossible to value.

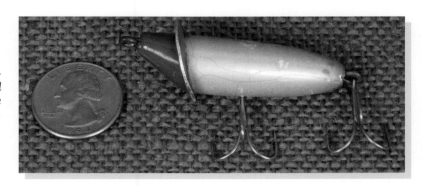

At some point in the company's lineage, this tiny fly rod-sized Slopenose or 200 Surface Bait was made and tested. This piece, also a factory prototype, cannot be valued.

The Zaragossa emerged in the 1920s. This tiny fly rod-sized Zaragossa likely dates to that period but was not produced commercially. Note the green scale finish and red chin blush. It is unique and impossible to value.

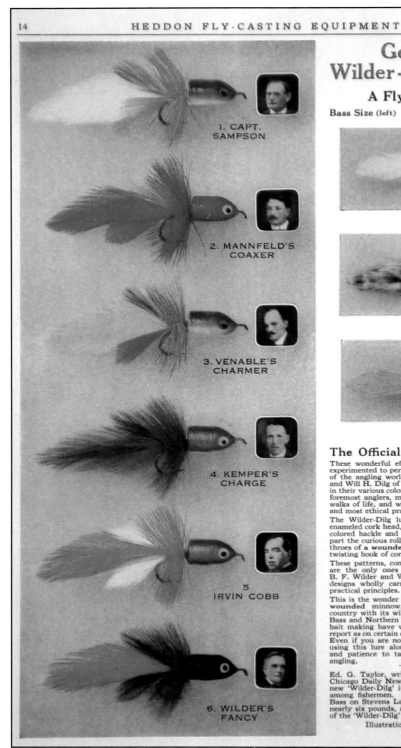

14   HEDDON FLY-CASTING EQUIPMENT

1. CAPT. SAMPSON

2. MANNFELD'S COAXER

3. VENABLE'S CHARMER

4. KEMPER'S CHARGE

5 IRVIN COBB

6. WILDER'S FANCY

Genuine Wilder-Dilg Lures

A Fly Rod Lure

Bass Size (left)   Trout Size (below)

No. 30, Irvin Cobb

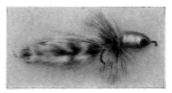

No. 31, Brann's Glory

No. 32, Wilder's Fancy

The Official Wilder-Dilg Lures

These wonderful effective new lures, successfully experimented to perfection by those two gentlemen of the angling world, B. F. Wilder of New York and Will H. Dilg of Chicago, have been christened, in their various colors, after twelve of the country's foremost anglers, men of national repute in other walks of life, and who stand for the highest ideals and most ethical practices in the Camp of Walton.

The Wilder-Dilg lure is made up from a light enameled cork head, brilliant eyes, a ruff of various colored hackle and fin-and-body-feathers that impart the curious rolling, dipping and depth-seeking throes of a wounded minnow, with a single non-twisting hook of correct size and shape.

These patterns, constructed and tied by Heddon, are the only ones authorized by the inventors, B. F. Wilder and Will H. Dilg, and are the only designs wholly carrying out their scientific and practical principles.

This is the wonder lure, imitating the action of a wounded minnow, that last year swept the country with its wildfire success in fly casting for Bass and Northern Pike. Never in our history of bait making have we received such unanimity of report as on certain qualities developed by this lure. Even if you are not a fly caster, the privilege of using this lure alone makes it worth your time and patience to take up this sporting phase of angling.

Ed. G. Taylor, writer of Woods and Waters in Chicago Daily News, writes us as follows: "This new 'Wilder-Dilg' is going to create a sensation among fishermen. I hooked a big Small-Mouth Bass on Stevens Lake, Wisconsin, which weighed nearly six pounds, also several others. I am sure of the 'Wilder-Dilg' Lure."

Illustrations nearly actual size.

Perhaps the most famous of Heddon's fly rod lures were the No. 910 and No. 930 Wilder-Dilg, made in an assortment of colors. Many were named in honor of the nation's foremost anglers. The most sought-after Heddon fly rod boxes are the rare "portrait" boxes with the anglers' faces adorning the boxtops.

The value for such boxes ranges from $150.00 to more than $400.00. The Wilder-Dilg lures were made in both a bass and trout size and were later made in plastic, under the "Spook" name.

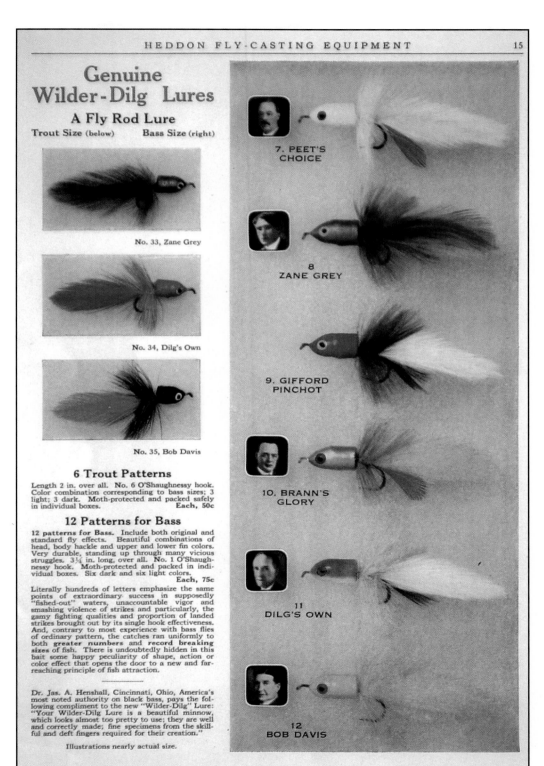

169

The No. 930 trout-sized Wilder-Dilg (above) and its bass-sized counterpart (below) are both new in the box. Value with box is $100.00 to $200.00.

Wilder-Dilg lures found with the spook finish will be made of plastic. Older cork-bodied versions, No. 910, are a little scarcer. Value: $15.00 to $40.00 for plastic versions; $20.00 to $50.00 for cork-bodied examples.

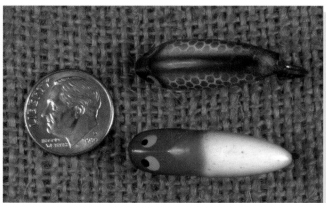

The No. 750 River Runtie (wooden and without a diving lip) and the No. 950 River Runtie Spook (plastic with a plastic diving lip) both were advertised as "new" in the 1937 catalog. Value range: $65.00 to $150.00. Unusual colors could be higher.

The No. 40 Westchester Bug is among Heddon's most handsome fly rod baits. This large lure is difficult to find in any condition. Value: $300.00 to $350.00.

Heddon's No. 80 Tiny Teaz lures are wooden and include a nicely countersunk cup in the belly to accept the recessed hook hanger. The lower lure is in a trout finish. These are hard to find and date to the 1920s. Value: $75.00 for common colors, up to $150.00 for the trout finish.

The No. 90 Bubbling Bug was a fat, noisy fly rod bait that could almost be cast with a regular rod and reel due to its size and weight. Most examples have a box swivel attachment at the line tie. These lures are from the 1920s and 1930s. Note the unusual bumble bee finish on the lower lure. They can be found with or without wings. Value range $150.00 to $200.00.

The New Heddon Bass Bugs

NO. 50
PEET'S FAVORITE

NO. 58
ST. JOHN'S PAL

NO. 54
BOB DAVIS

NO. 51
DILG'S GEM

NO. 59
CLARK'S FANCY

NO. 55
BUCKINGHAM'S GLORY

NO. 52
BRANN'S RANGER

NO. 60
WILDER'S FANCY

NO. 56
CHADWICK'S SUNBEAM

NO. 53
CARTER HARRISON

NO. 61
ALEX'S FRIEND

NO. 57
OZARK RIPLEY

The Bug with the Hackle   (Illustration ¾ actual size)

The new Heddon Bass Bug has solid cork body, a No. 1 Model Perfect Hook, with turned-down eye. Hook is firmly imbedded in the cork and tied securely, the whole body finished with Heddon's Superior Enamel. The wings, hackle and tail are securely tied. When in the water, the hackle spreads and serves to conceal the hook point. It also helps support the wings. Will light on the water in the proper position with the hook down.

For fish-getting qualities these Bass Bugs stand supreme, being personally endorsed by nationally known Fly Casters, for whom each of the twelve beautiful patterns is named.   **Each, 75c**

Mr. George M. A. Goetz, of New Palestine, Ind., writes on October 9, 1923, as follows: "I have just returned from my Kentucky fishing trip. Had a fine time. Your Bass Bug proved to be good. I caught bass with it. I tried it in the morning and at noon, and at night, and it is a good one. I fished all one day in the rain with this Bug and got six bass — one weighed 3½ lbs. They ride on the water as natural as a live fly."

The No. 50 Bass Bugs and their plastic counterpart, the No. 975 Bass Bug Spook, are among the most attractive of the Heddon fly rod lures. Value range: $15.00 to $40.00 for Spook versions, $20.00 to $75.00 for cork-bodied models.

Above and right: Bass bugs came in a wide array of colors and sizes, including the No. B-50 Baby Bass Bug.

The No. 720 and No. 710 panfish size fly rod Flaptail are much like their wooden bass-sized counterpart, complete with a brass flapper on the tail. Value range: $50.00 to $125.00.

Heddon's No. 85 Popeye Frog came in two finishes: yellow and green frog. Their distinct, bulging eyes make them easy to identify. Most have the name stenciled on the belly. Value range: $25.00 to $35.00.

The No. 980 fly rod Punkinseeds, or "Punkie Spooks," are highly sought after, even though they are later plastic lures. They can be found with a tail treble hook or the more common single hook. Value $75.00 to $225.00.

The No. 500 fly rod Stanley Ace spoon is difficult to find and shaped like its larger Queen and King Stanley lures of the same design. Value range: $20.00 to $40.00.

The Fly Rod Spoony Fish is a tiny metal fish-shaped lure. Note the single tail hook and the absence of a wire leader found on larger models. This factory prototype is too rare to value.

The No. 300 Widget is a small, wooden lure that resembles the Tango baits made by J.K. Rush of New York. They can be found in many unusual colors, such as the black spotted and salt flash finishes shown here. Value range: $25.00 to $50.00, depending on color.

Heddon's No. 940 Popper Spook lures were simple baits made of plastic. Many finishes were available. Note the long body and relatively short tail dressings. Value $15.00 to $35.00.

Some of the more obscure Heddon fly rod lures include the No. 960 Bug-A-Bee (bottom); and the Fuzzi-Bug (No. 75 bass and No. 74 small, top and middle, in two sizes). Value range for all: $35.00 to $45.00.

The classic Heddon lures sought by collectors today didn't just appear overnight in the company's production line. Each bait was the culmination of months — or even years — of diligent research and testing.

Factory engineers working with dozens of field testers built, discarded, revised, and tried out thousands of baits that never made it into the product catalog. Others that ultimately emerged as commercial baits had numerous ancestors whose action and performance helped shape the final product that anglers were asked to purchase to use at their favorite lake or stream.

The lures on the following pages are all factory pieces. Some are prototypes, some are experimental versions, and some are lures that were never placed into production for one reason or another. These baits, for the most part, are as unique as snowflakes and impossible to value. Therefore, no prices will be included for these lures.

This Underwater Expert style factory bait is cast from solid aluminum and has the circa 1902 propeller at the front. Note the formed fish tail and teardrop hook socket opening. The line tie is an extended loop. This unusual metal bait was obviously an experiment never placed into production.

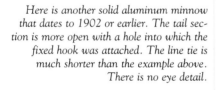

Here is another solid aluminum minnow that dates to 1902 or earlier. The tail section is more open with a hole into which the fixed hook was attached. The line tie is much shorter than the example above. There is no eye detail.

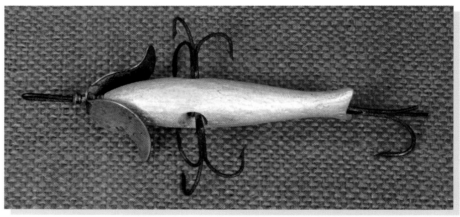

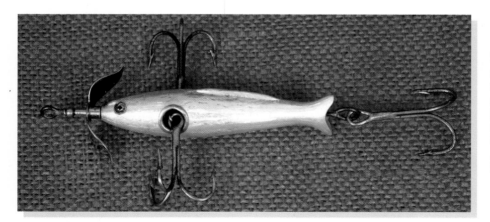

This solid metal, fish-tailed bait has a dorsal fin at the top and cups countersunk into the aluminum body. There are very tiny glass eyes and a more typical, unmarked propeller. Based on the parts and design, this bait likely dates to 1904 and would have been used at the time the first No. 100 Dowagiac Minnow was being placed into production.

This circa 1905 Smith Minnow (top) came from the Heddon Factory archives and belonged to Will Heddon, who thought enough of the mechanical bait to create his own version (bottom) with side hooks more typical of Heddon lures.

The only advertisement ever found for the Smith Minnow is in Will Heddon's personal scrapbook. The lure was made by Charles H. Smith, doing business as the LaGrange Bait Co. in LaGrange, Indiana, and featured a hinged dorsal fin and wiggling tail.

Will Heddon's handmade experimental copy of the Smith Minnow utilized an early wooden body for the 100 Dowagiac and a typical Heddon propeller and line tie. Like the Smith Minnow, Heddon's version included a dorsal fin and fish-shaped tail. The Smith Minnow has no tail hook, but Heddon's version has a wire clip likely intended as an extended hook hanger.

This oval-shaped, circa 1905 wooden minnow includes an unusual, pinned external belly-weight and experimental treble hooks. Predating the Dummy-Double by almost a decade, this lure illustrates James Heddon's perennial fascination with variations of the fish hook.

This wooden, glass-eyed lure has fixed metal wings and a pair of fixed, single hooks in the tail. The belly-weight is external. Dating to around 1904, it bears a striking resemblance to the Jamison Coaxer bait of the same year. The wood body likely was cut down from a blank for the 300 Surface lure, which was under development that year for the following season.

This is another circa 1904 bait, also likely cut from the body of a 300 Surface lure. The metal lip is similar to the one that appeared a decade later on the No. 1700 Near Surface Wiggler. It has opaque glass eyes and a pair of fixed single hooks mounted in the tail.

This 1904 or 1905 Dowagiac 100 has a unique, adjustable line tie. The lure has holes drilled along the top and bottom, enabling the long, clip-type line tie to be moved forward or backward to adjust the action of the lure.

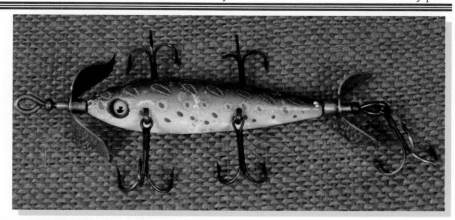

This 1904 or 1905 Dowagiac 100 body is equipped with four side hooks attached by hand-made staple rigs. The unusual paint job includes both red dots and teardrop-shaped spots.

This large, five-sided wooden minnow has a unique, fitted diving lip, hand-painted gills, a hand-set external belly-weight, a V-shaped belly, a very slender tail drilled for a hook that was never inserted, and many other idiosyncrasies that show the extent to which the Heddons went in developing their early lures.

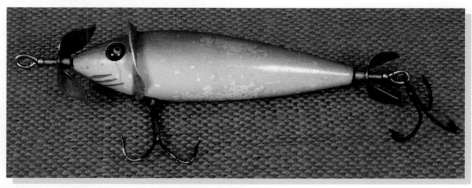

This lure has the body of the 1906 or later 300 Surface bait with the added feature of an aluminum, Slopenose-type collar on the front, in addition to the usual propellers fore and aft. Perhaps this experiment later yielded the Spindiver lure, which included both a diving lip and front propeller.

This slim-bodied Dowagiac 175 Heavy Casting Minnow in brown sienna is rigged with the staple hook attachments later found in the rare No. 1400 Single Hook Minnow.

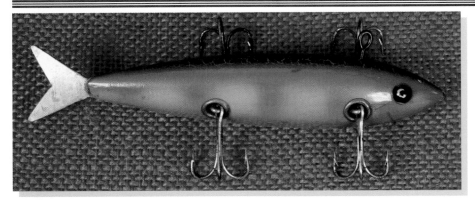

Decoy or lure? This large, wooden bait includes a forked metal tail reminiscent of early ice decoys but with the addition of four side-mounted trebles. The sienna rainbow finish is not found on early decoys. The line tie is on the top of the body.

This late 1800s, small-bodied Pardee Minnow was discussed by Charles Heddon during a 1920s patent infringement trial. Charles credited the Pardee as one of few underwater baits in actual production at the time his father was developing similar lures. This lure from the factory's own archives was in the possession of James Heddon and his sons at the time the Underwater Expert was created.

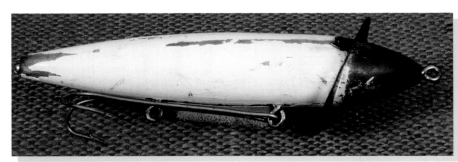

This Slopenose-like lure has a 200 Surface body with a 3″, double hook pinned to the belly, much like the No. 900 Swimming Minnow that emerged in 1910.

This mechanical weedless bait features a string line tie run through the nose, a copper belly plate attached with four pins, and a finely tooled, spring-loaded single hook. The weed guard recessed within the slot has similarities to the later Stanley Weedless Hook.

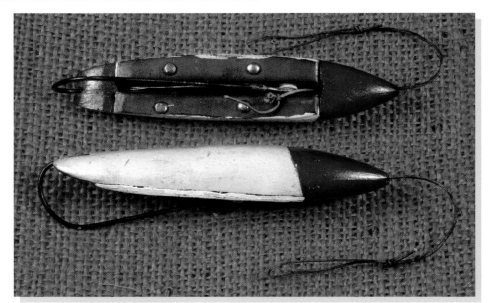

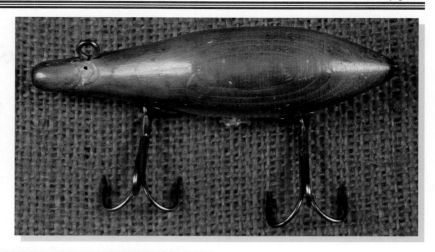

Collectors have long debated whether the "Bottle Nose Tadpolly" sold by Diamond Manufacturing of St. Louis is actually a Heddon product. We submit the following prototype from the factory archives to support the longstanding claim that Heddon indeed produced these unusual lures.

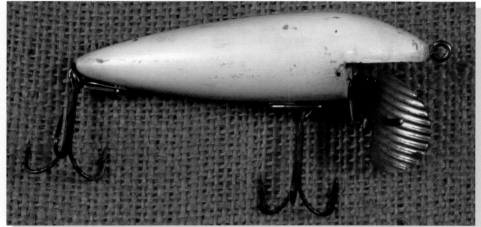

This lure has the body of a 210 Surface lure and two-piece hardware. It has a notched-out mouth much like a Pflueger Surprise and a corrugated diving lip suspended on a wire shaft out from the nose of the lure, apparently to allow it to wiggle in all directions. Perhaps this experiment was inspired by another Pflueger product, the All-in-One minnow that included four separate diving lips, one of which is similar to this one.

This early 900 Swimming Minnow prototype has a four-sided wooden body and a popper-type lip fashioned from a bottle cap, much like Will Heddon later described as having been used on his father's first homemade wooden lures. The bottle cap made the lure "spray" as it moved through the water. Handwritten in this bait is "AA-1." We wish this lure could talk.

This large forerunner of the No. 00 Underwater Minnow, circa 1910, has no eyes, hooks held by brass pins, and unmarked props. Heddon's early production years included many multi-sided baits. Few other makers attempted such products.

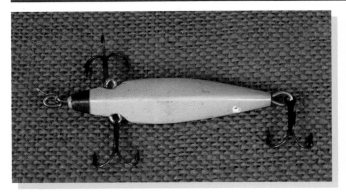

This prototype for the No. 800 Swimming Minnow likely dates to 1908 or 1909. The nose cap is machine-wound brass wire, perhaps an effort to better balance the bait. The forward-mounted side hooks are screw-eye fastened into the body without cups. The lure has one belly-weight.

This is another forerunner of the Swimming Minnow lures but with the hooks set farther back from the nose. It is almost a third larger than similar prototypes, has a wider back, and includes two belly-weights at the center and rear of the body.

This 2⅞" prototype of the No. 800 Swimming Minnow, circa 1908, has four tiny belly-weights nicely mounted in the body. The top of the lure is faintly lettered in pencil in James Heddon's own handwriting, "A Nice Darter — Runs Some to the Right."

This circa 1908 Swimming Minnow type lure is ⅜" longer than the example at the left. The four belly-weights are closely spaced this time. Heddon wrote, in pencil, on the side of this lure, "Favors Going to the Left. Darts Fair."

This wood-bodied lure is one of the most unusual in tackle history. Dating to around 1904 or 1905, it has four huge propellers, the same ones that later appear on the nose of the Musky 700 Underwater minnow lures. The bait has an external rear belly-weight, the same one used on early Underwater Expert lures. The side-mounted trebles are in tiny brass cups, and the extended front line tie and brass washer tail spacers are reminiscent of the first (circa 1904) Dowagiac 100 Minnow with the tail and line tie extensions. Measuring 3¾", this famous, glitter enameled lure was nicknamed "Star Wars" back in the 1970s by members of the National Fishing Lure Collectors Club.

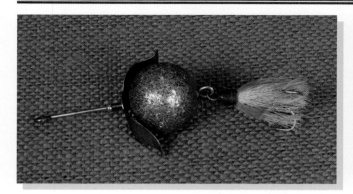

This 3", round bodied "spinner-ball" bait has two belly-weights and dates to around 1905. It has a large, unmarked propeller, wonderful glitter paint finish, and an extended wire shaft line tie. The ball is slightly more than 1" in diameter.

This nickel-plated, fish-shaped lure frame is outfitted with a trimmed down wood body of a Dowagiac #100 with five internal belly-weights. The wire shaft is inserted all the way through the body of this 4⅝" lure. This bait has features of the circa 1908 Multiple Metal Minnow. This prototype may have spawned the concept of a casting weight and also represents Heddon's early interest in the use of flat metal.

This glass-eyed, wood-bodied minnow has a metal keel mounted in the belly in lieu of belly-weights. The extra-wide back is 1" across, but the lure is barely ½" tall. It tapers to a machined brass tube mounted in the tail. The dressed tail treble is screwed on a long shaft through the tail tube into the wood body. Note the circa 1905 glitter finish and hand-painted gills.

This finely made brass spinner is mounted on a 4½" wire shaft and features an external belly-weight on the tail identical to those used on circa 1902 Underwater Expert lures. Note the nicely scalloped edges and dressed tail treble.

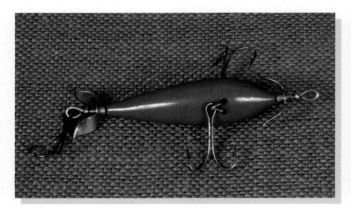

This early, all-red Dowagiac 100 wooden body is rigged with staple-type hardware later found on the Dowagiac #1400 Single Hook Minnow. The Heddons were fascinated by hook attachment hardware and experimented extensively in that area.

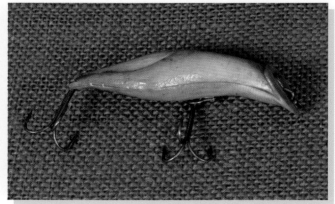

This is a Baby Luny Frog prototype with a two-piece molded, seamed body, and a celluloid "skull cap" attached to the nose. This bait is circa 1926, prior to the lure's official debut.

This circa 1926 prototype lure has been dubbed the "Gamefisher Luny Frog" and is specially painted with a unique, froglike finish. The front half is a Gamefisher lure, while the rear section has molded rubber frog legs attached with a metal harness that wraps through the frog's crotch. The rear has a fixed single hook.

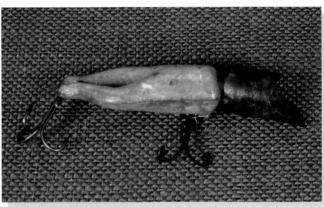

This circa 1926 prototype has been dubbed the "Zig-Wag Luny Frog" and features a two-piece molded, pyralin rear section, with a solid pyralin head similar to that of a Zig-Wag. The eyes are pinned beads, and the lure has two-piece hardware.

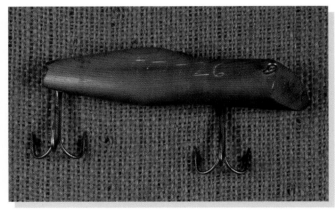

This Basser type lure body has been carved into a Luny Frog shape. The circa 1926 prototype is in natural wood finish and was an early effort at what later became the Luny Frog.

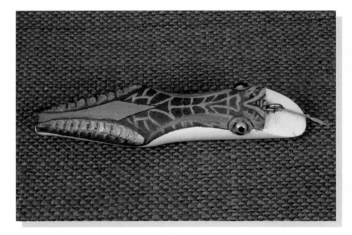

This is a wooden Basser lure made into a Luny Frog body and painted with oil paints in a beautiful frog finish. This circa 1926 prototype also features glass eyes and was never outfitted with hooks or hardware.

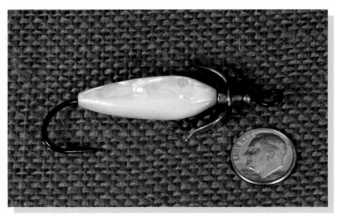

This fish-shaped, 1" long, mother-of-pearl lure is quite detailed, with carved fins and eyes. The shaft is drilled through and outfitted with an unmarked prop on the front and a fixed single hook on the rear. This lure dates to around 1907. It is called the "Pearl Minnow."

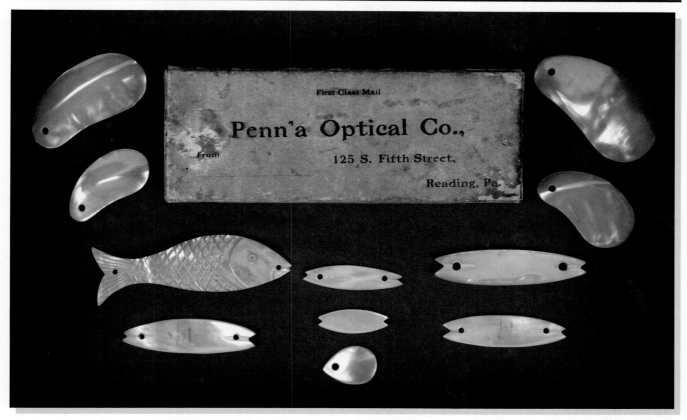

The Heddons experimented with mother-of-pearl baits during the early years of lure production. This assortment of pearl lure bodies in a box from Penn Optical Company came from the factory archives. Note the detailed workmanship on some of these lure bodies, including hand-etched scales on the fish-shaped form in lower left.

This Gamefisher prototype has a longer, thicker front section and shorter tail section and features an oversized, bell-shaped lip and partial, high-hump line-tie similar to what appears on the No. 6000 Tadpolly in 1918, its introductory year. The bait also has a large, crude, brass hook hanger that resembles — but likely predates — the famous L-rig hardware.

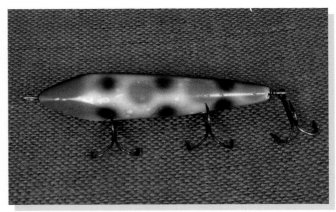

This prototype utilizes the wood body for a No. 1600 Deep Diving Wiggler. It has three hooks and was never outfitted with the typical diving planes found on production models. This lure, however, is pictured on the side panels of early Wiggler boxes.

This five-hook prototype for the No. 1600 Deep Diving Wiggler has a pinned, external belly-weight.

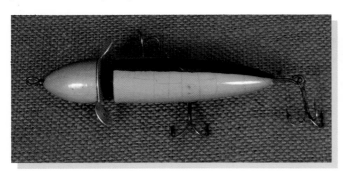

The No. 3000 Spindiver is one of Heddon's prettiest lures. This factory board prototype has a crudely made, plain diving lip but no propeller. The paint department gave the back of this lure an unusual pink finish. Their reasoning is unknown.

This musky-sized, revolving head lure illustrates Heddon's interest in the many revolving lures produced by Ans Decker, the Pfluegers and other makers. It is hand painted and has large cup hook hangers.

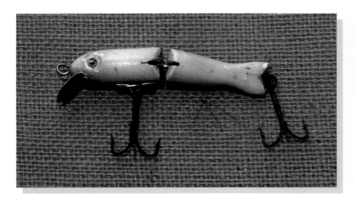

This lure appears to be a small Shakespeare Tantalizer body outfitted with Heddon two-piece hardware, a No. 110 River Runt lip, and a Gamefisher joint pinned from the top. The Heddons frequently experimented with competitors' products.

This pretty factory lure resembles the South Bend Baby Surf-Oreno, a possible inspiration for Heddon's No. 260 Surface Minnie. This lure has two-piece hardware, as did the Surface Minnie.

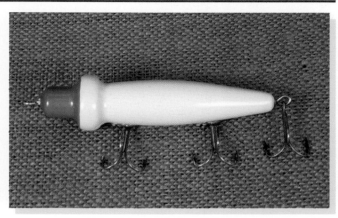

This brightly painted spoon with a recessed, single hook was dubbed the "Slick Trick Spoon" at the Heddon factory. It represents one of many efforts by the Heddons to develop what anglers wanted: lures that were weed proof.

This early collar bait has L-rig hardware and a much fatter head than is found on commercially produced lures. Competitors such as South Bend and Pflueger made similar lures, but the Moonlight Bait Co. of nearby Paw Paw, Michigan, likely made the first "peckerhead" baits.

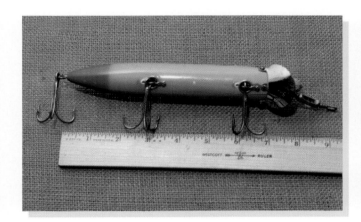

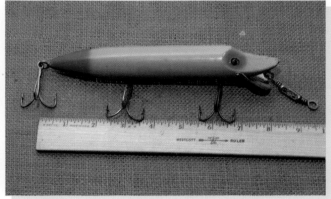

This 8" Musky Vamp from the factory board shows various experiments with the design and placement of the heavy-duty L-rig hook fasteners.

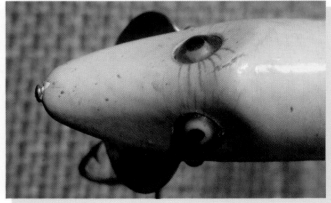

This early Vampire has hand-painted eyelashes. It is from the factory board. Perhaps someone at the factory was bored.

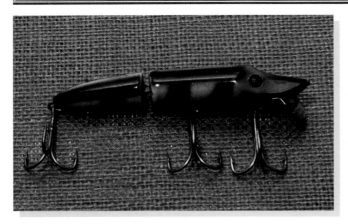

This glass-eyed Jointed Vamp from the factory board has a one-of-a-kind, but nonetheless beautiful airbrushed paint finish. This color resurfaced briefly in the 1970s and was called "tiger musky."

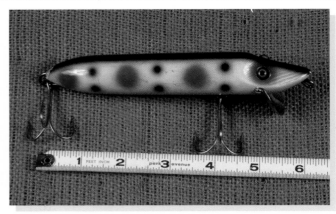

This 6" Musky Vamp from the factory board was rigged with only two hooks instead of the usual three.

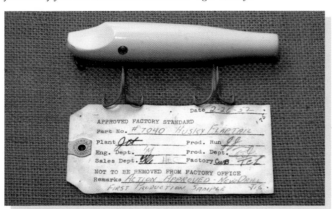

This "approved factory standard" tag from February 26, 1952, is for the No. 7040 Husky Flaptail and was signed by various factory production personnel. Remarks on the tag say, "action approved, new drill jig, first production sample."

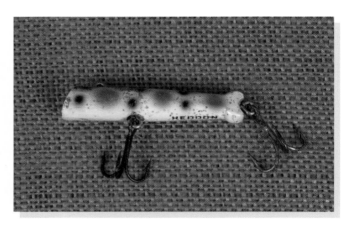

This strawberry spot pier bait is stamped "Heddon" but closely resembles lures made by other companies. However, it is identical in all respects to lure blanks found with other Heddon lure bodies in the workshop of Will and Laura Heddon in Minneola, Florida.

This wood-bodied, painted-eyed lure features a carved-down body of a No. 110 River runt rigged with a leader and spinners. It has two-piece hardware and a nose-mounted lead weight. It was an experiment that ultimately led to the introduction of the No. 9100 Dowagiac Spook made of pyralin.

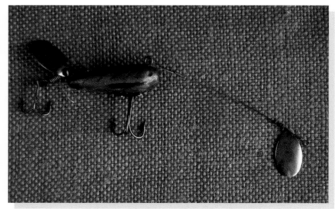

This crudely made and painted wooden prototype is another step in the process of developing the No. 9100 Dowagiac Spook, a Heddon favorite for many years.

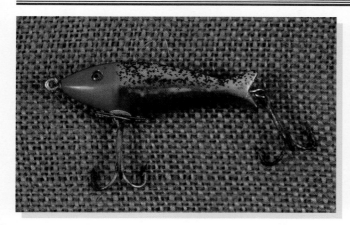

This pyralin forerunner of the Florida Special and Saltwater Special lures features glass eyes, two-piece hardware and a fish-shaped tail with a more pronounced fork than is found on commercially sold lures.

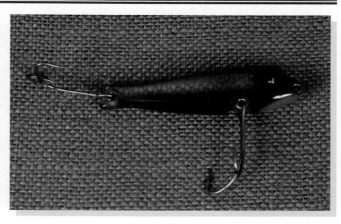

This prototype of the No. 9800 Dowagiac Sea Spook has a hole drilled in the nose for the line tie. Note the use of the metal plate hook hanger on the belly and a reinforced tail hook hanger. Neither fasteners were used in the final product.

This No. 110 River Runt prototype is painted in factory white and has a slightly different shaped body than production models. This body was being evaluated about the time two-piece hardware was adopted in the 1930s. It has no eyes.

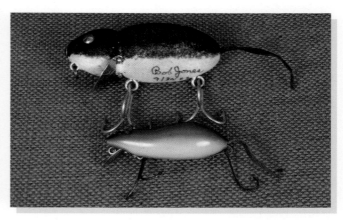

This Musky Mouse Heddon prototype is one of two made. It has the diving lip from an 8″ Musky Vamp and the general shape of a Musky Crazy Crawler body, although this mouse is much larger. It dates to the 1930s, but was signed on September 30, 1983, by Bob Jones, a management employee in charge of Heddon's historical section. The standard F4000 Meadow Mouse is shown for size comparison.

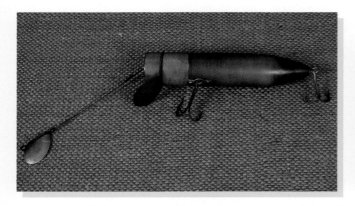

These two pyralin baits illustrate Heddon's brief interest in electric lighted lures that were popular in the 1920s and 1930s. The heads can be unscrewed, ostensibly for the insertion of a battery and light bulb. The brown one has toilet seat hardware, while the green lure has a bar-rig fastener. Unlike many of the prototypes discussed in this chapter, these lures never led to any future production baits.

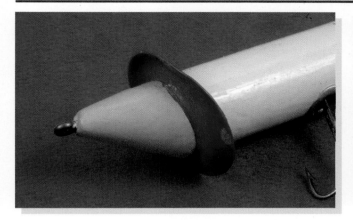

Early Slopenose lures had painted collars attached by pins.

The lure on the right has early "rimless cups" used on the first Slopenose baits, circa 1902. The example on the left is a later model with gold washed cups.

The earliest Underwater Expert lures had an external belly-weight and unusual floppy prop.

This long, sweeping prop was found on the 1903 Underwater Expert.

This brass tail rudder appeared on the 1903 Underwater Expert lures.

This very early Dowagiac Underwater Minnow has staple rig hardware.

Early Heddon minnows had pointed, unmarked props.

The large cup hook hangers appeared on the No. 175 Heavy Casting Minnow.

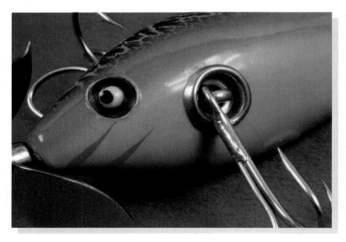

Early underwater minnows have nickel-plated "forward raised" cups.

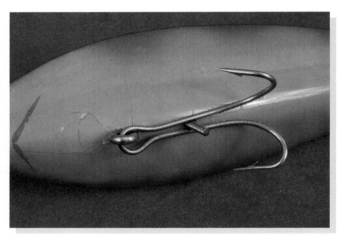

The No. 900 Swimming Minnow had a pin-mounted belly double hook.

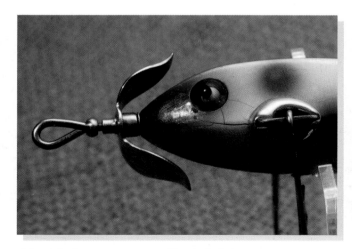

This is the famous Dummy-Double "football" hardware, circa 1913.

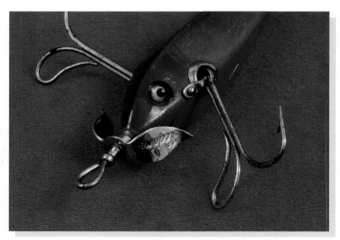

The Dummy-Double lure has distinct, specially made hooks.

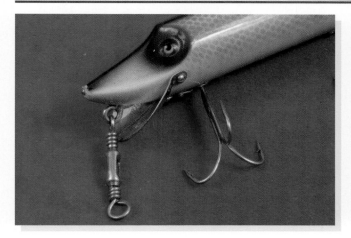

A large box swivel was attached to the 8" Musky Vamp which also has its own distinct diving lip.

The Stanley Weedless Pork Rind lure had marked Stanley props and a weedless attachment.

Early Darting Zara lures had a line tie on top of the head and a tiny tack in the notched mouth.

Musky Flaptail lures had a wire leader attached into a cup rig and heavy duty toilet seat hook fasteners.

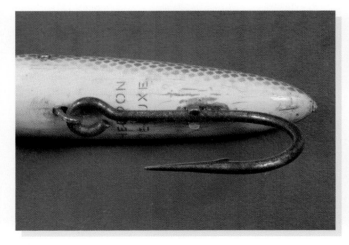

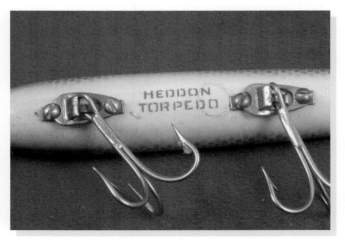

This single hook attachment was featured on the Deluxe Basser used for salmon.

This Torpedo has the two-piece flap hook fasteners.

Heavy duty toilet seat fasteners are found on Musky Crazy Crawler lures.

This Crazy Crawler has the "Donaly" rig hardware on the wing attachment.

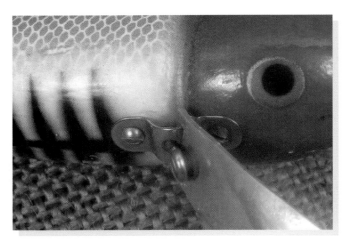

This Crazy Crawler has the more common Heddon wing attachment hardware.

A special "shoehorn lip" appears on this Salmon River Runt which also has "Teddy Bear" glass eyes.

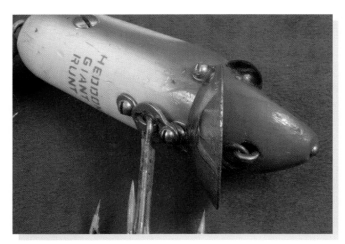

This Giant River Runt has heavy-duty diving lip fasteners, teddy bear eyes, and heavy duty toilet seat hardware.

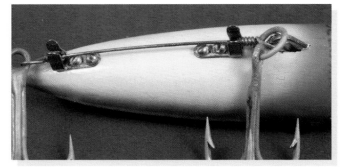

The Deluxe Salmon Basser featured a pull-away wire hook attachment.

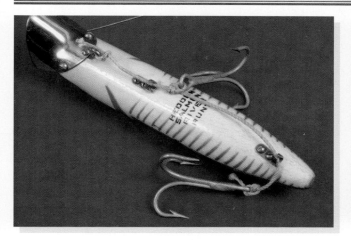

Salmon River Runts had a pull-away string hook attachment on the belly.

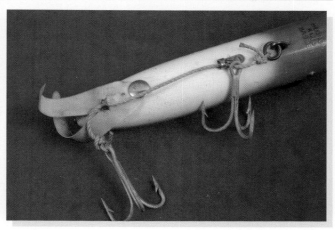

The belly of this Salmon Basser has a string rig for attaching hooks, and a thumbtack type attachment to secure the rubber skirt sold with this lure.

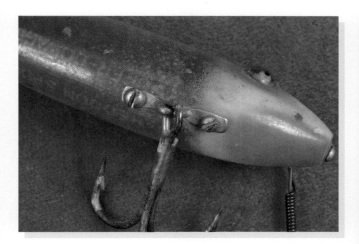

The bar rig appears on the belly hangers of this Dowagiac Spook.

This "scoop lip" appears on deep dive River Runts and some Vamps.

The No-Snag River Runt features a weedless nose guard.

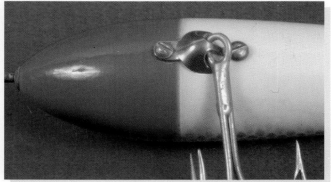

Surface rig hook hangers were used throughout the late 1940s and the 1950s on many Heddon lures.

Lure Boxes and Papers

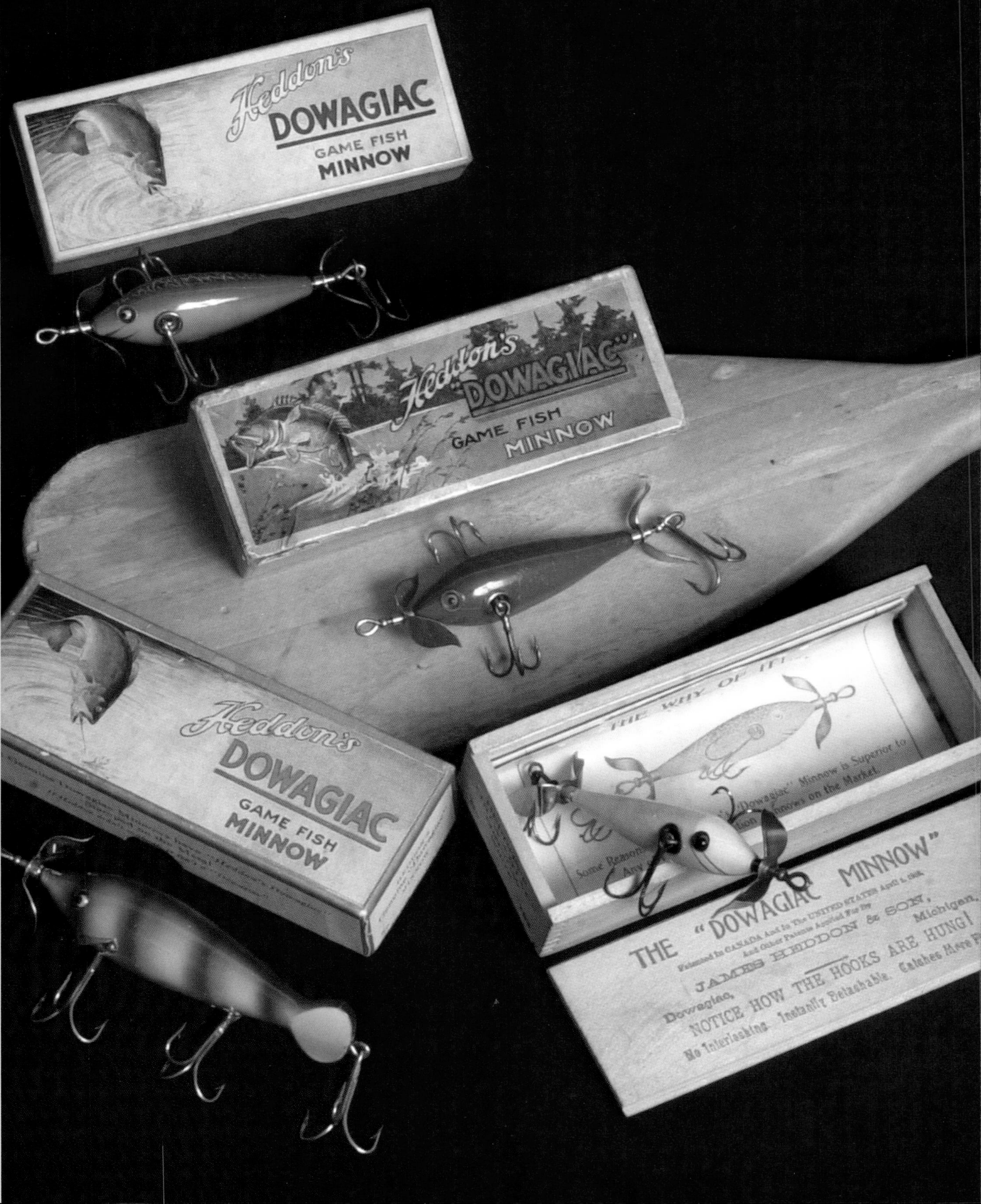

The exquisite wooden and cardboard boxes that held the Heddon lures were designed to do much more than protect the baits inside. The use of graphics, slogans, pictures, and insightfully composed paper inserts were all part of a grand scheme to lure anglers to the baits that caught the fish. The pages that follow trace the evolution of Heddon's boxes and paper lure box inserts from 1902 to the 1960s.

Introduced in 1902, this is the earliest box for the Dowagiac Perfect Surface Casting Bait. This box has a paper label with blue print and an oak leaf design along the border. There is no labeling on the endflaps.

The Dowagiac No. 2, introduced in 1902 and known to collectors as the Four-Hook Slopenose, came in this white pasteboard box with a lithograph picture of the lure it contained. The endflaps were marked Dowagiac No. 2.

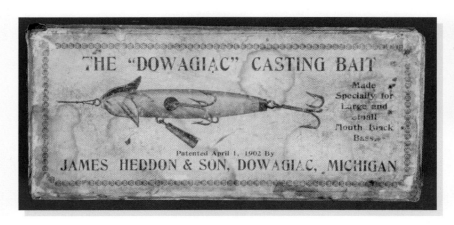

This is the earliest of the boxes for the Dowagiac Underwater, dating to spring 1902. It would hold what collectors refer to as the external belly-weight model Underwater Expert. Note the endflap with "Dowagiac" on one line and "Underwater" on the other.

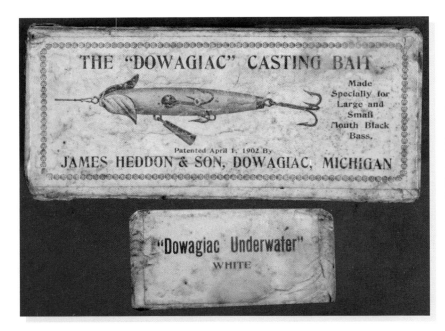

There were three different versions of the Dowagiac Underwater baits introduced in 1902, all made within a few months of each other. This box would hold the later version offered in fall of 1902, the only year these external belly-weight lures were produced. It is possible the 1903 and later Underwater Experts may have been packaged in the boxes with the picture of the external belly-weight models. The box papers, however, were changed to reflect the newer products.

This is the 1903 box for the Dowagiac Expert. The name "Dowagiac Perfect Surface Casting Bait" has been shortened to "Dowagiac Expert." Note that "No. 200" now appears on the end-flap.

This is the 1906 "Slopenose" box, with slightly different lettering than what is found on earlier models. Note the change to a double-line straight border in blue. Also in 1906, for the first time, all hardware on Dowagiac baits was nickel-plated.

The *"New Dowagiac Minnow"* box dates to around 1904 and would hold the very first three belly-weight lure. Note the rear extension tube in the illustration of the bait pictured on this rare box. This box, and the lure it held, was of very short duration. This is the only known example of this box.

This circa 1905 box is for the Dowagiac Killer. Note the use of the squiggly or wavy line border. This early box is overlabeled atop an older four-hook Slopenose box. This is believed to be the earliest of the Killer boxes, after which the company opted to stick with the oak leaf border design on other boxes of the era.

This Dowagiac Killer box also dates to 1905 and would hold a three belly-weight lure with brass hardware. Note the difference in the font style of the box top lettering.

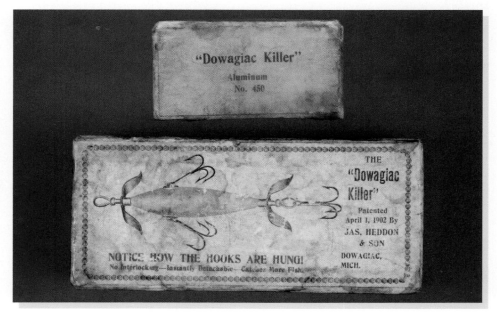

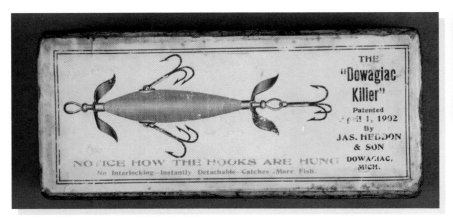

Here is the circa 1906 Dowagiac Killer box. The border has been changed to a straight, double line. Baits packaged in this box would have had nickel-plated hardware.

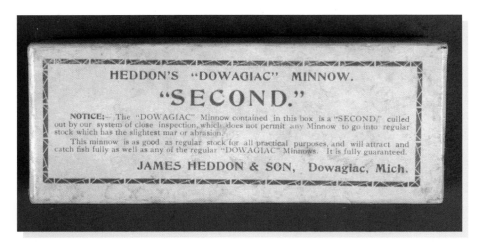

This is the only known example of the "second" box produced in spring of 1905. The box was part of an effort by James Heddon to market his "seconds," or slightly marred baits, at reduced prices. However, the factory later decided to sell its entire stock of "second" baits to a hardware store in Dowagiac, and the Heddon "second" boxes vanished forever.

The Jeanette Hawley Mohawk Sinking or Underwater Minnow was made in 1905, and this is one of two known examples of the beautiful boxes in which they were packaged. Sold in limited numbers by Will and Laura Heddon from their home in Mineola, Florida, the Mohawk boxes are very tall, well-made pasteboard creations. Jeanette Hawley, by the way, was Laura Heddon's pen-name.

This 1905 box is the introductory carton for the Dowagiac Surface Minnow, No. 300. Only a handful of these boxes are known, as most No. 300 lures were packaged in wooden boxes from 1905 to 1907.

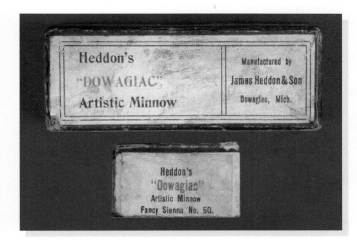

The Dowagiac Artistic Minnow was introduced in 1907 and came in this little maroon edge box. Note the label says "James Heddon & Son," which predates the change to "Sons" in 1908.

This is a circa 1907 Artistic Minnow box that has been overlabeled for the No. 11 Light Casting Minnow. The box now has a red edge rather than the earlier maroon edge.

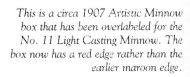

In 1908, the Artistic Minnow box was changed from "James Heddon & Son" to "James Heddon & Sons," reflecting Charles Heddon's decision to join his father and brother in their new enterprise. The company also devised special, small boxes with "Dowagiac Minnow" on them to hold the No. 20 Baby Dowagiac Underwater and No. 10 Light Casting Minnow, which previously were packaged in Artistic Minnow boxes. The second box in this photo says "James Heddon's Sons," circa 1912, was printed after James Heddon's death in 1911.

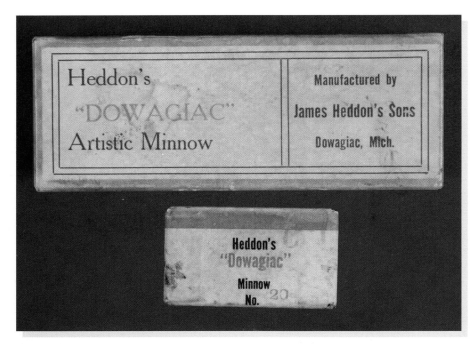

This is the 1912 version of the Artistic Minnow box. Note that it now says "James Heddon's Sons" on the label, reflecting James Heddon's death in 1911, leaving only sons Will and Charles running the company. The endflap on this box has been overlabeled for a No. 20 Baby Dowagiac Underwater, indicating, perhaps, that the supply of special boxes mentioned above for the No. 20 and No. 10 had been exhausted.

The Bucktail Surface Minnow dates to 1908, when this beautiful pasteboard box was offered. No other lures have been found sold with this box, which was made only a season or two.

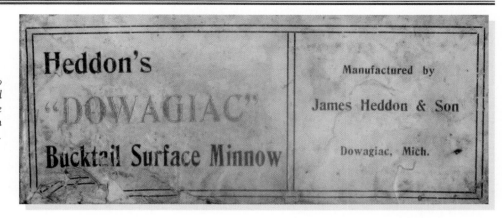

The Multiple Metal Minnow was introduced in 1908 and came in this special white pasteboard box, of which only a handful are known to have survived.

The Dowagiac Musky Minnow box held the huge No. 700 underwater minnow. This was the introductory box for the 700 series and dates to 1909. This white box has blue lettering.

This box for the Swimming Minnow was introduced in 1909 and held the No. 900 Swimming Minnow lure. The box was used a second year in 1910 for the introduction of its smaller cousin, the No. 800 Swimming Minnow. Collectors call this the "It Swims" box.

The Killer Wooden Minnow box dates to 1906 or 1907. The earlier version shown here is maroon with a label with a wavy border design. It would hold a round-bodied Heddon bait and likely was manufactured for sale to wholesalers like the Edward K. Tryon Co. and VL&A to repackage and sell under their own labels. The Heddon name is absent from these boxes.

This later version of the Killer Wooden Minnow maroon box dates to 1908 or 1910 and would hold a Heddon round-bodied minnow.

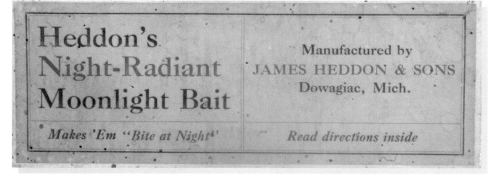

Heddon's Night-Radiant Moonlight Bait dates to 1910, the only year this bulbous classic was produced. Only a handful are known to have survived.

This black box with luminous white lettering is another version of the short-lived Night-Radiant bait produced in 1910. This box is the only known example.

Heddon's Dowagiac Minnow box with the "center bass" logo would contain circa 1910 Heddon wooden minnows. The white pasteboard box has a maroon outside border. The "center bass" picture was used in 1909 and 1910 Heddon product catalogs.

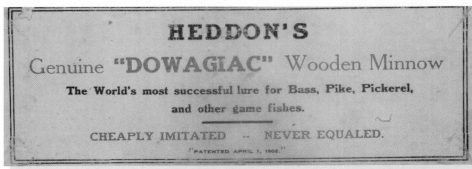

This is the standard white pasteboard box that Heddon used from 1906 to around 1911. It has red and blue lettering and was used for many baits of that era, including the No. 100, No. 150, No. 200, No. 300, and No. 900 Swimming Minnows.

The "left leaping bass" box, also known among collectors as the "Pine Tree Box," was used only in 1912. This colorful box is the only Heddon carton with the bass leaping to the left and the only box in which there is no lure in the fish's mouth. The side panels state that "All Genuine Dowagiac Minnows have Heddon's Dowagiac Stamped on the Spinners."

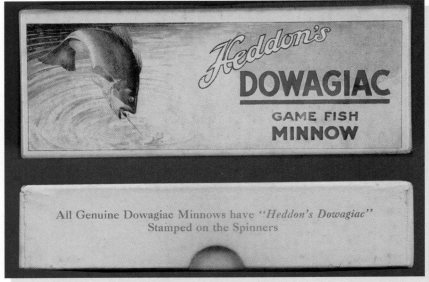

This circa 1912 white pasteboard box is the first "down leaping bass" box Heddon made. The box emphasizes the downward diving fish which by now has a Heddon lure in its mouth. The addition of the lure was an effective way to sell a product.

The blue-bordered downward leaping bass box also dates to 1912 and would be considered the second of such box versions. It is identical in all respects to the white border, with the exception of the blue border. It is harder to find than the white border box.

This large, white-bordered box with the downward leaping "Game Fish Minnow" logo dates to 1912 and was made for large baits such as the No. 700 Musky Underwater Minnow. The box has a double-thick red line around the border.

The white bordered, downward leaping bass "extended" box dates to 1912 – 1913 and was used to package the No. 1300 Black Sucker and three-hook No. 700 Musky Minnow lures.

The Diamond Submarine box holds the unusual lure also known as the Bottle Nosed Tadpolly, a Heddon product made for Diamond Manufacturing Co. of St. Louis. Submarine baits were made in the 1915 – 1917 era, predating by several years the introduction of Heddon's Tadpolly lure in 1918.

This is the Type I and Type II Heddon wooden box placed into production in 1904. The Type I box was smaller than its successors and made of thinner wood that was susceptible to warping. It had a one-way thumbnail slide and was marked for the "New Dowagiac Minnow." It contained the three belly-weight No. 150 with brass hardware. The Type II (shown in photo) is identical except it was made with thicker, more durable wood. Both boxes have the notation on top that says "Notice How the Hooks are Hung!" Note the exclamation mark after the word "Hung."

The Type III Heddon wooden box also says "New Dowagiac Minnow" and has a two-way slide top and no thumbnail. It would also have an exclamation mark after the word "Hung." The box would hold a two belly-weight, high-forehead minnow from the 1905 brass hardware era.

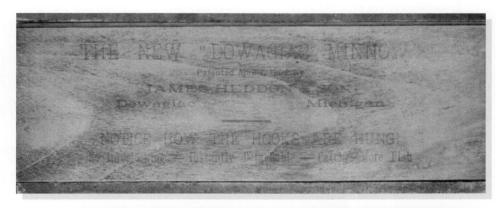

The Type IV Heddon wooden box is marked for the "Dowagiac Minnow" and features a two-way slide top. This box also mentions a Canadian patent on the lid and still has the exclamation point after the word "Hung." This box was in use in 1905 – 1906 and would hold the No. 100, No. 150, and No. 300 with brass or nickel hardware and one or two belly-weights. Some later Type IV boxes mention the Canadian patent but omit the exclamation point after the word "Hung."

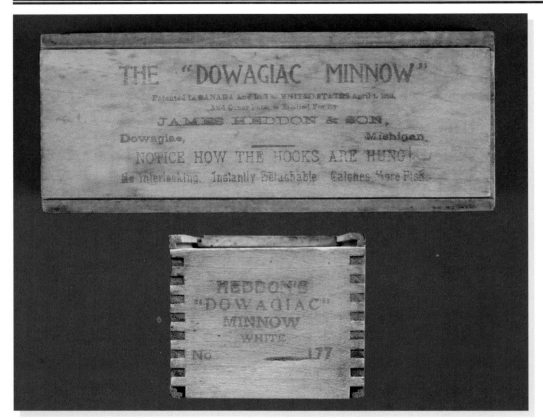

This extra large Type IV Heddon wooden box was made for the No. 175 Heavy Casting Minnow. It was taller to accommodate the big minnow's extra large hooks.

This Type IV Heddon wooden box was made for the No. 300 Surface Minnow and was marked on the endflap.

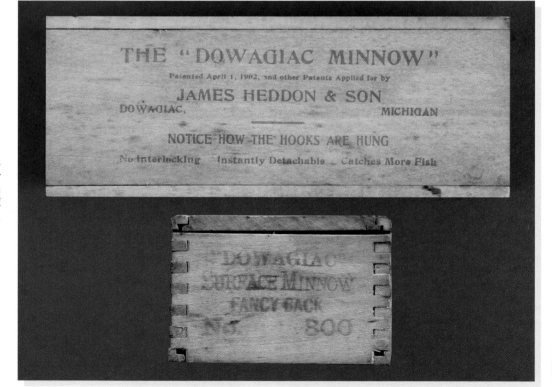

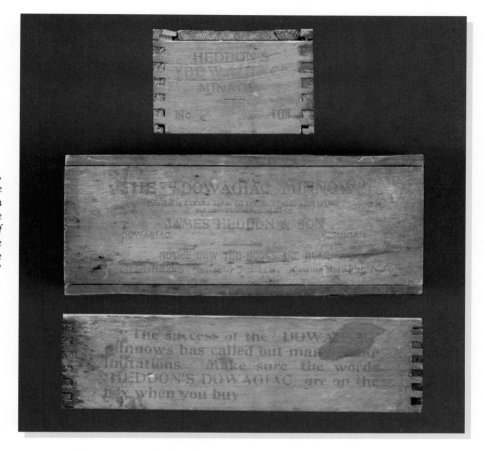

This is the Type V Heddon wooden box, circa 1907, which features a two-way slide and makes no mention of the Canadian patent. Baits found in this box include the single belly and nickel-hardware versions of the No. 100, No. 150, and No. 300. The box lid has no exclamation point after the word "Hung."

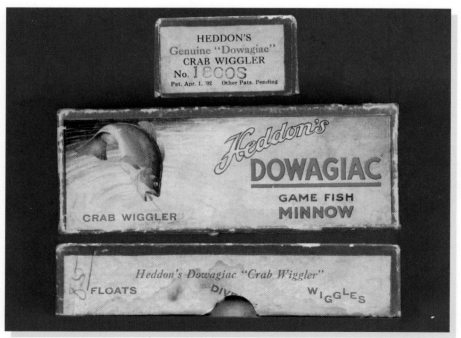

The downleaping Crab Wiggler box dates to 1915 and has typical "Game Fish Minnow" box features. The "Crab Wiggler" lettering is below the bass and the side panel graphics say, "Floats, Dives, Wiggles."

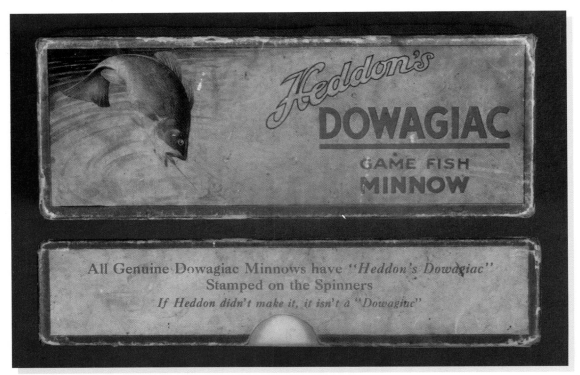

The downleaping "Game Fish Minnow" box with the red border would date to 1912 – 1915. Note that the bass has a red and white lure in its mouth. The slogan "Heddon's Dowagiac Stamped on the Spinners" is on the side panels.

This circa 1915 – 1920 downleaping "Game Fish Minnow" box will have the slogan "Heddon's Dowagiac Stamped on the Metal" on the box side panels. Note the bass still has a red and white lure in its mouth.

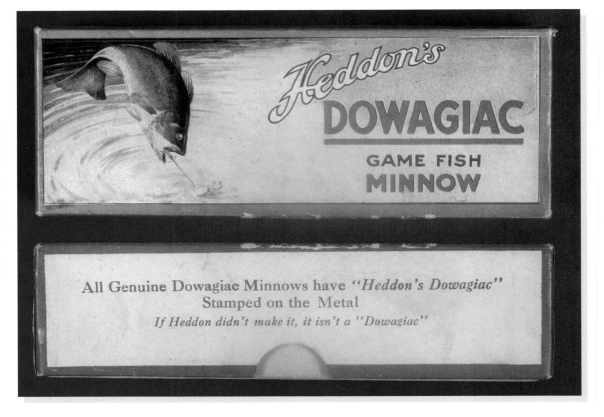

This red-bordered, extended down-leaping "Game Fish Minnow" box was made in the teen years for larger lures that were too long for standard boxes.

This is the circa 1915 Dowagiac Wiggler box, a downleaping carton used for the No. 1600 and No. 1700 Wiggler lures. Note the extra tall box construction and the graphics on the side that say "Floats Dives Wiggles."

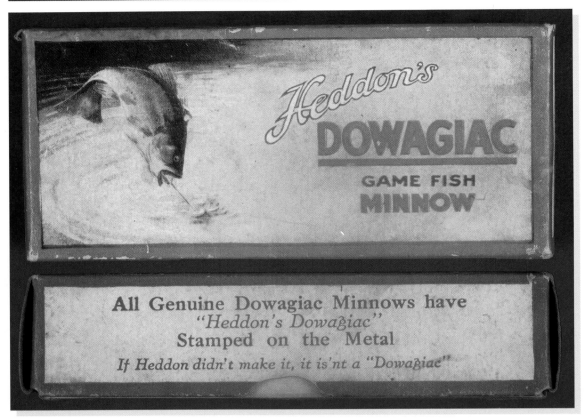

This is the last of the red border downleaping boxes that show the red and white lure in the fish's mouth. The box is also of the folded-style construction and the side of the box has a misspelled word in the slogan, "If Heddon Didn't Make It, it is'nt a Dowagiac." (The misspelled word is "is'nt.")

This is a newer downleaping bass box, circa 1924 – 1927. The box lid lettering has been changed to "Genuine Heddon Dowagiac minnow," and the lure in the fish's mouth is now solid red. The side panel slogan now reads, "Heddon Made – Well Made." This is the last of the downleaping bass boxes.

This downleaping bass box is another example of the "extended" carton used to hold some of the larger baits.

This is the circa 1925 extra large box for the 8" Musky Vamp. This one also can hold the No. 1300 Black Sucker.

This is the downward leaping bass box for the Weedless Porkrind Minnow, circa 1924.

The fly rod Wilder Dilg came in this circa 1924 downleaping bass box.

The first "upward leaping" bass box, circa 1927 – 1930, featured a new illustration of a bass leaping into the air with a red and white Vamp in its mouth. The script on the box remained the same as the last version of the downleaping bass boxes.

This upward leaping bass box held a Heddon Stanley Pork Rind Lure, circa 1928.

This upward leaping box held a fly rod Wilder-Dilg and dates to 1931.

This upward leaping bass box, circa 1931, has the inscription "Heddon Made, Well Made" added to the bottom of the boxtop below the bass. The company address has been added to the bottom right corner of the box lid and a color chart appears on the side panel.

Color Chart Last number and letter shows color: Example: Vamp 7500 in Rainbow is 7501; Pike Scale 7509M.

O Green crackle back	9A Yellow perch	9G All black	9P Shiner scale
OS White; red & green spots	9B Frog	9H Red scale	9R Natural scale
1 Rainbow	9BB Meadow frog	9J Frog scale	9SS Silver scale
2 White body, red head	9BF Bull Frog	9K Gold fish scale	9V Orange, black spots
4 All red	9BK Brook Trout	9L Yellow perch scale	9X Blue scale
8 White body, gold specks	9C Crab	9M Pike scale	9Z Rainbow scale
9 White silver specks	9D Green scale	9N Red Dace Scale	

RH Red head   BH Blue head   Lum Luminous

NP Nickle Plate   GP Gold Plate   CP Copper Plate

This circa 1934 upward leaping bass box includes references to the number of years of Field & Stream magazine fishing contests in which Heddon has excelled. Since the magazine began the competitions in 1911, these boxes are easily dated.

The circa 1932 "Fish-Flesh" box shows P.L. Waldrop of Clarksdale, Mississippi, with a string of bass caught on Fish-Flesh Heddon baits. This box would hold glass-eyed Spook lures, which were new in the Heddon line in 1932. Other angler testimonials decorate the rest of the side panels of this short-lived and important box. Unfortunately, most of the early "fish flesh" lures have disintegrated over the years.

This is the H.R. Brush box, circa 1934. Typically, it would contain lures of the two-piece hardware era. The lid shows H.R. Brush and his 17-pound, 5-ounce bass caught on a Vamp Spook at Florida's Lake Apopka in 1933. The bass won the Field & Stream Big Fish Contest that year.

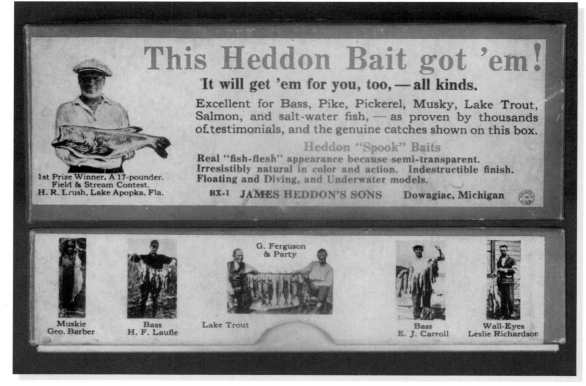

This is the introductory box for the circa 1918 Wiggle King lure. The gray textured box with red printing has a wonderful jingle: "The Wobble Makes 'Em Gobble."

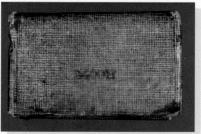

The introductory box for the Heddon Lucky 13 Junior, introduced in 1919, is almost identical to the Wiggle King box of the previous year, but with no lettering on the boxtop, only the number for the bait and color on the endflap.

The Tad-Polly was introduced in 1918 in its own beautiful black box with green lettering and pictures of the new lure on the cover. This box would hold either the No. 5000 or No. 6000 series Tad-Polly, but they would be the early versions with the heart-shaped lip and the high-hump line tie seen on the box illustration.

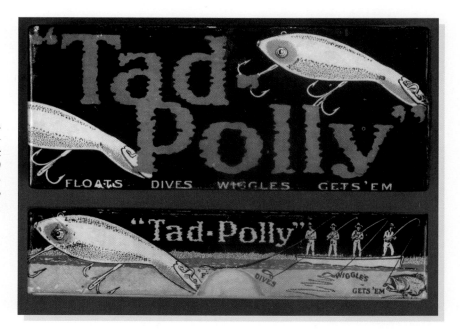

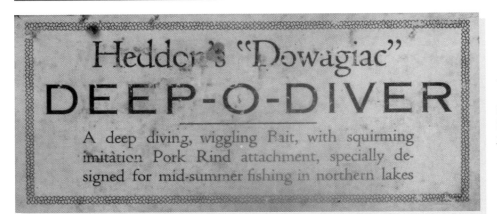

The Deep-O-Diver was introduced in 1919 as a baby cousin to Heddon's popular Crab Wiggler lures. The plain white box with black lettering was made solely for this bait.

The Heddon Musky Vamp box, circa 1925, was made for the 8" Musky Vamp. The large white box with red lettering is fashioned from heavy cardboard and the overhanging lid of the box is shorter than the bottom. The side panels have the slogan, "If Heddon Didn't Make it, it isn't a Dowagiac."

The circa 1923 Wilder-Dilg "portrait boxes" included pictures of a dozen famous anglers, to whom specific fly rod lures in the Heddon line were dedicated. It is difficult to amass a complete set.

The Bass Bug box, circa 1928, featured a see-through window. The side panels have a slogan promoting "splashy sports" using Genuine Heddon bugs and feathered lures.

This is a box for the standard tournament casting weight, circa mid-1920s. The attractive red-border design box would hold a competition certified weight acceptable for use in all National Association of Scientific Angling Clubs (NASAC) competition.

This is a box for Heddon "agatine" line guides used in rod-making and rod repairs. It dates to the 1930s.

This is the last cardboard-topped box, circa 1946 – 1954. It emerged after World War II and has a jumping bass on the lid with a yellow shore River Runt in its mouth, beside the later "wedge banner" logo.

This is the River Runt Spook box, made for the myriad of plastic "Spook" lures and variations marketed from the late 1930s into the 1950s. The box lid shows a jumping bass with a yellow shore River Runt Spook in its mouth.

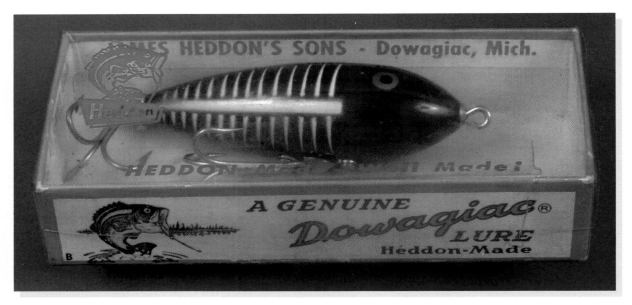

By 1955, most Heddon lures were packaged in this plastic top or "window" box that replaced the last "banner wedge" all-cardboard box. It offered the consumer a better view of the product, eliminating the need for the attractive graphics that had long been a Heddon tradition.

This is the box for the circa 2000 "Millennium Edition" Lucky 13, produced for sale during the National Fishing Lure Collectors Club national convention in Little Rock, Arkansas, that year.

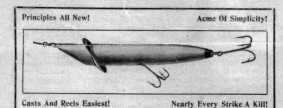

Principles All New!   Acme Of Simplicity!

Casts And Reels Easiest!   Nearly Every Strike A Kill!

INSTRUCTIONS

For Making Large Catches of Black Bass With the "DO-WAGIAC" Perfect Surface Casting Bait

The angler who would achieve the best success in casting any bait should bring to his aid a well balanced, elastic rod, (preferably 5½ or 6 feet in length) a fine silk line, and an easy-running, quadruple multiplying reel. When cast, the bait should drop lightly upon the surface of the water, rather than coming down with a "splash," then going below the surface and consuming time to rise. This is accomplished by casting the bait nearer in a direct line, rather than high into the air, and just before it strikes the surface shutting down on the reel with the thumb, quickly elevating the tip of the rod, (which should previously have been well lowered as the bait was going out.) This drops the bait artistically, with greater fascination for the fish and leaves it in the best possible condition to start and run in best form.

Rather than throwing the bait entirely by the law of centrifugal force, as would be done if using a lath or broom-handle, it should acquire its impetus principally from the elastic action of the rod, especially from the tip, by imparting to the rod much the same action given to a well balanced whip by an artistic driver when about to "crack the whip." With this instruction carefully observed the angler will cast with greater ease, pleasure and efficiency.

To avoid the ever-perplexing "back-lash," "runback," or over-running of the line, so frequent and annoying to the beginner, a firm pressure should be kept upon the spool with the thumb of the casting hand, especially during the last ten or fifteen feet of the bait's flight. Do not try to make long casts in the beginning, for neither then nor after you become expert will you find long casts most successful. An artistic bait-caster casts first in good style, second accurately, and third both of these with long range added, when advisable; i. e., when you wish to reach certain spots that look "fishy," without the necessity of running your boat out of its course. Usually short and frequent casts give the best results.

Slower reeling is gaining favor with experts, though the bait should be STARTED back at a rapid rate.

Should a hook be broken or the angler find himself among muskallonge, or for any other reason desire to change sizes, a few turns of the screw-eye to the left affords an opening by means of which he can detach and attach the treble.

When the fish rises to the bait and the sense of feeling tells you he is hooked, a gentle strike back with the rod is usually sufficient to hook the barbs into the flesh with certainty, when a taut line should be kept (protecting the line by the spring of the rod)

until your prize is safe within the landing net. The "Dowagiac" No. 1 bait contained in this box is intended primarily for use when bait-casting for black bass, although it can be used to fine advantage with other methods of fishing and when angling for other species of game fish. In all waters where bass rise to a floating bait it will prove the best attracter and surest but fairest killer. For ease of casting and steadiness, beauty and ease of running or reeling qualities, we feel confident the "Dowagiac" will win its way onto the end of the line of every judge of the artistic in tackle.

ELEVEN REASONS

Why the "Dowagiac" is the Best Surface Casting Bait Ever Tied to a Line.

1. It always runs the same side up, thus admitting of perfect hook presentment, where long experience teaches they are most needed.

2. The sockets or in-sets into which the hooks are fastened keep them **Always Outward** and presented to the fish.

3. The "Dowagiac" creates more commotion in the water than any other bait, (and reels easier,) which is a strong point in attracting game fish.

4. It casts nicely, because of fine relation between size, weight and buoyancy.

5. It reels in easily, (offering only that resistance necessary to "make a good spool,") and is therefore not tiring to the nerves nor wearing on the tackle.

6. It has no whirling parts, thus insuring against weakening and twisting the line and consequent "runbacks" or "back-lashes."

7. Its colors excite the beligerency of the bass and attract him at a greater distance than any other lure.

8. It cannot leak or soak water and thus always remains of proper weight.

9. By virtue of the collar it is less liable to catch weeds and rushes than any other bait possessing reasonable killing qualities.

10. It always remains on the surface, whether moving or still, floating the line and avoiding weeds below the surface.

11. All hooks are so fastened as to be instantly removed in case of breakage or should other sizes be preferred by the angler.

Besides the above points of superiority, many objections usually found in the construction of artificial baits have been entirely eliminated from the "Dowagiac."

The "Dowagiac" is **Patented**, (date of April 1, 1902,) and the patent covers the angling collar, independent, the socket, independent, the screw-eyes, independent, (that is when used in any fish bait,) and the elevated fore-end, when used in combination with any collar or any bait. Liberal rewards will be paid for information leading to the conviction of anyone found illegally selling or using any bait containing any of the patented features of the "Dowagiac."

There are some lakes, where the black bass keep in the deeper water, especially early in the season, being, like pickerel, reluctant to rise to the surface in response to the most tempting lure, and for use under these conditions we have devised an under-water bait that is a wonderful killer, a beautiful bait to cast, and which is protected by our patent, and will soon be placed upon the market.

Price, sent postpaid   75 Cents

JAMES HEDDON & SON
Makers
DOWAGIAC,   ·   ·   ·   MICHIGAN

This is the box paper insert for "The Dowagiac Perfect Surface Casting Bait," circa 1902. On the backside of the paper it says, "The Dowagiac No. 1 Bait Contained in this box..." This would be the very first Heddon box paper. The bottom of the backside of the paper mentions that Heddon has devised a new underwater bait that would soon be placed on the market. This box paper also was used for the Dowagiac No. 2. On the backside, Heddon changed the flyer to read, "The Dowagiac No. 2 Bait..." The factory also modified the bottom of the back side of the flyer to say they have an underwater bait protected by their patent. This would validate the theory that the Underwater Expert was the second bait produced by Heddon. Lastly, this box paper was again used in 1903 when Heddon changed the name from the "Dowagiac Perfect Surface Casting Bait" to the "Dowagiac Expert." The backside of the flyer was changed again from "The Dowagiac No. 1 Bait" to "The Dowagiac Expert," further reflecting the name change.

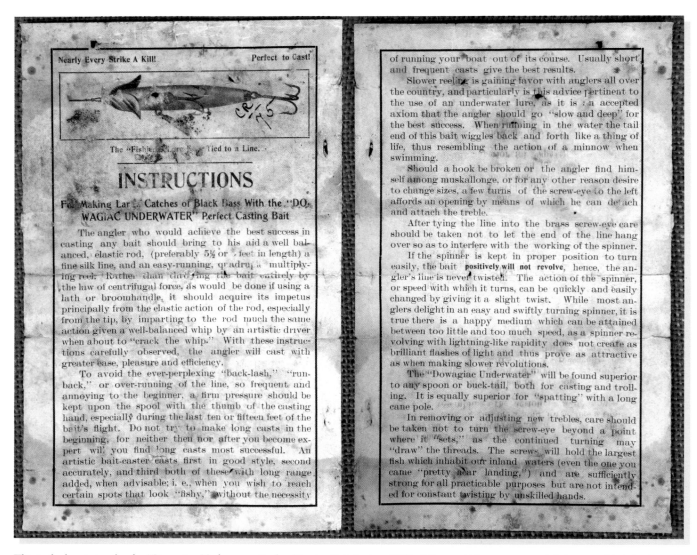

Nearly Every Strike A Kill!   **Perfect to Cast!**

The "Fishing Lure" as Tied to a Line.

INSTRUCTIONS

For Making Large Catches of Black Bass With the "DO-WAGIAC UNDERWATER" Perfect Casting Bait

The angler who would achieve the best success in casting any bait should bring to his aid a well balanced, elastic rod, (preferably 5½ or 6 feet in length) a fine silk line, and an easy-running, quadruple multiplying reel. Rather than directing the bait entirely by the law of centrifugal force, as would be done if using a lath or broomhandle, it should acquire its impetus principally from the elastic action of the rod, especially from the tip, by imparting to the rod much the same action given a well-balanced whip by an artistic driver when about to "crack the whip." With these instructions carefully observed, the angler will cast with greater ease, pleasure and efficiency.

To avoid the ever-perplexing "back-lash," "run-back," or over-running of the line, so frequent and annoying to the beginner, a firm pressure should be kept upon the spool with the thumb of the casting hand, especially during the last ten or fifteen feet of the bait's flight. Do not try to make long casts in the beginning, for neither then nor after you become expert will you find long casts most successful. An artistic bait-caster casts first in good style, second accurately, and third both of these with long range added, when advisable; i. e., when you wish to reach certain spots that look "fishy," without the necessity

of running your boat out of its course. Usually short and frequent casts give the best results.

Slower reeling is gaining favor with anglers all over the country, and particularly is this advice pertinent to the use of an underwater lure, as it is an accepted axiom that the angler should go "slow and deep" for the best success. When running in the water the tail end of this bait wiggles back and forth like a thing of life, thus resembling the action of a minnow when swimming.

Should a hook be broken or the angler find himself among muskallonge, or for any other reason desire to change sizes, a few turns of the screw-eye to the left affords an opening by means of which he can detach and attach the treble.

After tying the line into the brass screw-eye care should be taken not to let the end of the line hang over so as to interfere with the working of the spinner. If the spinner is kept in proper position to turn easily, the bait **positively will not revolve**, hence, the angler's line is never twisted. The action of the spinner, or speed with which it turns, can be quickly and easily changed by giving it a slight twist. While most anglers delight in an easy and swiftly turning spinner, it is true there is a happy medium which can be attained between too little and too much speed, as a spinner revolving with lightning-like rapidity does not create as brilliant flashes of light and thus prove as attractive as when making slower revolutions.

The "Dowagiac Underwater" will be found superior to any spoon or buck-tail, both for casting and trolling. It is equally superior for "spatting" with a long cane pole.

In removing or adjusting new trebles, care should be taken not to turn the screw-eye beyond a point where it "sets," as the continued turning may "draw" the threads. The screws will hold the largest fish which inhabit our inland waters (even the one you came "pretty near landing,") and are sufficiently strong for all practicable purposes but are not intended for constant twisting by unskilled hands.

This is the box paper for the "Dowagiac Underwater Perfect Casting Bait," circa 1902. This would have accompanied the second bait in the early Heddon line. The same Underwater Expert picture was used for the 1903 box papers, but the weight was eliminated from the paper, and the brass tailpiece was added. The write-up also was revised to include the aluminum underwater baits added that season.

This is the very first box paper for the No. 100 "New Dowagiac Minnow," circa 1904. This paper is the only one known and was inserted in Will Heddon's scrapbook long ago. Note the tail tube extension at the rear of the bait. This paper would have been folded into a white pasteboard box with the same picture on the lid as is shown in this paper.

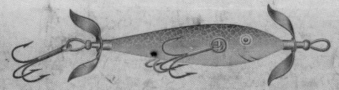

THE WHY OF IT!

Why the "Dowagiac" Minnow is Superior to Any of the Many Imitation Minnows on the Market

Because—It is small and of perfect casting weight.

Because—It will not soak water, being covered with six coats of water proof enamel which cannot be worn off.

Because—Its glistening white belly is easily seen and most attractive in the water.

Because—The patented Dowagiac method of attaching the hooks enables you to take off the trebles and to attach others by giving the screw-eye a few turns to the left.

Because—Our patented Dowagiac method of adjusting the trebles in a socket holds the points of the hooks outwardly, toward the fish, and therefore makes the killing qualities more certain.

Because—The Dowagiac method of hanging the hooks prevents them from interlocking or becoming tangled into each other, a feature so disagreeable and encountered upon other baits.

Because—The Minnow is strong and durable and has an elegance of design and workmanship possessed by no other bait.

Price, in wooden box, prepaid - - - - - 75c

JAMES HEDDON & SON

DOWAGIAC   MICHIGAN

HINTS FOR SUCCESS

Cast or troll the bait near lily pads and other aoquatic vegetation where bass usually abound.

Adjust the speed of retrieving to the depth of water and other prevailing conditions. Slow reeling wins the most strikes.

Always strike your fish as soon as it strikes the bait.

A drop of oil upon the spinders helps them to revolve more freely.

Your success in hooking fish depends largely upon keeping the points of the hooks sharp. Don't allow them to get rusty and dull. A few minutes' work with a file upon the points may prevent your losing "that big one."

This is the second box paper produced for the new No. 100 Dowagiac Minnow in 1904. This paper would accompany a lure packaged in a one-way slide-top wooden box that says, "The New Dowagiac Minnow"on the lid. The box would hold a three belly-weight No. 100 or No. 150. The paper is identifiable by the caption, "The Why of It" at the top of the sheet. In the left margin the word "Because" is printed seven times in red ink. There is no writing on the back.

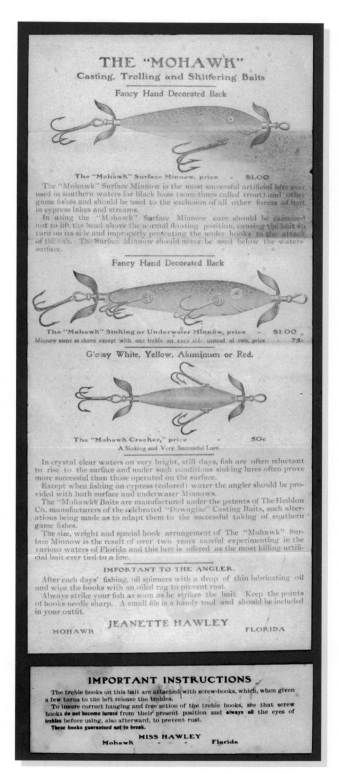

This is the box paper for the Jeanette Hawley or "Mohawk" casting, trolling, and skittering baits, circa 1905. The flyer shows the three baits produced by Will Heddon and his wife, Laura Heddon, who used Hawley as a pen-name. The second paper offers instructions for the care of this important bait.

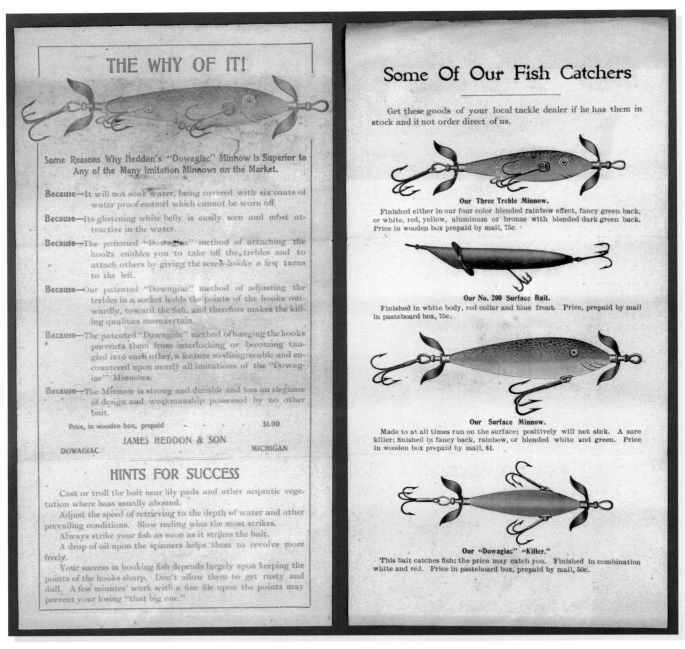

THE WHY OF IT!

Some Reasons Why Heddon's "Dowagiac" Minnow is Superior to Any of the Many Imitation Minnows on the Market.

Because—It will not soak water, being covered with six coats of water proof enamel which cannot be worn off.

Because—Its glistening white belly is easily seen and most attractive in the water.

Because—The patented "Dowagiac" method of attaching the hooks enables you to take off the trebles and to attach others by giving the screw-hooks a few turns to the left.

Because—Our patented "Dowagiac" method of adjusting the trebles in a socket holds the points of the hooks outwardly, toward the fish, and therefore makes the killing qualities more certain.

Because—The patented "Dowagiac" method of hanging the hooks prevents them from interlocking or becoming tangled into each other, a feature so disagreeable and encountered upon nearly all imitations of the "Dowagiac" Minnows.

Because—The Minnow is strong and durable and has an elegance of design and workmanship possessed by no other bait.

Price, in wooden box, prepaid $1.00

JAMES HEDDON & SON
DOWAGIAC   MICHIGAN

HINTS FOR SUCCESS

Cast or troll the bait near lily pads and other acquatic vegetation where bass usually abound.

Adjust the speed of retrieving to the depth of water and other prevailing conditions. Slow reeling wins the most strikes.

Always strike your fish as soon as it strikes the bait.

A drop of oil upon the spinners helps them to revolve more freely.

Your success in hooking fish depends largely upon keeping the points of the hooks sharp. Don't allow them to get rusty and dull. A few minutes' work with a fine file upon the points may prevent your losing "that big one."

Some Of Our Fish Catchers

Get these goods of your local tackle dealer if he has them in stock and if not order direct of us.

Our Three Treble Minnow.
Finished either in our four color blended rainbow effect, fancy green back, or white, red, yellow, aluminum or bronze with blended dark green back. Price in wooden box prepaid by mail, 75c.

Our No. 200 Surface Bait.
Finished in white body, red collar and blue front. Price, prepaid by mail in pasteboard box, 75c.

Our Surface Minnow.
Made to at all times run on the surface; positively will not sink. A sure killer; finished in fancy back, rainbow, or blended white and green. Price in wooden box prepaid by mail, $1.

Our "Dowagiac" "Killer."
This bait catches fish; the price may catch you. Finished in combination white and red. Price in pasteboard box, prepaid by mail, 50c.

This is the third Heddon box paper produced and would have come in a two-way, slide-top wooden box for "The New Dowagiac Minnow" or "The Dowagiac Minnow." The circa 1905 – 1906 boxes also would have the exclamation mark after the word "Hung" on the boxtop. The box paper has "The Why of It" at the top and the word "Because" in red ink in the margin six times. The back has advertisements for the No. 100, the Slopenose, the Killer, and the No. 300 baits.

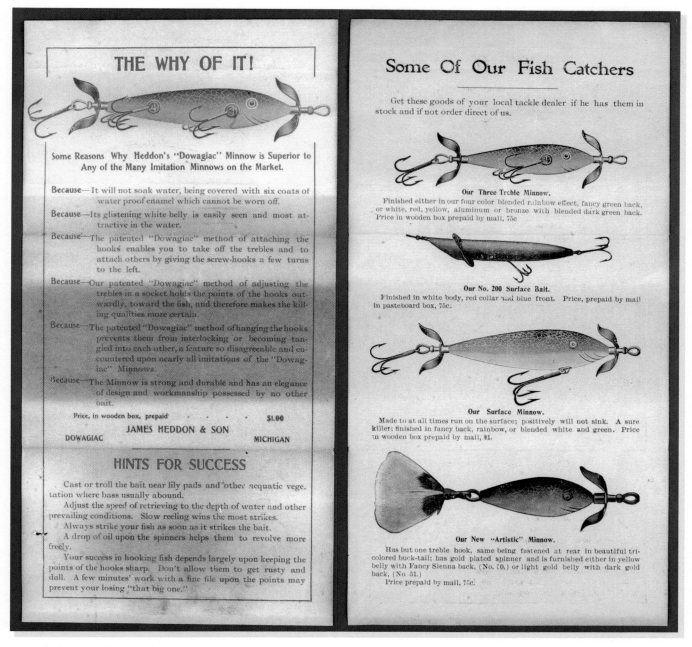

THE WHY OF IT!

Some Reasons Why Heddon's "Dowagiac" Minnow is Superior to Any of the Many Imitation Minnows on the Market.

Because— It will not soak water, being covered with six coats of water proof enamel which cannot be worn off.

Because—Its glistening white belly is easily seen and most attractive in the water.

Because—The patented "Dowagiac" method of attaching the hooks enables you to take off the trebles and to attach others by giving the screw-hooks a few turns to the left.

Because—Our patented "Dowagiac" method of adjusting the trebles in a socket holds the points of the hooks outwardly, toward the fish, and therefore makes the killing qualities more certain.

Because—The patented "Dowagiac" method of hanging the hooks prevents them from interlocking or becoming tangled into each other, a feature so disagreeable and encountered upon nearly all imitations of the "Dowagiac" Minnows.

Because—The Minnow is strong and durable and has an elegance of design and workmanship possessed by no other bait.

Price, in wooden box, prepaid · · · · $1.00

JAMES HEDDON & SON

DOWAGIAC   MICHIGAN

HINTS FOR SUCCESS

Cast or troll the bait near lily pads and other aquatic vegetation where bass usually abound.

Adjust the speed of retrieving to the depth of water and other prevailing conditions. Slow reeling wins the most strikes.

Always strike your fish as soon as it strikes the bait.

A drop of oil upon the spinners helps them to revolve more freely.

Your success in hooking fish depends largely upon keeping the points of the hooks sharp. Don't allow them to get rusty and dull. A few minutes' work with a fine file upon the points may prevent your losing "that big one."

Some Of Our Fish Catchers

Get these goods of your local tackle dealer if he has them in stock and if not order direct of us.

Our Three Treble Minnow.
Finished either in our four color blended rainbow effect, fancy green back, or white, red, yellow, aluminum or bronze with blended dark green back. Price in wooden box prepaid by mail, 75c.

Our No. 200 Surface Bait.
Finished in white body, red collar and blue front. Price, prepaid by mail in pasteboard box, 75c.

Our Surface Minnow.
Made to at all times run on the surface; positively will not sink. A sure killer; finished in fancy back, rainbow, or blended white and green. Price in wooden box prepaid by mail, $1.

Our New "Artistic" Minnow.
Has but one treble hook, same being fastened at rear in beautiful tricolored buck-tail; has gold plated spinner and is furnished either in yellow belly with Fancy Sienna back, (No. 70,) or light gold belly with dark gold back, (No 51.)
Price prepaid by mail, 75c.

This is the fourth and last of "The Dowagiac Minnow" wooden box papers, circa 1906 – 1907. This paper would show the No. 100, the Slopenose, the No. 50 Artistic Minnow, and either the No. 300 Surface or the No. 400 Bucktail Surface lure. This paper also would have "The Why of It" at the top and the "Because" in red ink in the margin six times.

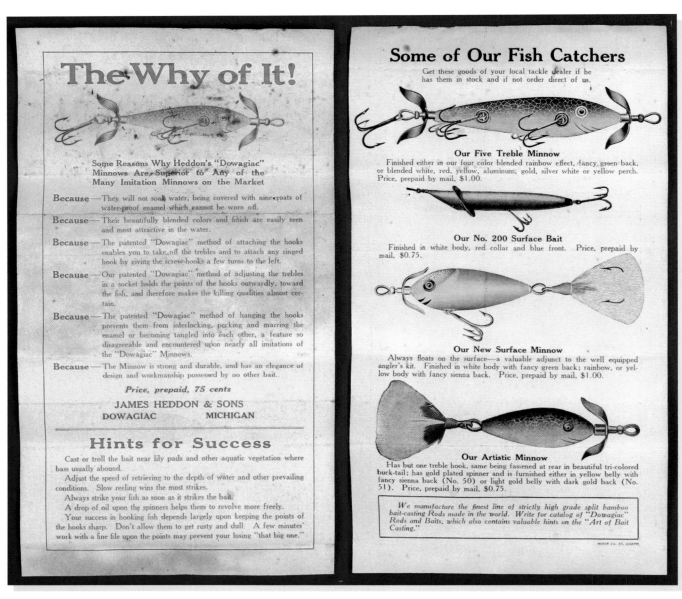

The Why of It!

Some Reasons Why Heddon's "Dowagiac" Minnows Are Superior to Any of the Many Imitation Minnows on the Market

Because—They will not soak water, being covered with nine coats of water-proof enamel which cannot be worn off.

Because—Their beautifully blended colors and finish are easily seen and most attractive in the water.

Because—The patented "Dowagiac" method of attaching the hooks enables you to take off the trebles and to attach any ringed hook by giving the screw-hooks a few turns to the left.

Because—Our patented "Dowagiac" method of adjusting the trebles in a socket holds the points of the hooks outwardly, toward the fish, and therefore makes the killing qualities almost certain.

Because—The patented "Dowagiac" method of hanging the hooks prevents them from interlocking, pecking and marring the enamel or becoming tangled into each other, a feature so disagreeable and encountered upon nearly all imitations of the "Dowagiac" Minnows.

Because—The Minnow is strong and durable, and has an elegance of design and workmanship possessed by no other bait.

Price, prepaid, 75 cents

JAMES HEDDON & SONS
DOWAGIAC   MICHIGAN

Hints for Success

Cast or troll the bait near lily pads and other aquatic vegetation where bass usually abound.

Adjust the speed of retrieving to the depth of water and other prevailing conditions. Slow reeling wins the most strikes.

Always strike your fish as soon as it strikes the bait.

A drop of oil upon the spinners helps them to revolve more freely.

Your success in hooking fish depends largely upon keeping the points of the hooks sharp. Don't allow them to get rusty and dull. A few minutes' work with a fine file upon the points may prevent your losing "that big one."

Some of Our Fish Catchers

Get these goods of your local tackle dealer if he has them in stock and if not order direct of us.

Our Five Treble Minnow
Finished either in our four color blended rainbow effect, fancy green back, or blended white, red, yellow, aluminum, gold, silver white or yellow perch. Price, prepaid by mail, $1.00.

Our No. 200 Surface Bait
Finished in white body, red collar and blue front. Price, prepaid by mail, $0.75.

Our New Surface Minnow
Always floats on the surface—a valuable adjunct to the well equipped angler's kit. Finished in white body with fancy green back; rainbow, or yellow body with fancy sienna back. Price, prepaid by mail, $1.00.

Our Artistic Minnow
Has but one treble hook, same being fastened at rear in beautiful tri-colored buck-tail; has gold plated spinner and is furnished either in yellow belly with fancy sienna back (No. 50) or light gold belly with dark gold back (No. 51). Price, prepaid by mail, $0.75.

We manufacture the finest line of strictly high grade split bamboo bait-casting Rods made in the world. Write for catalog of "Dowagiac" Rods and Baits, which also contains valuable hints on the "Art of Bait Casting."

MOORE CO. ST. JOSEPH

This is the last of "The Why of It" papers, circa 1908 – 1911. This paper would be found in the white pasteboard boxes of the era showing blue and red lettering on the box lids. Note that on this paper, the prices of the baits have been reduced from $1.00 to 75¢ to make room for new stock.

This is the very rare paperwork for the No. 300 Surface Minnow of the wooden box era. This dates to 1907, and the paperwork includes mention of the No. 100, No. 150, and the "new" Artistic Minnow.

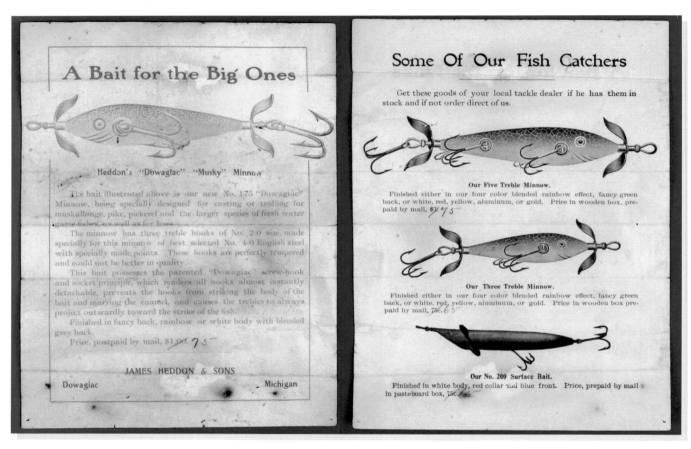

This is a very rare paper flyer for the No. 175 Heavy Casting Minnow, circa 1906 – 1907. These papers would be found in wooden boxes only.

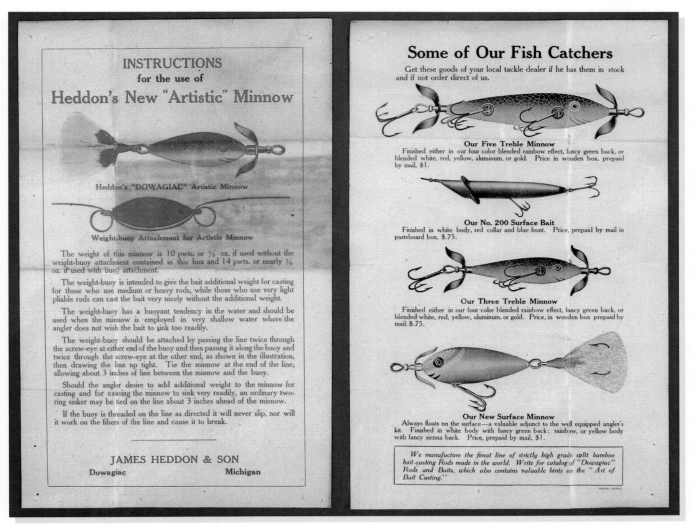

INSTRUCTIONS
for the use of
Heddon's New "Artistic" Minnow

Heddon's "DOWAGIAC" Artistic Minnow

Weight-buoy Attachment for Artistic Minnow

The weight of this minnow is 10 pwts. or ½ oz. if used without the weight-buoy attachment contained in this box and 14 pwts. or nearly ¾ oz. if used with buoy attachment.

The weight-buoy is intended to give the bait additional weight for casting for those who use medium or heavy rods, while those who use very light pliable rods can cast the bait very nicely without the additional weight.

The weight-buoy has a buoyant tendency in the water and should be used when the minnow is employed in very shallow water where the angler does not wish the bait to sink too readily.

The weight-buoy should be attached by passing the line twice through the screw-eye at either end of the buoy and then passing it along the buoy and twice through the screw-eye at the other end, as shown in the illustration, then drawing the line up tight. Tie the minnow at the end of the line, allowing about 3 inches of line between the minnow and the buoy.

Should the angler desire to add additional weight to the minnow for casting and for causing the minnow to sink very readily, an ordinary two-ring sinker may be tied on the line about 3 inches ahead of the minnow.

If the buoy is threaded on the line as directed it will never slip, nor will it work on the fibers of the line and cause it to break.

JAMES HEDDON & SON
Dowagiac   **Michigan**

Some of Our Fish Catchers

Get these goods of your local tackle dealer if he has them in stock and if not order direct of us.

Our Five Treble Minnow
Finished either in our four color blended rainbow effect, fancy green back, or blended white, red, yellow, aluminum, or gold. Price in wooden box, prepaid by mail, $1.

Our No. 200 Surface Bait
Finished in white body, red collar and blue front. Price, prepaid by mail in pasteboard box, $.75.

Our Three Treble Minnow
Finished either in our four color blended rainbow effect, fancy green back, or blended white, red, yellow, aluminum, or gold. Price, in wooden box prepaid by mail, $.75.

Our New Surface Minnow
Always floats on the surface—a valuable adjunct to the well equipped angler's kit. Finished in white body with fancy green back; rainbow, or yellow body with fancy sienna back. Price, prepaid by mail, $1.

We manufacture the finest line of strictly high grade split bamboo bait-casting Rods made in the world. Write for catalog of "Dowagiac" Rods and Baits, which also contains valuable hints on the "Art of Bait Casting."

This is the introductory paperwork for the Artistic Minnow and would have been folded into the small, maroon boxes that contained the buoy weight attachment.

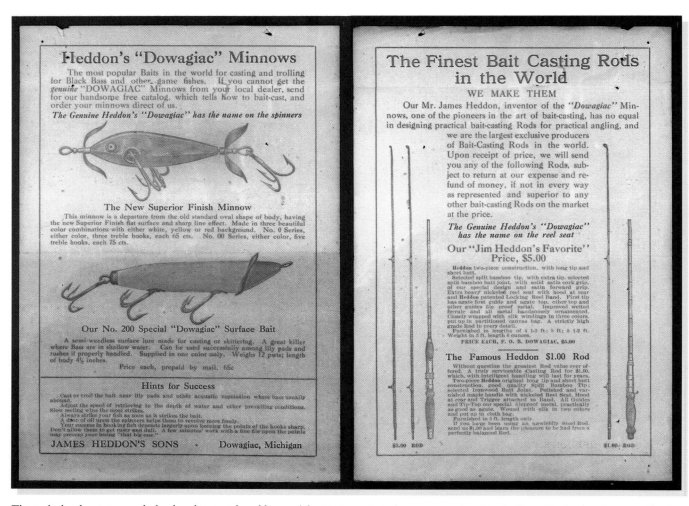

Heddon's "Dowagiac" Minnows

The most popular Baits in the world for casting and trolling for Black Bass and other game fishes. If you cannot get the genuine "DOWAGIAC" Minnows from your local dealer, send for our handsome free catalog, which tells how to bait-cast, and order your minnows direct of us.

The Genuine Heddon's "Dowagiac" has the name on the spinners

The New Superior Finish Minnow

This minnow is a departure from the old standard oval shape of body, having the new Superior Finish flat surface and sharp line effect. Made in three beautiful color combinations with either white, yellow or red background. No. 0 Series, either color, three treble hooks, each 65 cts. No. 00 Series, either color, five treble hooks, each 75 cts.

Our No. 200 Special "Dowagiac" Surface Bait

A semi-weedless surface lure made for casting or skittering. A great killer where Bass are in shallow water. Can be used successfully among lily pads and rushes if properly handled. Supplied in one color only. Weighs 12 pwts; length of body 4½ inches.

Price each, prepaid by mail, 65c

Hints for Success

Cast or troll the bait near lily pads and other aquatic vegetation where bass usually abound.

Adjust the speed of retrieving to the depth of water and other prevailing conditions. Slow reeling wins the most strikes.

Always strike your fish as soon as it strikes the bait.

A drop of oil upon the spinners helps them to revolve more freely.

Your success in hooking fish depends largely upon keeping the points of the hooks sharp. Don't allow them to get rusty and dull. A few minutes' work with a fine file upon the points may prevent your losing "that big one."

JAMES HEDDON'S SONS · Dowagiac, Michigan

The Finest Bait Casting Rods in the World

WE MAKE THEM

Our Mr. James Heddon, inventor of the "Dowagiac" Minnows, one of the pioneers in the art of bait-casting, has no equal in designing practical bait-casting Rods for practical angling, and we are the largest exclusive producers of Bait-Casting Rods in the world. Upon receipt of price, we will send you any of the following Rods, subject to return at our expense and refund of money, if not in every way as represented and superior to any other bait-casting Rods on the market at the price.

The Genuine Heddon's "Dowagiac" has the name on the reel seat

Our "Jim Heddon's Favorite" Price, $5.00

Heddon two-piece construction, with long tip and short butt.

Selected split bamboo tip, with extra tip, selected split bamboo butt joint, with solid satin cork grip, of our special design and satin forward grip. Extra heavy nickeled reel seat with hood at rear and Heddon patented Locking Reel Band. First tip has agate first guide and agate top, other top and other guides file proof metal. Improved welted ferrule and all metal handsomely ornamented. Closely wrapped with silk windings in three colors, put up in partitioned canvas bag. A strictly high grade Rod in every detail.

Furnished in lengths of 4 1-2 ft.; 5 ft.; 5 1-2 ft. Weight in 5 ft. length 6 ounces.

PRICE EACH, F. O. B. DOWAGIAC, $5.00

The Famous Heddon $1.00 Rod

Without question the greatest Rod value ever offered. A truly serviceable Casting Rod for $1.00, which, with intelligent handling will last for years.

Two-piece Heddon original long tip and short butt construction, good quality Split Bamboo Tip; selected Ironwood Butt Joint. Polished and varnished maple handle with nickeled Reel Seat, Hood at rear and Trigger attached to Band. All Guides and Tip-Top our special fileproof metal, practically as good as agate. Wound with silk in two colors and put up in cloth bag.

If you have been using an unwieldy Steel Rod, send us $1.00 and learn the pleasure to be had from a perfectly balanced Rod.

$5.00 ROD $1.00 ROD

This is the last box paper made for the white pasteboard boxes of the 1911 era. It is also sometimes found in the first white-border, downward leaping bass boxes of 1911 – 1912. The boxes would have the phrase "Heddon's Dowagiac Stamped on the Spinners."

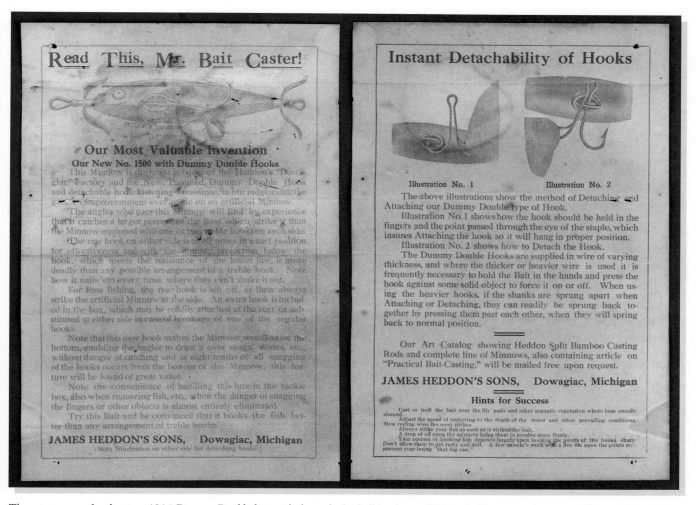

Read This, Mr. Bait Caster!

Our Most Valuable Invention
Our New No. 1500 with Dummy Double Hooks

This Minnow is the latest product of the Heddon's "Dowagiac" Factory and the New, Patented, Dummy Double Hook and detachable hook fastening constitute, in our judgement, the greatest improvement ever made on an artificial Minnow.

The angler who uses this Minnow will find by experience that it catches a larger percent of the Bass which strike it than the Minnow equipped with one or two treble hooks on each side.

The one hook on either side is at all times in exact position for effectiveness and with the dummy projection below the hook, which meets the resistance of the lower jaw, is more deadly than any possible arrangement of a treble hook. Note how it nails 'em every time, where they can't shake it out.

For Bass fishing, the rear hook is left off, as Bass always strike the artificial Minnow at the side. An extra hook is included in the box, which may be readily attached at the rear or substituted at either side in case of breakage of one of the regular hooks.

Note that this new hook makes the Minnow weedless on the bottom, enabling the angler to draw it over snags, stones, etc., without danger of catching and as eight-tenths of all snagging of the hooks occurs from the bottom of the Minnow, this feature will be found of great value.

Note the convenience of handling this lure in the tackle box, also when removing fish, etc., when the danger of snagging the fingers or other objects is almost entirely eliminated.

Try this Bait and be convinced that it hooks the fish better than any arrangement of treble hooks.

JAMES HEDDON'S SONS,   Dowagiac, Michigan

Note Illustration on other side for detaching hooks.

Instant Detachability of Hooks

Illustration No. 1   Illustration No. 2

The above illustrations show the method of Detaching and Attaching our Dummy Double type of Hook.

Illustration No. 1 shows how the hook should be held in the fingers and the point passed through the eye of the staple, which insures Attaching the hook so it will hang in proper position.

Illustration No. 2 shows how to Detach the Hook.

The Dummy Double Hooks are supplied in wire of varying thickness, and where the thicker or heavier wire is used it is frequently necessary to hold the Bait in the hands and press the hook against some solid object to force it on or off. When using the heavier hooks, if the shanks are sprung apart when Attaching or Detaching, they can readily be sprung back together by pressing them past each other, when they will spring back to normal position.

Our Art Catalog showing Heddon Split Bamboo Casting Rods and complete line of Minnows, also containing article on "Practical Bait-Casting," will be mailed free upon request.

JAMES HEDDON'S SONS,   Dowagiac, Michigan

Hints for Success

Cast or troll the bait near the lily pads and other acquatic vegetation where bass usually abound.

Adjust the speed of retrieving to the depth of the water and other prevailing conditions. Slow reeling wins the most strikes.

Always strike your fish as soon as it strikes the bait.

A drop of oil upon the spinners helps them to revolve more freely.

Your success in hooking fish depends largely upon keeping the points of the hooks sharp. Don't allow them to get rusty and dull. A few minute's work with a fine file upon the points may prevent your losing "that big one."

These papers are for the circa 1914 Dummy-Double bait with the early football hardware. This is the "long paper" version. There is also a "short paper" version for the 1915 Dummy-Double, also with football hardware.

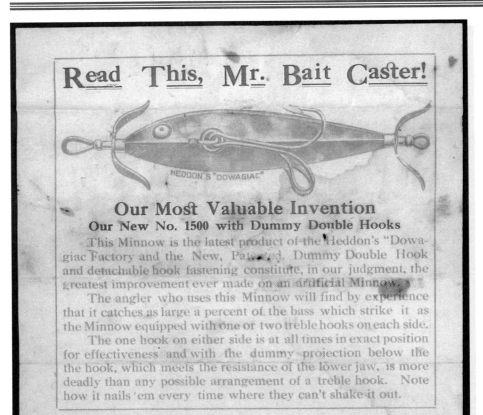

This is a circa 1916 – 1918 paper flyer for the L-rig version of the Dummy-Double.

This circa 1918 color flyer promoting the Baby Crab Wiggler was inserted into Heddon boxes containing many other lures — all part of an effort by Heddon to promote its Crab Wiggler baits. This flyer was used for several years thereafter and priced the bait at 95¢.

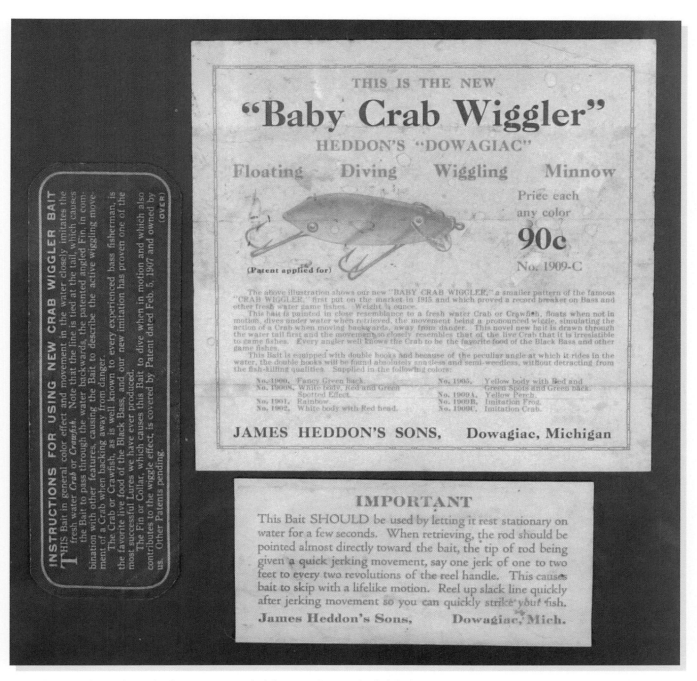

INSTRUCTIONS FOR USING NEW CRAB WIGGLER BAIT

THIS Bait in general color effect and movement in the water closely imitates the fresh water *Crab* or *Crawfish*. Note that the line is tied at the tail, which causes the Bait to pass through the water backwards, the patented angled Fin, in combination with other features, causing the Bait to describe the active wiggling movement of a Crab when backing away from danger.

The Crab or Crawfish, as is well known to every experienced bass fisherman, is the favorite live food of the Black Bass, and our new imitation has proven one of the most successful Lures we have ever produced.

The Fin or Collar, which causes this Bait to dive when in motion and which also contributes to the wiggle effect, is covered by Patent dated Feb. 5, 1907 and owned by us. Other Patents pending.

(OVER)

THIS IS THE NEW

"Baby Crab Wiggler"

HEDDON'S "DOWAGIAC"

Floating   Diving   Wiggling   Minnow

Price each
any color

90c

No. 1909-C

(Patent applied for)

The above illustration shows our new "BABY CRAB WIGGLER," a smaller pattern of the famous "CRAB WIGGLER," first put on the market in 1915 and which proved a record breaker on Bass and other fresh water game fishes. Weight ½ ounce.

This bait is painted in close resemblance to a fresh water Crab or Crawfish, floats when not in motion, dives under water when retrieved, the movement being a pronounced wiggle, simulating the action of a Crab when moving backwards, away from danger. This novel new bait is drawn through the water tail first and the movement so closely resembles that of the live Crab that it is irresistible to game fishes. Every angler well knows the Crab to be the favorite food of the Black Bass and other game fishes.

This Bait is equipped with double hooks and because of the peculiar angle at which it rides in the water, the double hooks will be found absolutely snagless and semi-weedless, without detracting from the fish-killing qualities. Supplied in the following colors:

No. 1900,	Fancy Green Back.	No. 1905,	Yellow body with Red and
No. 1900N,	White body, Red and Green		Green Spots and Green back.
	Spotted Effect.	No. 1909A,	Yellow Perch.
No. 1901,	Rainbow.	No. 1909B,	Imitation Frog.
No. 1902,	White body with Red head.	No. 1909C,	Imitation Crab.

JAMES HEDDON'S SONS,   Dowagiac, Michigan

IMPORTANT

This Bait SHOULD be used by letting it rest stationary on water for a few seconds. When retrieving, the rod should be pointed almost directly toward the bait, the tip of rod being given a quick jerking movement, say one jerk of one to two feet to every two revolutions of the reel handle. This causes bait to skip with a lifelike motion. Reel up slack line quickly after jerking movement so you can quickly strike your fish.

James Heddon's Sons,   **Dowagiac, Mich.**

The first Baby Crab Wiggler flyer, circa 1916, had the price of 90¢ and called the bait "new." The red cardboard hang tag was included.

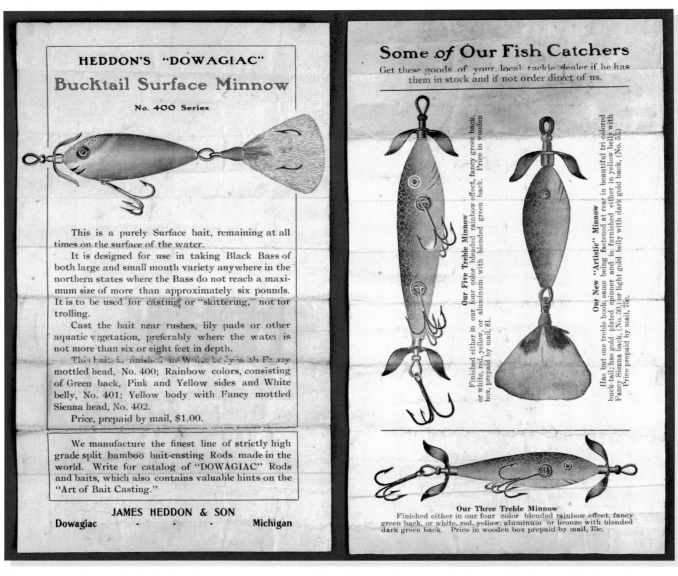

HEDDON'S "DOWAGIAC"
Bucktail Surface Minnow
No. 400 Series

This is a purely Surface bait, remaining at all times on the surface of the water.

It is designed for use in taking Black Bass of both large and small mouth variety anywhere in the northern states where the Bass do not reach a maximum size of more than approximately six pounds. It is to be used for casting or "skittering," not for trolling.

Cast the bait near rushes, lily pads or other aquatic vegetation, preferably where the water is not more than six or eight feet in depth.

This bait is finished in White body with Fancy mottled head, No. 400; Rainbow colors, consisting of Green back, Pink and Yellow sides and White belly, No. 401; Yellow body with Fancy mottled Sienna head, No. 402.

Price, prepaid by mail, $1.00.

We manufacture the finest line of strictly high grade split bamboo bait-casting Rods made in the world. Write for catalog of "DOWAGIAC" Rods and baits, which also contains valuable hints on the "Art of Bait Casting."

JAMES HEDDON & SON
Dowagiac · · · Michigan

Some of Our Fish Catchers
Get these goods of your local tackle dealer if he has them in stock and if not order direct of us.

Our Five Treble Minnow
Finished either in our four color blended rainbow effect, fancy green back, or white, red, yellow, or aluminum with blended green back. Price in wooden box, prepaid by mail, $1.

Our New "Artistic" Minnow
Has but one treble hook, same being fastened at rear in beautiful tri-colored buck-tail; has gold plated spinner and is furnished either in yellow belly with Fancy Sienna back, (No. 50,) or light gold belly with dark gold back, (No. 5½.) Price prepaid by mail, 75c.

Our Three Treble Minnow
Finished either in our four color blended rainbow effect, fancy green back, or white, red, yellow, aluminum or bronze with blended dark green back. Price in wooden box prepaid by mail, 75c.

This paper is for the No. 400 Bucktail Surface Minnow, circa 1908. This would be found in the special white pasteboard box made for this early minnow.

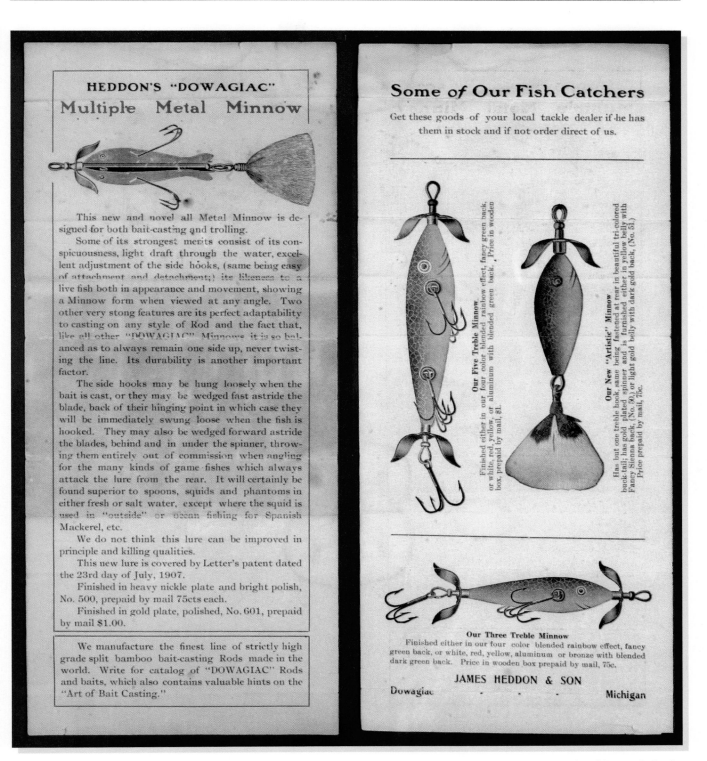

HEDDON'S "DOWAGIAC"
Multiple Metal Minnow

This new and novel all Metal Minnow is designed for both bait-casting and trolling.

Some of its strongest merits consist of its conspicuousness, light draft through the water, excellent adjustment of the side hooks, (same being easy of attachment and detachment;) its likeness to a live fish both in appearance and movement, showing a Minnow form when viewed at any angle. Two other very stong features are its perfect adaptability to casting on any style of Rod and the fact that, like all other "DOWAGIAC" Minnows it is so balanced as to always remain one side up, never twisting the line. Its durability is another important factor.

The side hooks may be hung loosely when the bait is cast, or they may be wedged fast astride the blade, back of their hinging point in which case they will be immediately swung loose when the fish is hooked. They may also be wedged forward astride the blades, behind and in under the spinner, throwing them entirely out of commission when angling for the many kinds of game fishes which always attack the lure from the rear. It will certainly be found superior to spoons, squids and phantoms in either fresh or salt water, except where the squid is used in "outside" or ocean fishing for Spanish Mackerel, etc.

We do not think this lure can be improved in principle and killing qualities.

This new lure is covered by Letter's patent dated the 23rd day of July, 1907.

Finished in heavy nickle plate and bright polish, No. 500, prepaid by mail 75cts each.

Finished in gold plate, polished, No. 601, prepaid by mail $1.00.

We manufacture the finest line of strictly high grade split bamboo bait-casting Rods made in the world. Write for catalog of "DOWAGIAC" Rods and baits, which also contains valuable hints on the "Art of Bait Casting."

Some of Our Fish Catchers

Get these goods of your local tackle dealer if he has them in stock and if not order direct of us.

Our Five Treble Minnow — Finished either in our four color blended rainbow effect, fancy green back, or white, red, yellow, or aluminum with blended green back. Price in wooden box, prepaid by mail, $1.

Our New "Artistic" Minnow — Has but one treble hook, same being fastened at rear in beautiful tri-colored buck-tail; has gold plated spinner and is furnished either in yellow belly with Fancy Sienna back, (No. 50,) or light gold belly with dark gold back, (No. 51.) Price prepaid by mail, 75c.

Our Three Treble Minnow — Finished either in our four color blended rainbow effect, fancy green back, or white, red, yellow, aluminum or bronze with blended dark green back. Price in wooden box prepaid by mail, 75c.

JAMES HEDDON & SON
Dowagiac · · · Michigan

Here is the box paper for the No. 500 Multiple Metal Minnow, circa 1908. This would be found in the special white pasteboard box made for this early minnow.

Heddon's "DOWAGIAC"
Night-Radiant or Moonlight Bait
Makes 'Em Bite At Night

In reponse to requests from our many friends, who have asked us to make a Night-Radiant or Moonlight bait, one which would possess the characteristic high grade construction, finish and durability of the "DOWAGIAC" Baits, we offer herewith the new Heddon's "DOWAGIAC" Night-Radiant or Moonlight Bait, a surface or floating lure, designed for catching Bass and other surface biting game fishes which are well known night feeders.

This Bait is the strongest self-radiant or self-glowing lure ever produced, being coated with a special preparation for absorbing either daylight or bright artificial light, radiating same for many hours when exposed at night.

This bait is equally successful for daytime fishing and is so constructed as to give it peculiar attractive motions and make it a practically sure killer.

The constant use of it in the daytime in no way detracts from the result at night or self-glowing properties. Several features of this bait are under our patent.

How to Use the Bait
Cast it near aquatic vegetation the same as any other Surface lure. The darker the night the better the bait will show.

Care of the Bait
The bait should be exposed to daylight or a bright artificial light for a half hour or more before using. A fresh exposure is necessary for every fishing trip. The radiant properties will last for years.

Price postpaid by mail, $1.00.
Dealers should write to their jobbers or direct to us for special prices.

We manufacture the finest line of strictly high grade split bamboo bait-casting rods made in the world. Write for catalog of "DOWAGIAC" rods and baits, which also contains valuable hints on the "Art of Bait Casting."

JAMES HEDDON & SONS
Dowagiac - - - - Michigan

Special Notice
We advise the use of a bright lantern or lamp in the boat and two of the Night-Radiant lures, frequently alternated, one to secure a recharge of light while the other is being used. This insures strong luminosity.
JAMES HEDDON & SONS

This rare paper accompanied the No. 1000 Night-Radiant, or "Moonlight" bait, circa 1909 – 1910. It came with a second paper with instructions on "How to Use the Bait."

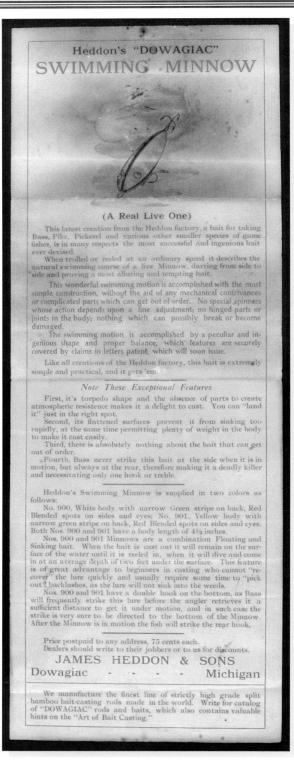

Heddon's "DOWAGIAC"
SWIMMING MINNOW

(A Real Live One)

This latest creation from the Heddon factory, a bait for taking Bass, Pike, Pickerel and various other smaller species of game fishes, is in many respects the most successful and ingenious bait ever devised.

When trolled or reeled at an ordinary speed it describes the natural swimming course of a live Minnow, darting from side to side and proving a most alluring and tempting bait.

This wonderful swimming motion is accomplished with the most simple construction, without the aid of any mechanical contrivances or complicated parts which can get out of order. No special spinners whose action depends upon a fine adjustment; no hinged parts or joints in the body; nothing which can possibly break or become damaged.

The swimming motion is accomplished by a peculiar and ingenious shape and proper balance, which features are securely covered by claims in letters patent, which will soon issue.

Like all creations of the Heddon factory, this bait is extremely simple and practical, and it gets 'em.

Note These Exceptional Features

First, it's torpedo shape and the absence of parts to create atmospheric resistence makes it a delight to cast. You can "land it" just in the right spot.

Second, its flattened surfaces prevent it from sinking too rapidly, at the same time permitting plenty of weight in the body to make it cast easily.

Third, there is absolutely nothing about the bait that can get out of order.

Fourth, Bass never strike this bait at the side when it is in motion, but always at the rear, therefore making it a deadly killer and necessitating only one hook or treble.

Heddon's Swimming Minnow is supplied in two colors as follows:

No. 900, White body with narrow Green stripe on back, Red Blended spots on sides and eyes; No. 901, Yellow body with narrow green stripe on back, Red Blended spots on sides and eyes. Both Nos. 900 and 901 have a body length of 4½ inches.

Nos. 900 and 901 Minnows are a combination Floating and Sinking bait. When the bait is cast out it will remain on the surface of the water until it is reeled in, when it will dive and come in at an average depth of two feet under the surface. This feature is of great advantage to beginners in casting who cannot "recover" the lure quickly and usually require some time to "pick out" backlashes, as the lure will not sink into the weeds.

Nos. 900 and 901 have a double hook on the bottom, as Bass will frequently strike this lure before the angler retrieves it a sufficient distance to get it under motion, and in such case the strike is very sure to be directed to the bottom of the Minnow. After the Minnow is in motion the fish will strike the rear hook.

Price postpaid to any address, 75 cents each.
Dealers should write to their jobbers or to us for discounts.
JAMES HEDDON & SONS
Dowagiac - - - - Michigan

We manufacture the finest line of strictly high grade split bamboo bait-casting rods made in the world. Write for catalog of "DOWAGIAC" rods and baits, which also contains valuable hints on the "Art of Bait Casting."

This introductory box paper accompanied the Swimming Minnow lures and can be found in the circa 1909 No. 900 Swimming Minnow and circa 1910 No. 800 Swimming Minnow boxes. These are the "Swims Swims Swims" boxes.

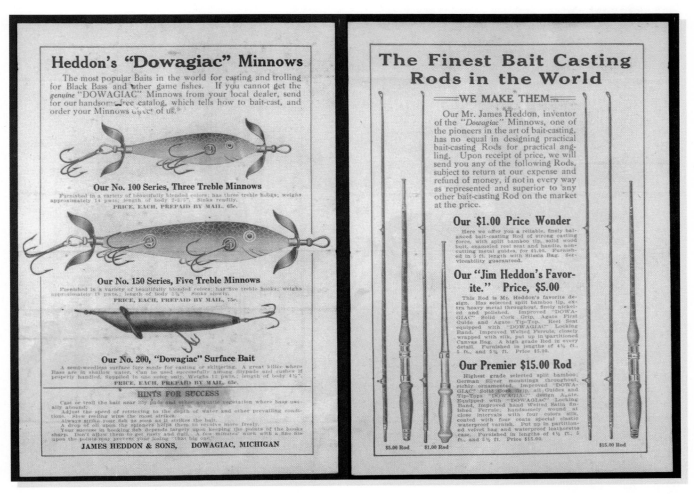

This box paper was inserted into the circa 1909 – 1911 white pasteboard boxes, into the circa 1909 – 1910 "center bass" logo boxes, and into white pasteboard boxes with Swimming Minnow lures.

Lure Boxes and Papers

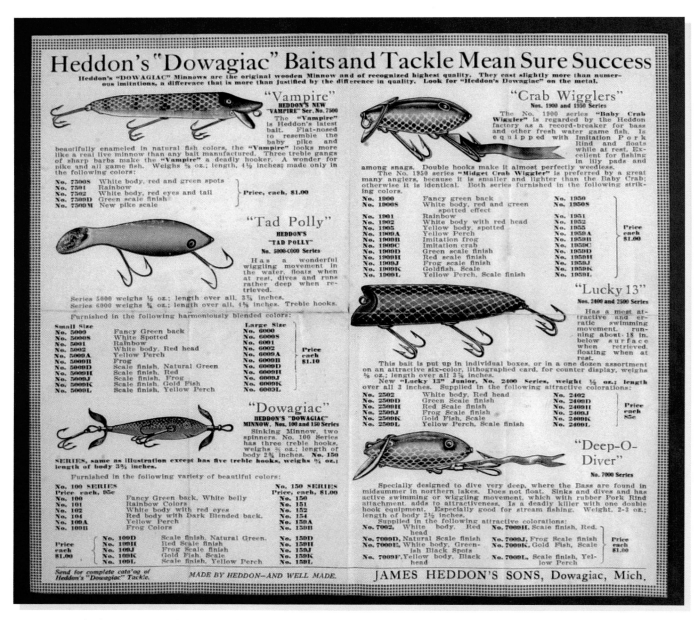

This box paper is for the circa 1919 – 1922 folded type downward leaping bass boxes. It mentions the "Vampire Vamp."

244

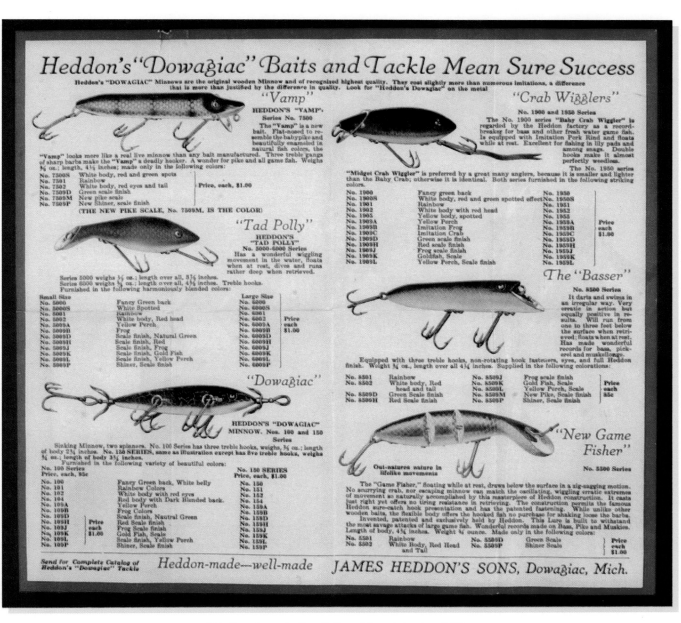

This flyer shows the "new" Gamefisher, dating it to 1923.

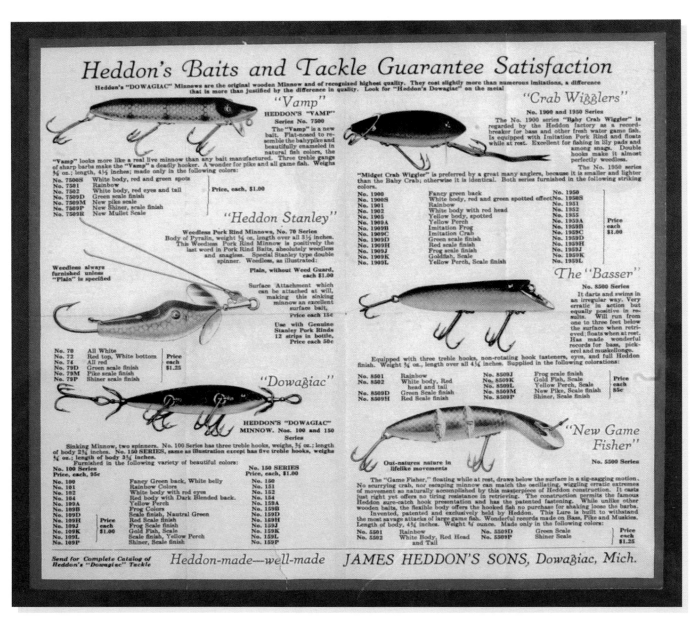

This flyer shows the Pork Rind Minnow, dating it to 1923.

(Facing page) Top: Heddon's Six First Choices, circa 1923. Bottom: This is the last of the foldout-style box paperwork from the 1920s, but shows up in boxes from 1926 and afterwards.

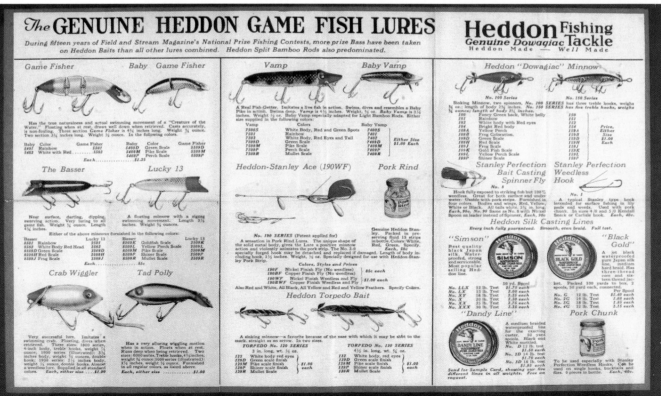

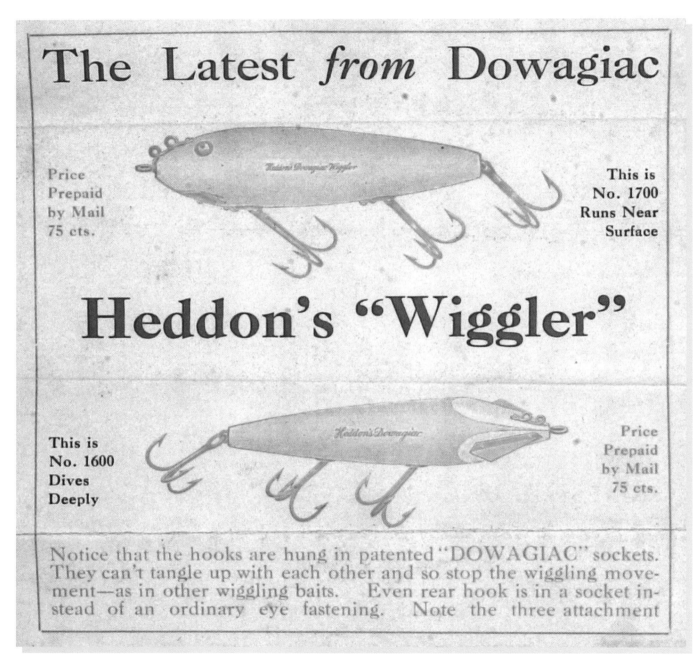

The Latest *from* Dowagiac

Price
Prepaid
by Mail
75 cts.

This is
No. 1700
Runs Near
Surface

Heddon's "Wiggler"

This is
No. 1600
Dives
Deeply

Price
Prepaid
by Mail
75 cts.

Notice that the hooks are hung in patented "DOWAGIAC" sockets. They can't tangle up with each other and so stop the wiggling movement—as in other wiggling baits. Even rear hook is in a socket instead of an ordinary eye fastening. Note the three attachment

This is the introductory flyer for the No. 1600 Wiggler, circa 1915.

WHAT OLD "JOHN T. FACT" SAYS:

When you're buying fishing tackle, here's Old John T. Fact himself to back you up in buying Heddon Rods, Reels and Baits for both Bait and Fly Casting.

Heddon Tackle has dominated in fourteen years of Field & Stream's National Prize Fishing Contests. Our last published record:

Out of 24 prize Bass caught on Wooden Baits, 13 were Heddon—the other eleven of all different makes. 20 Split Bamboo Rods were used—15 were Heddon.

We are justly proud of the above record, indicating the effectiveness of Heddon Tackle and the preference of the most successful fishermen in the country.

James Heddon's Sons   **Dowagiac, Mich.**

This interesting paper is found in some boxes dating to the late 1920s.

This tissue paper stamped with the Heddon logo is sometimes found with baits in downleaping boxes through 1920.

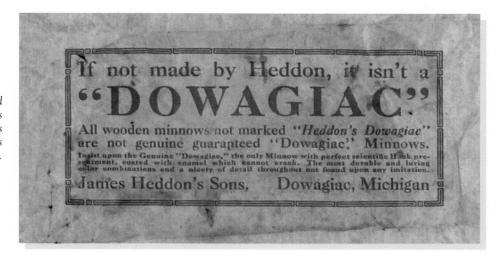

If not made by Heddon, it isn't a
"DOWAGIAC"
All wooden minnows not marked *"Heddon's Dowagiac"* are not genuine guaranteed *"Dowagiac"* Minnows.
Insist upon the Genuine "Dowagiac," the only Minnow with perfect scientific Hook pre-parement, coated with enamel which cannot crack. The most durable and luring color combinations and a nicety of detail throughout not found upon any imitation.
James Heddon's Sons,   Dowagiac, Michigan

Heddon Baits

(Genuine Dowagiacs)

Thousands upon thousands of all kinds of Game-Fish are caught each year on these "old reliable" Dowagiacs. All kinds for ALL purposes.

Floating — Diving — Swimming — Deep-Running — Action

Swimming Baits

Vamp

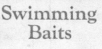

VAMP—7500 Series. A proven fish-getter. Imitates a live fish; swims and dives and resembles a Baby Pike. Made in three sizes. All favorite colors and finishes. 7500, size, 4½ inches.
BABY VAMP—7400 Series. A smaller bait for lighter rods. Length, 3½ inches. Price each $1.00.

Basser

BASSER—8500 Series. Near surface lure. Extremely erratic action, side-darting and dipping. Very luring to all game-fish. All popular colors and finishes. Length, 4½ inches. Price $1.00.

Game Fisher

GAME FISHER—5500 Series. Has a triple compound flexing movement in graceful, serpentine curves. Floats and draws well down in deep course according to speed. Casts accurately, is non-fouling and always works. All game-fish getter. Various colors and scale finish. Length, 4¾ inches. Price $1.25.
BABY GAME FISHER — 5400 Series. Similar action. Two joints. Length, 4 inches. Price $1.25.

Tad-Polly

TAD-POLLY—5000 Series. Deepest running of all floating baits. Deep diver when pulled in, with wonderful wiggling motion. A favorite for Wall-Eyed Pike and Small-Mouth Bass. All popular colors. 5000 Series, length 3¾ inches. 6000 Series, length 4⅝ inches. Price $1.00.

Lucky 13

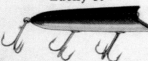

LUCKY 13—2500 Series. Another floating minnow of great merit. Draws slightly below surface with very effective zigzag swimming movement. A very popular lure. All colors and finishes. Length, 4 inches. Price $1.00.

Crab Wiggler

CRAB WIGGLER. Three sizes. Regarded as a superior achievement in casting baits. The special double-hook design has made this bait practically weedless and yet a great fish-getter. A surface lure exclusively of great attractiveness and wiggling movement. All desirable colors. Series 1800 Crab Wiggler, length 4 inches. 1900 Baby Crab, length 3½ inches. 1950 Midget Crab, length 2½ inches. Price each $1.00.

Sinking Baits

Torpedo

TORPEDO. A sinking minnow with slight body and revolving spinners. A great favorite for deep trolling and stream fishing. Excellent caster and a great favorite. All popular colors. 120, length 3 inches; 130, length 4½ inches. Price each $1.00.

"Dowagiac" Minnow

"DOWAGIAC" MINNOW. The original Heddon bait. A sinking minnow and an excellent caster. All popular colors. No. 100 Series, three treble hooks, length 2¾ inches. No. 150 Series, five treble hooks, length 3¾ inches.

Ace

ACE. A sensation in pork rind lures. Casts like a bullet, gives revolving appearance without line twisting. Practically weedless. Nickel, Copper, or Gold finish with bright feather. Length, 1¾ inches. Weight, ½ oz. Price $1.00.

Stanley Perfection Weedless Hooks

STANLEY PERFECTION WEEDLESS HOOKS. With and without spinner or flies. Can be used with pork rind. No. 8 Spinner Fly great for surface and underwater use. Several styles. Four colors. Price each 90 cents.

No. 1 Weedless Hook

No. 1 WEEDLESS HOOK. Single hook. Also made with Tandem hooks for pork strips. Also with Frog Tandem. Just the thing for weedy places, as they are 100% weedless. Price each 40 cents to 60 cents.

Pork Rind

PORK RIND. Packed in preserving fluid. 15 strips. Colors: White, Red and Green. Per bottle 50 cents. Also Pork Chunks, six pieces in bottle. Per bottle each 60 cents.

JAMES HEDDON'S SONS • Dowagiac, Michigan

This is a circa 1927 box paper.

This paper accompanies the Kinney Bird lure, sold in Florida but painted by Heddon in Dowagiac.

KINNEY'S BIRD LURES
FOR GAME FISH
Anglers, This Bird Don't "Sing"—It's a "Thriller"

This "BIRD" a fishing lure
Patented by Herbert A. Kinney Sept. 2C-1927 73503
HEDDON FINISH

THE WORLD'S FIRST BIRD LURE
For All Game Fish

ANGLERS know that a fluttering bird or fledgling on the water, is "desert" for all game fish. They strike it savagely. Our BIRD LURES positively imitate a fluttering bird on the water, when retrieved slowly, in short, "choppy" jerks, and if MR. BASS is around, "you got him." He don't "strike it," he "KILLS IT." **(No mistake about this.)**

Our BIRDS are each one finished and decorated in true AMERICAN BIRD colors, by one of the best artists in the Country.

PRICE $1.00 EACH, Postpaid
[STATE COLOR]

THE BEST DOLLAR'S WORTH YOU EVER GOT

This lure is the most expensive one made to sell at $1.00, but, anticipating an enormous sale—you get quality —we get ours in quantity.

Kinney's Famous BIRD LURES are proven BIG FISH GETTERS, and will give you Anglers "thrills" aplenty.

"THRILLS THAT LAST"

Just slip us a Dollar Bill, and get yours. State color of BIRD wanted, and pass this along to your fishing Buddy, (a sportsman's favor.) He will thank you.

ADDRESS
Old Hickory Rod & Tackle Company
Route No. 1, Box 137 A   Tampa, Florida

Heddon
WINONA
Tackle
Here's something good:

A gearless, easy running, casting and trolling Reel.

A "Keep - Fish - Alive" Stringer.

A Stringer-Holder to fasten onto boat seat.

A Float for Still-Fishing.

A pair of Serviceable Row Locks.

Ask your dealer, if he will not supply you, they will be sent direct on receipt of price and dealer's name.

JAMES HEDDON'S SONS
Dowagiac, Mich.

This advertising flyer is found in some lure boxes from the late 1920s.

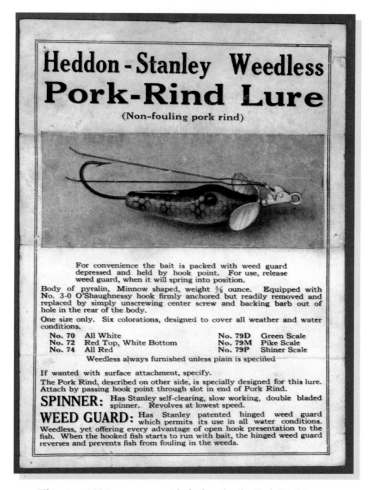

This circa 1924 paper goes with the box for the Pork Rind Lure.

This box flyer accompanied the Crazy Crawler, circa 1940s – 1950s.

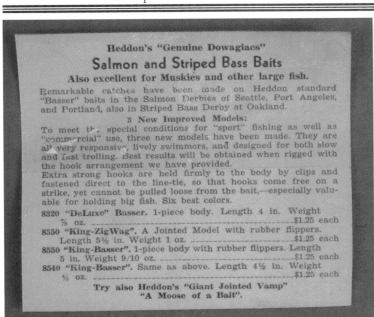

This 1936 box paper accompanied Heddon's rather extensive line of salmon baits.

These pocket catalogs were used from the 1940s into the early 1950s.

These pocket catalogs were used in the 1950s.

This older product catalog was added to lure boxes in the 1920s.

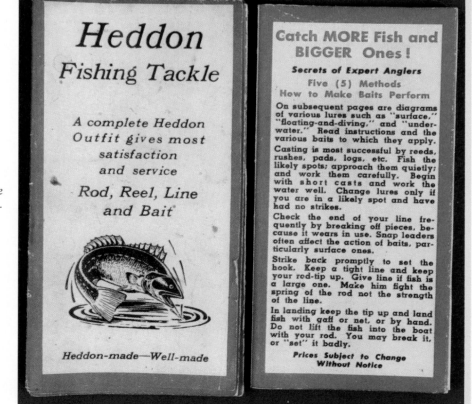

James Heddon's Sons first added reels to their product catalogs in 1912, a year after James Heddon's death left sons Will and Charles at the helm of what was destined to become the nation's most famous tackle company.

The earliest Heddon reels were actually the products of another well-known reel company – B.F. Meek & Sons of Kentucky. Heddon also marketed its own line of reels, manufactured at first by the Meisselbach Co.

Heddon soon realized the importance of reels to their overall image and marketing success and set out to recruit the top makers of the day to produce and manage that important aspect of their operation.

One of the new recruits was William Carter, who had owned a substantial interest in B.F. Meek & Sons prior to that company's sale to the Horton Manufacturing Co. in the summer of 1916. He joined Heddon the following year.

In 1919, Jack Welch became the factory superintendent at Heddon, having worked in previous years for B.F. Meek & Sons and another well-known reelsmith from Missouri, W.H. Talbot.

The years that followed included the introduction of some of the finest reels ever made. The pages that follow will cover some of the classics that have become favorites among collectors.

Summary of Heddon Reels

Model Number	Years Made
No. 30	1918 – 1919
No. 35	1918 – 1919
No. 40	1918 – 1919
No. 45	1918 – 1919
No. 3-15	1920 – 1927
No. 3-24	1920 – 1924
No. 3-30	1920 – 1924
No. 4-15	1922
No. 4-18	1923 – 1925
No. 3-35	1922 – 1926
No. 3-25	1926 – 1930

The Heddon Dowagiac No. 1 reel actually is a Meisselbach Takeapart, circa 1912 – 1915. Value range: $500.00 to $600.00. The Dowagiac No. 2 is rarer and worth more.

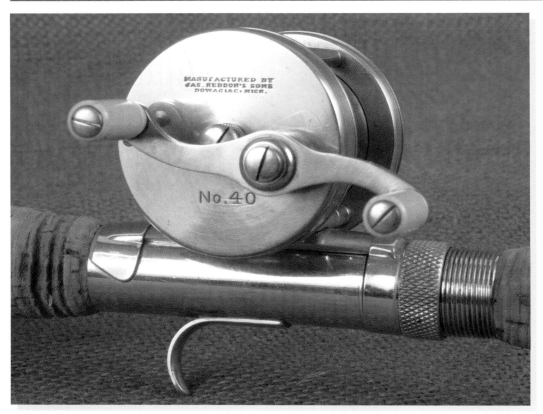

The No. 40 Kentucky pattern Takeapart dates to 1918 – 1919. Note the extra large handle found in many Heddon reels. It resembles the Bluegrass No. 25 reel of the same era. The No. 30 (not shown) is another high quality reel from the same era. Value range: $600.00 to $800.00. The No. 30 (not shown) is rarer and worth more.

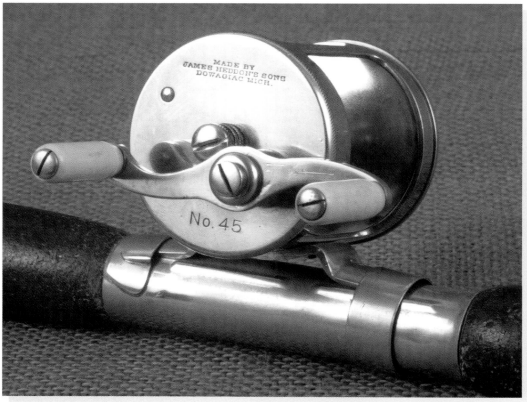

The No. 45 reel features a tubular frame and is a take-apart style reel. Its original price in the Heddon catalog was $9.00. It resembles the Bluegrass Simplex No. 33 in design and appearance. Value range: $200.00 to $300.00.

The No. 35 is an early Kentucky pattern reel, circa 1918 – 1919. Value range: $1,000.00+.

This is the Heddon 3-30 reel, circa 1920 – 1924. This was one of Heddon's finest reels, ranging from $30.00 to $60.00 in price, depending on which features it included. Value range: $500.00 to $600.00.

The Heddon 4-15 is an auto-spooler, circa 1922, with no patent date on the sideplates. This is the one known as the "windshield wiper" model due to the unusual level wind mechanism. Value range: $1,000.00+.

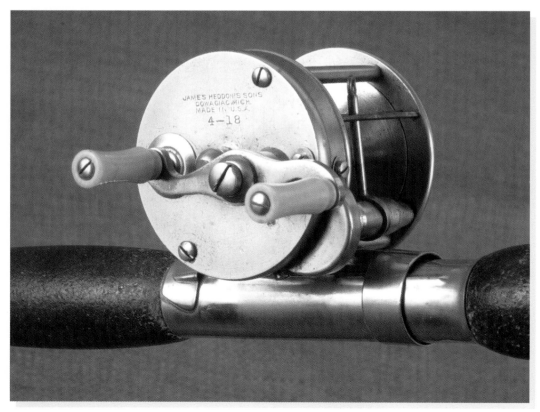

The Heddon 4-18 auto-spooler, circa 1923 – 1925, also has the "windshield wiper" feature that makes these reels so collectible. Value range: $1,000.00+.

The Heddon 3-35, circa 1922 – 1926, is a finely made level-winder. This is one of the many reels for which designer Jack Welch received a patent. Value range: $200.00 to $300.00.

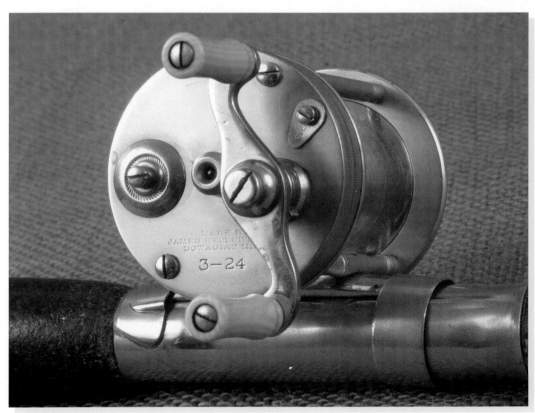

This is the Heddon Model 3-24, circa 1920 – 1924. It is hard to find, despite being carried in catalogs for a number of years. Value range: $1,000.00+.

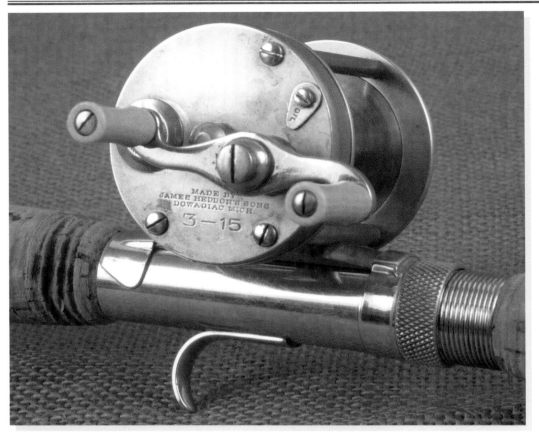

The Heddon Model 3-15,
circa 1920 – 1927, was a
favorite among anglers.
Value range: $200.00 to
$250.00.

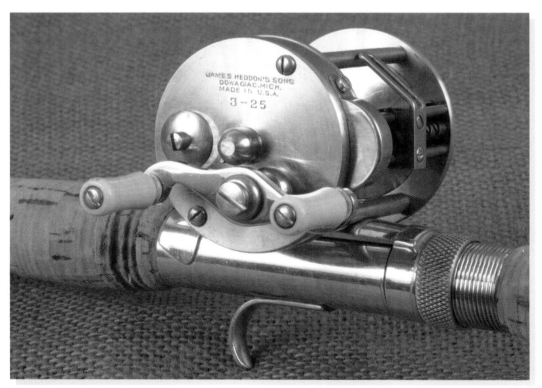

This is the Heddon Model
3-25, circa 1926 – 1930.
Reelsmith Jack Welch
received a patent for the
design of this reel. Value
range: $200.00 to
$350.00.

This is the finely made Jack Welch Tournament Casting Reel, stamped "hand made." Circa 1930. Value range: $1,000.00+.

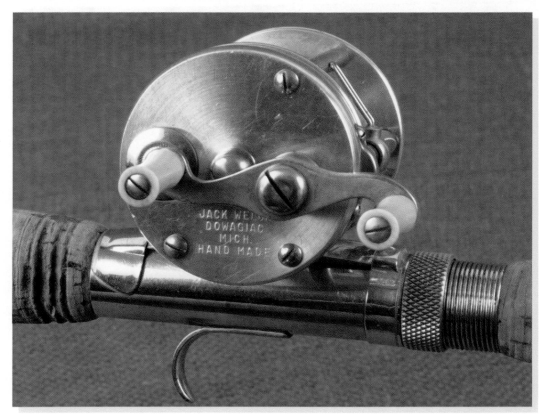

This is another Jack Welch reel, a level-winder, circa 1930, and stamped "Dowagiac, Mich." Value range: $1,000.00+.

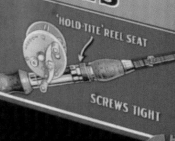

James Heddon and his sons took full advantage of their successful backgrounds in newspaper publishing and marketing when it came to promoting their products. The finest baits in the world were of little value unless anglers could be convinced to buy them, and the Heddons rapidly perfected the art of promotion. The following pages trace the lineage of Heddon's advertising campaigns from the early years into the 1960s.

Early product catalogs included finely lithographed color plates of Heddon's growing number of paint finishes. This 1906 page from a Belknap Hardware catalog certainly helped sell some Dowagiac minnows!

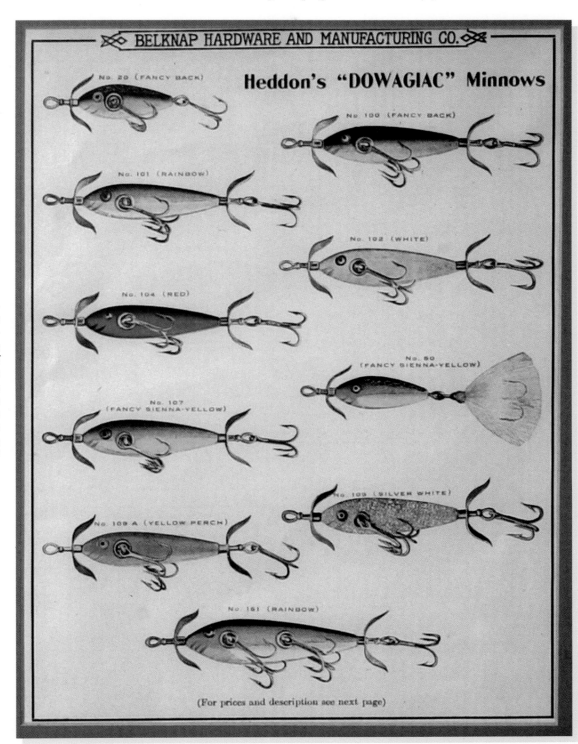

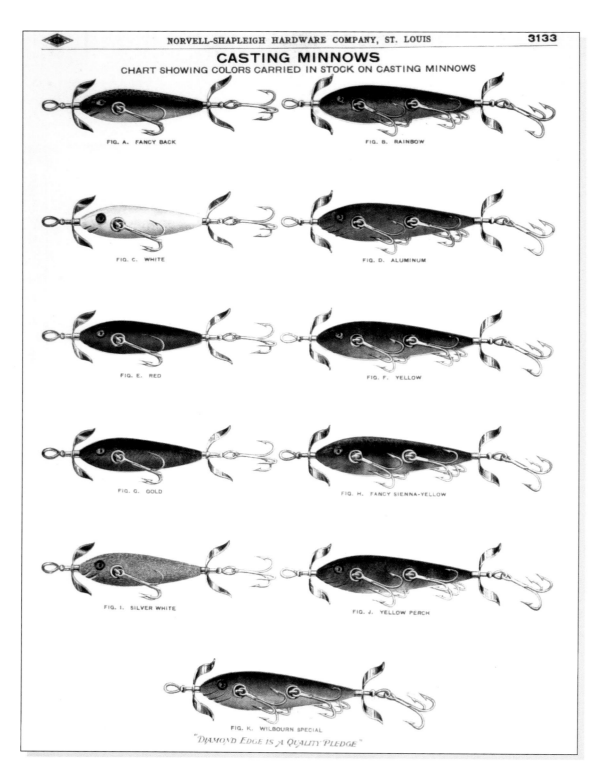

NORVELL-SHAPLEIGH HARDWARE COMPANY, ST. LOUIS   3133

CASTING MINNOWS
CHART SHOWING COLORS CARRIED IN STOCK ON CASTING MINNOWS

FIG. A. FANCY BACK

FIG. B. RAINBOW

FIG. C. WHITE

FIG. D. ALUMINUM

FIG. E. RED

FIG. F. YELLOW

FIG. G. GOLD

FIG. H. FANCY SIENNA-YELLOW

FIG. I. SILVER WHITE

FIG. J. YELLOW PERCH

FIG. K. WILBOURN SPECIAL

"DIAMOND EDGE IS A QUALITY PLEDGE"

This 1907 – 1908 page from the Norvell-Shapleigh Hardware Co. of St. Louis was used to promote Heddon's "casting minnows" to retailers and wholesalers.

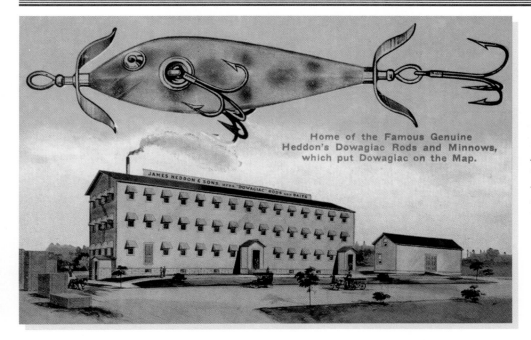

Home of the Famous Genuine
Heddon's Dowagiac Rods and Minnows,
which put Dowagiac on the Map.

This rare postcard — one of three known — is dated 1913, but the James Heddon & Son logo would date its origins to pre-1911, when James Heddon died and the company name became James Heddon's Sons.

"JIM" HEDDON'S LAST INVENTION

REFINING THE WOODEN MINNOW

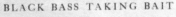

BLACK BASS TAKING BAIT

This illustration shows how the black bass, of all varieties and in all climates, always attacks the wooden minnow at the side, taking it between the jaws, not in the gullet. Note how effectively the one single hook is placed to engage the upper jaw and how the dummy portion will prevent the hook from dropping down and sliding out of the mouth without engagement. The dummy projection comes in contact with the lower jaw, forcing the hook point into the upper jaw. The old style of single hook is not efficient when attached to a wooden minnow, as the jaws of the fish are opened so widely by the wooden body of the minnow that the single hook readily slips out of the mouth when the angler strikes.

This Minnow and Hook gained a record last season of hooking nineteen bass without a miss.

It is not the number of hooks on the lure, but the character and presentation of them to the fish which insures the catch.

NEW DUMMY-DOUBLE MINNOW
No. 1300

(Above illustration shows the preferred coloration of this new Minnow, which will also be supplied in other standard color combinations upon special order.)

Equipped with two spinners; body portion, 3¾"long; weight, 13 pwts. Body shaped in our new flat surface and sharp line superior finish pattern, being our most artistic and beautifully finished product.

Hooks are fastened with a modified and improved construction of our patented socket principle, which holds the hook out away from the body of the bait and prevents the point from coming in contact with the body of the Minnow. This new style of socket, used only on this bait, gives maximum freedom of action to the hook, a very desirable feature. Equipped with one Dummy-Double on either side and without hook at rear. Leaving off rear hook does not decrease the certainty of the catch when fishing for bass. However, an extra hook, which may be instantly attached, is given with each bait, and may be put on at the rear or substituted for either of the side hooks, all hooks being readily detachable and interchangeable.

Price, each, prepaid by mail, $1.00, and worth much more
(Special colors without extra charge.)

HEDDON DUMMY-DOUBLE HOOK
PATENT APPLIED FOR

Jim Heddon, whose name is inseparably interwoven with the early development of the art of practical bait-casting, died December 7th, 1911.

One of his last ambitions was to rid the "*Dowagiac*" Minnows of the multiplicity of triple hooks, which have formed the only logical basis of objection ever urged against the wooden minnow.

He talked much of the advantages of the wooden minnow over the various forms of live bait, as specially adapted to bait-casting, and no feature was more often dwelt upon in his chats with sportsman companions than the fact that the wooden minnow rendered it no longer necessary to impale a live minnow upon a hook, or that still higher form of animal life, the frog.

He spoke often of the convenience of the artificial bait, and to the question of what, if any, objection could be urged against it aside from the multiplicity of hooks, he never received an answer.

His latest fishing days were devoted to experiments looking toward the elimination of the many hooks, and as a result of his tireless and painstaking efforts we are now enabled to offer the bait-casting world a type of wooden minnow which eliminates this last objection, and at the same time increases the certainty of the catch, but always in a truly sportsmanlike manner.

The invention consists of the new and singularly original Heddon Dummy-Double Hook, the advantages of which are effectively set forth on this page.

SOME ADVANTAGES OF THE NEW DUMMY-DOUBLE

First.—The one hook with the Dummy reinforcement is always in perfect position for engaging the upper jaw of the fish, and the strike of the angler is all centered on driving home the one point, instead of being divided over several points, thereby meeting less resistance and increasing the certainty of penetration.

Second.—Many fish are lost where treble hooks are used because of one hook engaging the upper jaw, another the lower jaw, enabling the fish to secure resistance and disengaging both hooks. The Dummy-Double eliminates this.

Third.—The elimination of the treble hooks makes the wooden minnow semi-weedless. The bait can be drawn over snags, stones and many forms of aquatic vegetation without danger of catching.

Fourth.—In handling minnow and especially when removing fish, the old danger of engaging hooks into fingers is almost entirely eliminated.

Fifth.—The elimination of the multiplicity of trebles greatly lessens the liability of the bait becoming fast to weeds or snags when the fish is trying to eject it, offering a resistance which enables the fish to tear loose from the hooks.

This is an ad for "Jim Heddon's Last Invention," the Dummy Double. This centerfold sales flyer was an effort by sons Charles and Will to capitalize on their late father's reputation.

Heddon's "Dowagiac" Minnows

No. 1500

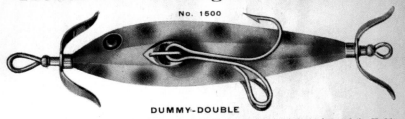

DUMMY-DOUBLE

This is Heddon's latest product, having new style of detachable hook fastening and the Heddon new patented Dummy-Double type of hook, doing away with treble hooks and guaranteed to increase killing certainty. Sinking Bait, two spinners, three Dummy-Double Hooks, length of body 3 in. No. 1500, White body with Red, Green and Yellow Spotted effect. No. 1501, Yellow body with Red, Green and Yellow Spotted effect.

No. 1400

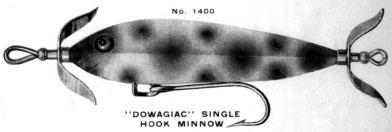

"DOWAGIAC" SINGLE HOOK MINNOW

This is a new type of Minnow, which has but one single detachable hook on the belly, being designed for compliance with State Laws prohibiting the use of more than one hook, or, for the use of anglers who prefer to use only one hook on a Bait. The one hook is located in the best possible position for effectiveness and an extra detachable hook is included in the box which may be put on at the rear if desired. Sinking Bait, two spinners, length of body 3 in. No. 1400, White body, with Red, Green and Black Spotted effect. No. 1401, Yellow body, with Red, Green and Black spotted effect.

HEDDON'S "DOWAGIAC" DECOY ICE MINNOW
For Fishing through the Ice

Length over all 5¼ inches; weight 2 1-2 ounces. Has metal fin on either side and at top and bottom, of nickeled and polished brass. Made of Wood, with twisted tail, which gives it a decidedly lifelike swimming motion when raised and lowered in the water. Has glass eyes and is enameled and finished with the same excellence of the Heddon's Bass Minnows. Finished in either Fancy Green back with White belly or imitation Perch colors.

No. 701

"DOWAGIAC" MUSKOLLONGE MINNOW, No. 700 SERIES

Designed specially for catching Muskollonge. Weighs nearly 3 ounces and is too heavy for bait-casting. Designed to hold and attract the big ones and the Bait should be properly used for trolling. Equipped on either side with a specially designed No. 1-0 extra heavy hollow point treble hook, and at the rear with a specially designed hollow point treble hook No. 8-0 size. Both sizes of hooks are of the finest possible quality. Has two spinners; body portion 5 1-2 in. long. Furnished in the following colors: No. 700, Fancy Green back, White belly; No. 701, Rainbow Colors; No. 709-A, Green back, White belly, sides Yellow with Perch Stripes.

This 1913 color insert was made by Heddon for insertion into distributor and wholesaler catalogs. The use of color and quality printing helped guarantee attention from buyers. This page is from an H.H. Michaelson catalog.

Company
letterheads
were changed
through the
years to reflect
new products
soon to hit the
market. This
1916 example
features the
Baby Crab
Wiggler that
was new that
year.

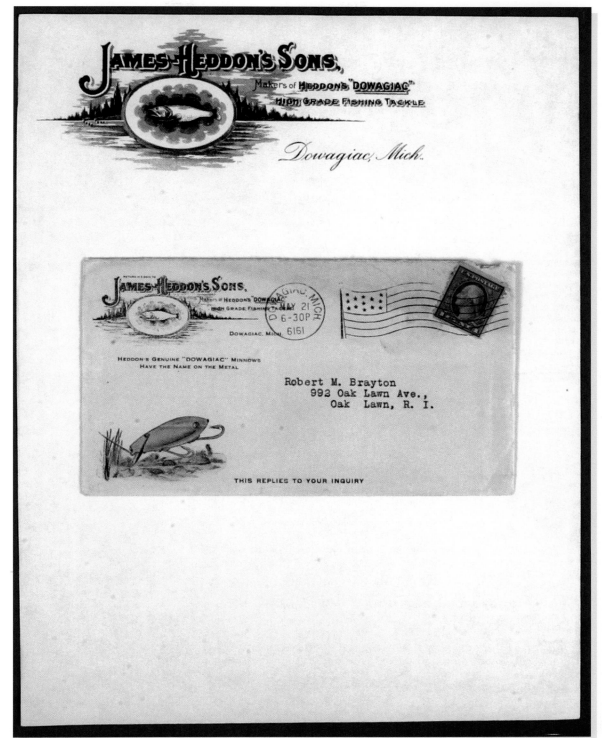

Try Out This New Dowagiac 'Wiggler'

FLOATS when at rest—swims, dives darts and zig-zags like a wounded minnow, when reeled in. Depth and amount of "wiggle" regulated by three points of attachments for line. Can run very deep, still retaining pronounced wobbling motion, impossible with other diving baits. Peculiar movements and attractive coloring irresistible to game fish. Non-tangling hooks; can't twist line. Uncrackable enamel finish; white with green and yellow spots or three other attractive color schemes.

Prepaid 75c.

If you want the real fun out of bait-casting, go to your dealer's and get better acquainted with the splendid

Genuine Heddon

Dowagiac

Casting Rods and Minnows

Heddon Dowagiac's are the acknowledged standard in Artificial Lures—wonderful in attractiveness and perfect in manufacture. Exactly right in weight and buoyancy; Heddon patent hook-fastening, insures deadliest presentation of hooks. Dozens of shapes, sizes and color effects, scientifically tested and proved to be the most attractive and enticing lures for their particular purposes. Comfortable to fish with, best balanced, and finished in our exclusive porcelain enamel, positively guaranteed not to check, flake, peel, crack or wear off in use.

JIM HEDDON Split Bamboo Casting Rods are first in their class. Two-piece construction makes casting easy and cuts out danger of breakage. Perfect in weight, balance, resiliency and spring. $1.50 to $15.00 and the only rods of their quality at anywhere near the price—particularly the "Jim Heddon Special" at $6.00.

This Handsomest of Fishing Books Free

Probably the largest, richest fishing book ever printed, showing you all the Heddon tackle in actual colors and dozens of practical hints and short cuts toward perfect casting and more successful fishing.

It's a book that you'll treasure so send for your free copy today!

James Heddon's Sons, Box 4, **Dowagiac, Mich.**

(Pronounce it "Doe-wah'-ji-ack")

We guarantee advertising on this page provided you mention FIELD AND STREAM

This advertisement from the May 1914 Field & Stream magazine announced the new Dowagiac Wiggler lures destined for sporting goods stores the following season. Such promotions helped build excitement for new lures.

This full-sized 1913 pamphlet was a supplement to catalogs of that year and included an article on "practical bait-casting" authored by the late Jim Heddon.

PRACTICAL BAIT-CASTING
"Jim Heddon's Fishing Tackle"

"JIM" HEDDON

JAMES HEDDON'S SONS

MANUFACTURERS

"DOWAGIAC"

RODS AND MINNOWS

Dowagiac   Michigan

This wooden, folk-art sign from the Treml Brothers bait and tackle shop in upstate New York featured an ad for Heddon lures on one side and an early three-digit phone number on the other.

DOWAGIAC MASCALLONGE MINNOW

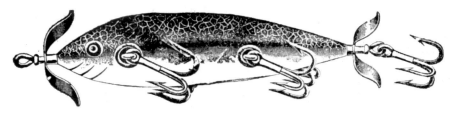

This is the only known ad for the No. 7000 Dowagiac Mascallonge Minnow, marketed through VL&A around 1916. Collectors call this 8", nine-ounce monster the "747" minnow. It was listed in two colors.

T13341 This minnow is designed especially for catching mascallonge and it is entirely too heavy for casting, unless thrown with a great deal of care upon a very heavy stiff rod. Its weight and general construction are designed to attract and hold the "big ones" and the bait should more properly be used by trolling. Has two spinners and five extra large and extra strong treble hooks. Weight, approximately 3 ounces; length of body, 5½ inches. Made in three colors only.

No. 700. White body, fancy green back.

No. 701. Rainbow, green back, red sides, blending into white belly.

No. 707. Yellow body with fancy mottled back.

Price, each (postpaid)................................$1.00 net

DOWAGIAC V. L. & A. MODEL MASCALLONGE MINNOW

T13342 These minnows are made by hand and are the finest enamel. The hooks are extra strong, the length of body 8 inches; otherwise constructed same as Dowagiac Regular Mascollonge Minnow.

No. 7000. White body, fancy green back.

No. 1001. Rainbow, green back, red sides, blending to white belly.

Price, each..$2.50 net

Weight, 9 oz.

This advertising pamphlet was created to introduce the "new" Luny Frog, circa 1927. It is shown here with a Little Luny and a rare red and white Luny Frog lure.

This colorful lithographed poster promoting the 200 Surface lure shows a bass jumping to the left. It is interesting to note that the rare "Pine Tree" box of the same era is the only Heddon box featuring a left-jumping bass. This poster is 14" x 21".

This magazine-sized catalog cover features a bass with Heddon's Basser in its mouth. The Head-On Basser appeared that year, 1921.

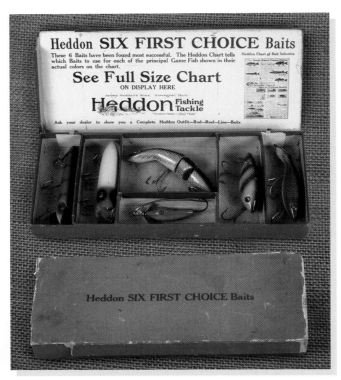

Beer sells well in six-packs, so why not lures? Heddon's Six First Choice Baits, circa 1923, featured (left to right) the Vamp, Basser, Gamefisher, Stanley Weedless Pork Rind Lure, Crab Wiggler, and Tadpolly. Heddon knew it was better to sell six baits than one!

This 1923 supplemental advertising kit included fish pictures and fishing tips. It opened into a full-color poster with plenty of things to interest an angler.

This rare flyer was offered to dealers to announce the introduction of what became one of Heddon's most famous lures: the Lucky 13, new in 1920.

The New Heddon "Lucky 13"

Zig-zag Swimming Minnow

Runs
Below
Surface

No. 2509 J

85c

Floats
while
at rest

In all scale finishes and two sizes. Illustration shows the exclusive Frog Scale Finish, new for 1920

Wouldn't You Hit at It Yourself?

AS the season's addition to the Heddon Dowagiac line one or more new baits are selected and developed each year from the vast number of suggestions, improvements and ideas submitted by our angling friends and our own experts.

This selection is made only after long and careful sifting down of comparative tests. Countless experimental models are taken to various parts of the country and tried under all manner of varying conditions. Experiences, recommendations and results are checked against each other and from this record the best is chosen. The last touches of Heddon refinement are applied, and the angling world is richer by one more approved, tested, fish-sure Heddon Dowagiac Bait to be safely added to the season's kit.

This Year The Heddon Spot Light Points Out The "Lucky 13"

While resembling, in appearance and principle, baits of standard popular acceptance, the "Lucky 13" possesses certain subtle improvements in balance, stream-outline and head-planes that result in radically intensifying the erratic swimming movement associated with baits of similar type. Only life itself could rival its peculiar action in the water.

This bait casts straight and true and floats on the surface until retrieved. Under the line pull, it drops to an average level of eighteen inches below the surface and comes in with an undulating, weaving motion, interrupted by short, scintillating darts that cannot fail to excite the hungry attention of the crustiest old bachelor bass within eye-shot. Biff! And the Heddon specialized hook-presentment has made him yours.

"Lucky 13" appears in the usual range of Heddon, crack-proof superfinishes, all but the standard red-and-white being in the popular and lifelike "scale" effect. The most noteworthy of these is the wonderful "Yellow Perch Scale Finish," new for 1920.

How to Use It

This Bait should not be retrieved when it first strikes the water, but should be allowed to rest for at least ten or fifteen seconds, excepting as to a slight wiggle, accomplished by jerking the tip of the Rod. Then commence to reel very slowly, loafing the Bait and giving a slight jerk every foot or so.

"Lucky 13" is made in two sizes, packed in individual boxes or found on handsomely lithographed display cards at dealers.

2500 Series, Large Size weighs 5-8 oz. Length, 3 7-8 inches over all.

85c

2400 Series, Junior Size weighs 1-2 oz. Length, 3 inches over all.

No. 2502	White body, Red head	No. 2402
No. 2509D	Green Scale finish	No. 2409D
No. 2509H	Red Scale finish	No. 2409H
No. 2509J	Frog Scale finish	No. 2409J
No. 2509K	Gold Fish, Scale	No. 2409K
No. 2509L	Yellow Perch Scale finish	No. 2409L

James Heddon's Sons - - **Dowagiac, Michigan**

(Facing page) This 1923 cardboard counter display advertising the new Gamefisher measures 10" x 14".

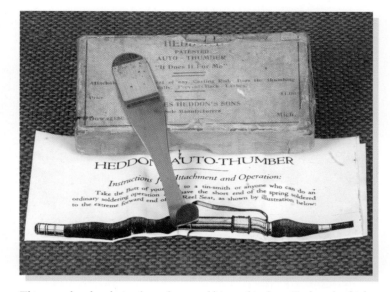

This auto-thumber device for reels was sold in a white box. "It does the thinking automatically, preventing backlash," the flyer claimed. This dates to the pre-1920 era.

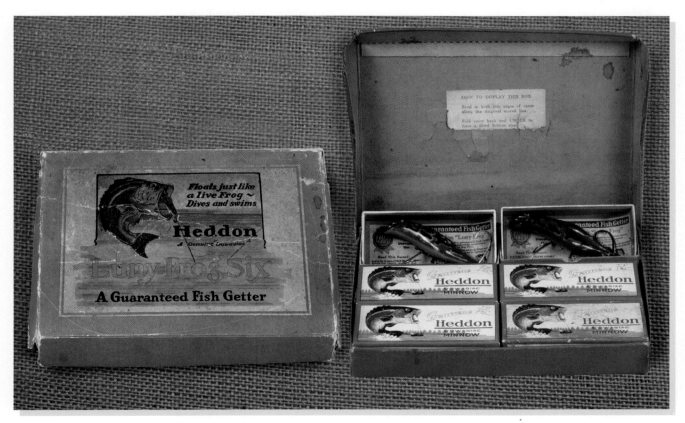

The Heddon Luny Frog was offered in an attractive six-pack box. A similar box was made for the Little Luny.

This supplemental flyer, the "Angler's Manual," was sent to retailers in 1930, when a new slogan, "The Rod with the Fighting Heart," was introduced.

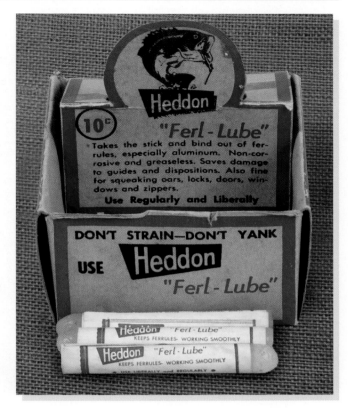

(Right) This counter display for
Ferl-Lube dates to the 1940s.

(Below) This colorful cardboard wall poster, measuring 28" x 32",
features a downward leaping bass box in the lower left corner. Note
the Vamp in the fish's mouth.

This six-pack presentation box was offered in 1928 to help sell the Spoon-Y Frog, which came in four colors.

This "Fisherman's Headquarters" poster was made for retailers to use in attracting business. The hope was that all who saw it would buy Heddon lures. It is cardboard and measures 4" x 16". It has "the box with the red edge," made famous by Heddon.

This Heddon flyer offered Outing Manufacturing Co. lures at reduced prices, dating this paperwork to 1928, a year after Heddon purchased Outing in 1927.

This unique, foldout box paper featured a Heddon-Outing tackle box that "pops up," much like the character's in today's "pop-up" children's books and greeting cards. It dates to the late 1920s.

This ad for Waltonian and Indian Chief reels dates to 1928.

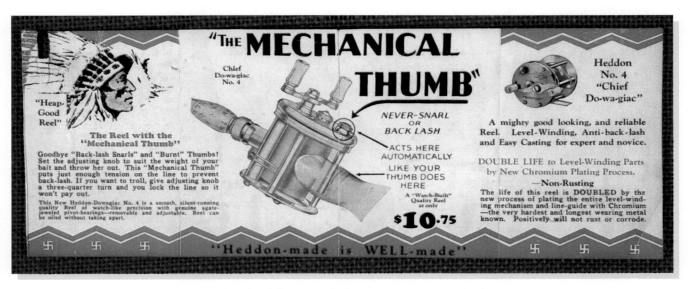

This ad promoted the No. 4 Chief Dowagiac, a "Heap good reel!"

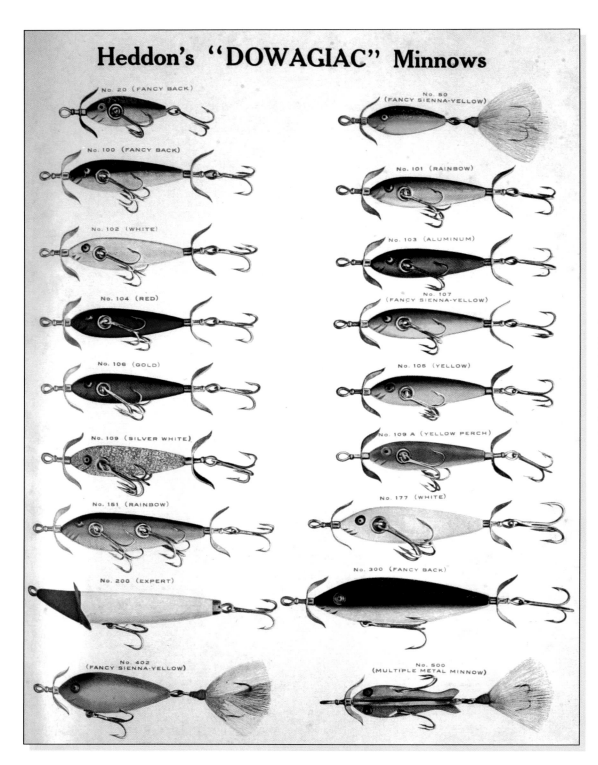

Heddon's "DOWAGIAC" Minnows

No. 20 (FANCY BACK)

No. 50 (FANCY SIENNA-YELLOW)

No. 100 (FANCY BACK)

No. 101 (RAINBOW)

No. 102 (WHITE)

No. 103 (ALUMINUM)

No. 104 (RED)

No. 107 (FANCY SIENNA-YELLOW)

No. 106 (GOLD)

No. 105 (YELLOW)

No. 109 (SILVER WHITE)

No. 109 A (YELLOW PERCH)

No. 151 (RAINBOW)

No. 177 (WHITE)

No. 200 (EXPERT)

No. 300 (FANCY BACK)

No. 402 (FANCY SIENNA-YELLOW)

No. 500 (MULTIPLE METAL MINNOW)

This 1908 color plate of Dowagiac Minnows appeared in an Edward K. Tryon Co. catalog. The Philadelphia company carried many Heddon products in its early years.

Regulations

1. Lies may be told at any place or time without notice. (Note: Not advisable to Game Wardens.)

2. Cameras may be used, scales doctored, and elastic rulers employed.

3. Borrowed or rented fish may be used at all times.

4. Guides or others may be bribed or otherwise induced to corroborate all good lies.

5. No lies may be retracted, but may be added to, at will.

6. An extra quarter pound or half inch will improve all lies.

7. This license is null and void if used for any other purpose, including:
    (a) Weight of babies.
    (b) Tire and gasoline mileage.
    (c) Golf scores.
    (d) Prohibition matters.
    (e) All private or business purposes.

The greatest TRUTH ever told is that Heddon Tackle catches MORE fish, and hooks and holds the BIG ones!

The "Liar's License" and accompanying counter display date to 1928.

LIARS' LICENSES *for your* Fishermen Friends FREE *Here!*

Users of Heddon Tackle *never need them*

INSTRUCTIONS: All Cheerful Liars should be licensed. Use your own judgment.

Liar's License for Fishermen
Issued by Heddon-Dewagiac Dealers and Boosters

THE BEARER _____ having, by reputation and long practice, coupled with a vivid imagination, exhibited all of the proper requirements therefor, is hereby empowered to Lie, Prevaricate, and show every other recklessness with the Truth, considered expedient by him, in connection with all matters relative to Fish and Fishing, for the current Season, subject however to the regulations on the back hereof.

Seal of Ananias
Prince of Liars

IN WITNESS HEREOF is attached the Grand Seal of Ananias, Prince of Liars.

Signed:

"I lie cheerfully"

Grand Muskellunge and Heddon Booster

Read the regulations on the other side

(Above) This was a promotion for the "frog card." The featured lures are all in Luny Frog finish.

(Facing page) Advertising for 1928: a frog year!

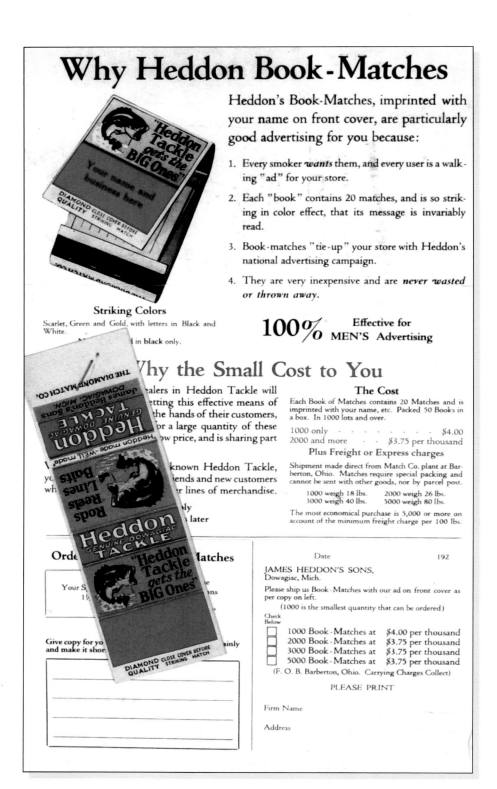

Why Heddon Book-Matches

Heddon's Book-Matches, imprinted with your name on front cover, are particularly good advertising for you because:

1. Every smoker *wants* them, and every user is a walking "ad" for your store.

2. Each "book" contains 20 matches, and is so striking in color effect, that its message is invariably read.

3. Book-matches "tie-up" your store with Heddon's national advertising campaign.

4. They are very inexpensive and are *never wasted or thrown away.*

Striking Colors

Scarlet, Green and Gold, with letters in Black and White.

...d in black only.

100% Effective for MEN'S Advertising

Why the Small Cost to You

...alers in Heddon Tackle will ...tting this effective means of ...the hands of their customers, ...r a large quantity of these ...w price, and is sharing part

...known Heddon Tackle, ...ends and new customers ...r lines of merchandise.

...ly ...later

The Cost

Each Book of Matches contains 20 Matches and is imprinted with your name, etc. Packed 50 Books in a box. In 1000 lots and over.

1000 only - - - - - - - $4.00
2000 and more - - $3.75 per thousand

Plus Freight or Express charges

Shipment made direct from Match Co. plant at Barberton, Ohio. Matches require special packing and cannot be sent with other goods, nor by parcel post.

1000 weigh 18 lbs. 2000 weigh 26 lbs.
3000 weigh 40 lbs. 5000 weigh 80 lbs.

The most economical purchase is 5,000 or more on account of the minimum freight charge per 100 lbs.

Order ...atches

Your S... ...e
1... ...ns

Give copy for yo... ...inly
and make it shor...

Date   192

JAMES HEDDON'S SONS,
Dowagiac, Mich.

Please ship us Book-Matches with our ad on front cover as per copy on left.

(1000 is the smallest quantity that can be ordered)

Check Below

☐ 1000 Book-Matches at $4.00 per thousand
☐ 2000 Book-Matches at $3.75 per thousand
☐ 3000 Book-Matches at $3.75 per thousand
☐ 5000 Book-Matches at $3.75 per thousand

(F. O. B. Barberton, Ohio. Carrying Charges Collect)

PLEASE PRINT

Firm Name

Address

A handsome color combination in Gold, Scarlet, Green, Black, and White

"Give Me a Match"

A request made by millions of men each day.

That's why Book-Matches are an excellent advertising medium for your store.

What can you give a fisherman that will be more appreciated?

Your store advertisement imprinted on the FRONT cover

The cost to you is *very* little under Heddon's co-operative plan.

(Right and on facing page) Like most other retailers, Heddon used matchbooks to promote its products.

This Heddon "match safe" is shown with a book of the company's paper matches.

Free Window Display Cards in Nine Colors

These expensive cards are supplied in keeping with a Dealer's sales on Heddon Tackle

Bait Displays

Your windows are the eyes of your store and one of your best assets. Nothing is more compelling than an attractive window display of tackle.

Heddon Window Display Cards catch the eye, stop the passerby and bring him into your store.

Other Cards

| Rod Card | Tackle Box | Liars License |
| Reel Card | Feather Lures | Sportsman Headquarters |

These cards are supplied only to those dealers who sell the respective items of Heddon Tackle, advertised by the cards.

10
Liars License

Fishermen's Headquarters

| 6 | 7 | 8 | 9 | 11 |
| Rod Card | Reel Card | Tackle Box Card | Feather Lures | Fisherman's Headquarters |

Counter Display Cards with Baits Attached

This modern method of merchandising shows these baits so your customer can easily examine them. A great convenience and sales booster. After baits are removed, the cards are still very attractive, as beneath each bait, is a full color reproduction of the bait. Printed in 6 colors with easel backs. Baits at regular prices.

Meadow Mouse

A mouse that is a mouse, even to bead-eyes and flexible tail. 3 colors—Brown, Grey, and White.
Card with 6 Baits (2 each) $6.00

Tiny Teaz

A light fly-rod lure for rainbows, bass, etc. 6 assorted colors.
Card with 6 Baits_____ $4.50

Tripple Teazer

A new weedless bait. Three tiny minnows flash and glitter. Single hook, feathered bucktail. 4 colors.
Card with 6 Baits_____ $6.00

(Left and facing page) This 1928 flyer offers wholesalers and retailers Heddon's line of colorful window posters that promoted everything the company made that year. The counter display cards mentioned in this ad even had baits attached!

Bait Display Cards--Baits Attached--Cont'd

S. O. S. Wounded Minnow. New!
The last word in a helpless minnow. "Sells-On-Sight" and "Swims-On-Side." Two sizes: No. 170 three trebles; No. 160 two trebles.
Three Baits on Card_____$3.00

Bull Frog Card
Bull Frog Card consists of one each of "Luny," "Little Luny" and "Spoon-y Frog," also one "Vamp," "Zig Wag" and "Weedless Widow" in new natural "Frog" finish.
Six Baits on Card_____$6.75

Spoon-y Frog Card
An all metal bait, frog shaped, in Frog color, Red-and-White, Nickel and Gold. A sure hooker and a good seller.
Card with Six Baits_____$6.00

Weedless Widow. New!
Here at last is a surface lure with excellent action. Brand new and one every angler will want. Colors: Frog, Red-and-White, and four other big selling colors.
Card with Six Baits_____$6.00

"Ace," "King," "Queen"
All metal baits that are big sellers. Card contains two Ace, two Kings and two Queens in Nickel finish only, red feather, single hooks.
No. 1 Card with Six Baits__$6.00

"King" and "Queen"
Two popular sellers. Four Kings and two Queens. Single hooks. Put up three ways: All Gold; all Nickel; and Red-and-White and Scale finishes.
No. 2 Card with Six Baits___$6.00

Other Merchandise Display Cards

Stanley Weedless Hook Card

An excellent means to show these standard weedless hooks. Furnished 3 each of the 4 big sellers. Priced at regular list price. No charge for the card.

3 No. 1 Hooks @ $.40	$1.20
3 No. 2 Hooks @ .45	1.35
3 No. 6 Hooks @ .55	1.65
3 No. 50 Hooks @ .50	1.50
	Total $5.70

Rod Cement Card

Shows Ferrule Cement in such a way that every fisherman will want one. To retail at 23 cents each. Per card (12 cartridges of cement)_____$2.76

Feather Lure Card

Contains one dozen Wilder-Dilg or Bass Bugs in either size. Also can be supplied with ½ dozen of each. Priced at regular list price for lures alone. No charge for the card. See page 11 for prices.

"No-Skeeto" Card

No-Skeeto is a "fly-dope" every fisherman will buy if it is shown. Kills all kinds of insect pests. Will not soil clothing or skin. Put up in small screw-top cans, to retail at 43 cents each. A striking card holder of 6 cans to card. Per card_____$2.58

This deck of playing cards, from the 1940s, is another effort to promote Heddon products.

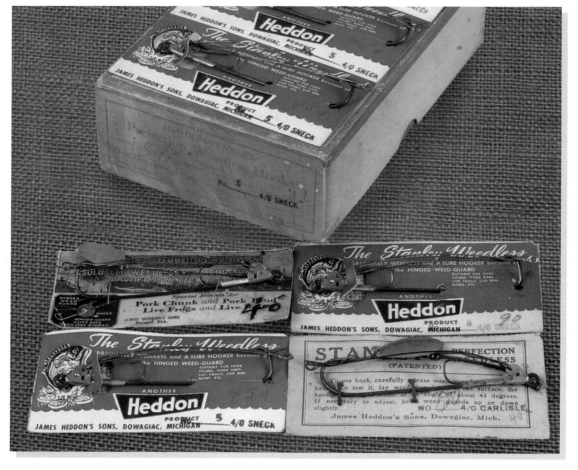

Stanley hooks were sold on colorful cards and came in large boxes. This piece dates to the 1940s.

This is the largemouth bass Heddon plaque, the most popular among a series of eight that featured various gamefish. They date to the 1940s and are labeled "Heddon" on the back.

(Left) This counter display card was supposed to say "Weedless Wizard," but part of the word was blacked out, possibly because the name was, at that time, undergoing a change to the Weedless Widow. This dates to 1927 or 1928.

(Right) This counter display for the Heddon SOS wounded minnow dates to 1928.

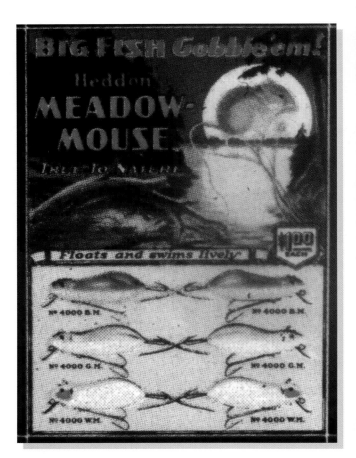 

(Left) This counter display helped promote the Meadow Mouse in 1928.

(Right) The Tiny Teaz fly rod lures were new in 1928, and this colorful counter display helped get them off to a great start.

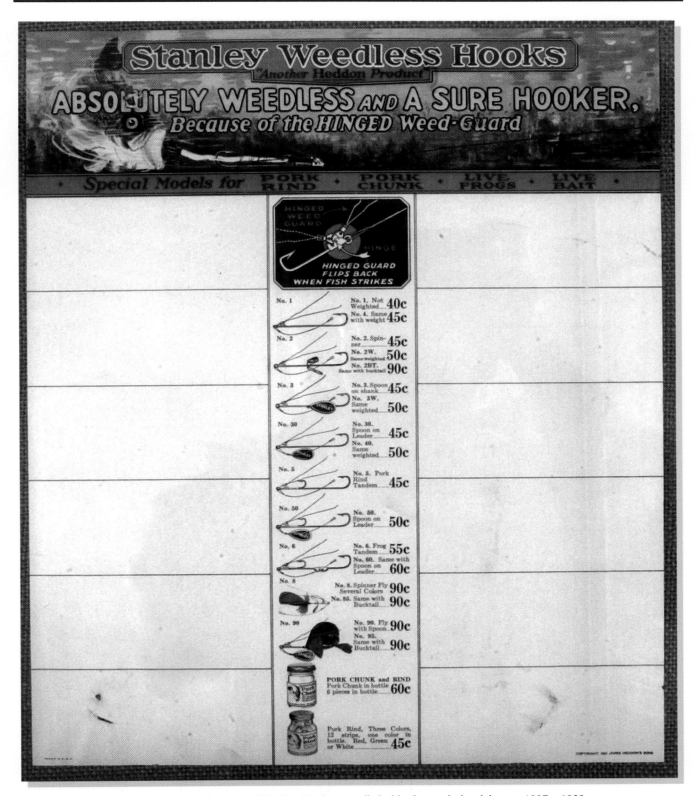

This counter display for Stanley Weedless Hooks originally had hooks attached and dates to 1927 – 1928.

Life!   Action!   Color!

Beautiful Designs! Handsome Lettering!

Slide No. 1

Short, snappy, up-to-date copy that **sells tackle.**

Here are slides that theatre-goers actually enjoy reading, and on which you will be proud to have your name.

They are real business getters.

TRY THEM!

Slide No. 2

Slide No. 3

Slide No. 4

Slide No. 5

Heddon offered dealers these slides to promote their products in movie theaters.

This beautiful color poster from 1929 featured Heddon fly rod lures. A counter display also was made in the same design.

Heddon's marketing department created dozens of ready-to-print newspaper ads that were used nationwide. Here are some examples from the late 1920s. Stores that carried lures in this period included drug stores, hardware stores, barber shops, and even salvage and auto supply stores!

*This counter display for "No-Skeeto" is shown
with a rare can of the product, circa 1927.*

This Heddon Luny Frog cardboard counter display dates to 1928.

(Near right) This is a Heddon mirror, shown with a black background to make the etchings legible. It has a banner logo from the 1940s.

(Far right) This cardboard counter display was made to sell Heddon bamboo rods in the late 1920s.

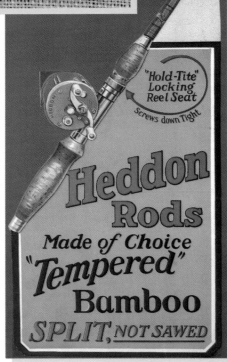

This Heddon pamphlet was produced to promote its Pal fishing rods, new in 1930.

Heddon encouraged major retailers to create elaborate window displays of tackle using Heddon products supplied by the factory. The photos on the following pages are examples of some of the best such displays, all dating to the 1920s. The captions that accompany them are from a Heddon sales kit.

"Eyes" of Your Store USE THEM!

"Tackle like ties, is sold by the window". Nothing appeals more to a fisherman than an attractive tackle window and no article of merchandise lends itself better to display than tackle.

To help dealers improve their windows and build up a profitable tackle business, we are showing herewith, several different sizes and styles of windows featuring tackle. We hope that they will be of help to you in trimming yours.

When a dealer features Heddon Tackle, he ties up his store with Heddon National Advertising, and brings into his store, old friends and new trade. The result is, that he sells more tackle of ALL kinds.

Be sure to have the new Merchandise Display Cards with Baits attached. They make a valuable addition to the regular free Window Display Cards and are suitable for use in both window and on counter. They are a modern method of merchandising, as they show the Baits and sell them too.

"Frogs for '28" are featured in Heddon's Advertising. Be sure to have the Big Bull-Frog Card and FROG Baits.

James Heddon's Sons

Dowagiac, Michigan

M. F. Jaman Jr

Manager Advertising and Sales Promotion.

"To Sibley, Lindsay and Curr Company of Rochester, New York, goes the credit for this handsome display. The round panels covered with cloth make an excellent background for the tackle shown. The actual amount of tackle in the window is not large, but the effect is very strong."

"This striking window of Knowlton & Bennett, Urbana, Illinois, shows nice balance. Note the handsome Heddon display boxes and box assortments. All small items are in the foreground. This window sold a lot of tackle."

"The Bishop-Kennedy Company of Columbus, Ohio, report that this handsome window blocked traffic in front of their store. The photo does not do justice to a very handsome and complete display of all kinds of sporting equipment."

"Another small display window, showing how the big Heddon leaping bass cut-out shows up in a window. Few sportsmen can pass this giant bass without the thought 'Maybe I can hook one also, with Heddon tackle.'"

"A small window but very effective. This was a 100 percent Heddon display and has, as a background, a minnow net. Some dealers have used the net as a background for having a large amount of baits. The six new Heddon display cards would have added materially to this window."

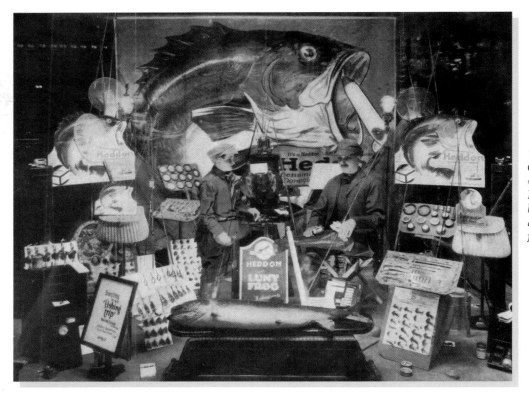

"A handsome window of the May Company, Cleveland, Ohio, which produced exceptional results. Note the use of the large Heddon bass cut-outs and the attractive arrangement of the tackle. Also the father and son idea."

"A corner window by F.L. Bartholomew, Cordele, Georgia. Note the orderly arrangement and the use of all of Heddon's window display. A 100 percent Heddon window in a small store that enjoyed a profitable business."

This counter display promoting the "Three Pals" includes the Pal tubular rods, the popular reels, and the line that went with them. This dates to the 1940s.

This cardboard counter display is for the Spoon-Y Frog, circa 1928.

This is a full-color cardboard poster for the No. 4 Chief Dowagiac reel, circa 1928.

This 1927 pamphlet with "suggestions and secrets of experts" was distributed to dealers.

This 14" x 18" cardboard poster was made to promote the Triple Teazer lure in the 1920s.

This cardboard poster measures 14" x 15" and promoted the "Shrimpy" lures.

This is a very early advertising piece: a sign made from a porcelain-type material featuring a life-sized Dummy-Double. It came from a New York sporting goods store that was being demolished. The sign was hidden behind an old wall. It likely dates to 1913.

This 1930 cardboard counter display features the Super Dowagiac Spook and the Floating Vamp Spook, two of Heddon's earliest pyralin and plastic baits.

This cardboard counter poster features the popular Crazy-Crawler lure, introduced in 1940.

This 30" x 42" poster for Heddon's River Runt lures dates to around 1939.

This rare cardboard counter display was made in 1925 to promote the famous Vamp lure, being made by then in four sizes.

This cardboard counter display features a Heddon tackle box and dates to 1927.

At left, this 1937 cardboard poster introduced six new shore finishes for River Runt Spook lures. Below is the actual oil painting John Heddon commissioned for this campaign. This painting hung over John's desk at the factory while he was president.

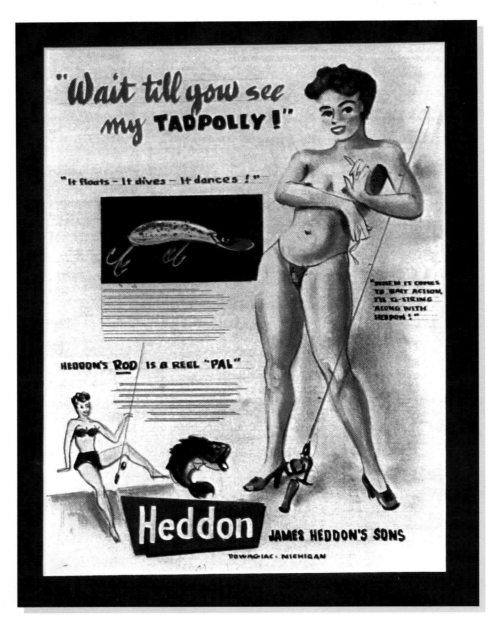

Although never placed into distribution, this adult-oriented ad for Heddon's Tadpolly Spook lures was proposed in 1952. Factory folklore holds that the wives of several prominent Heddon principals quietly vetoed the campaign.

This full-color ad appeared in Field & Stream magazine in 1913, promoting the new Dummy-Double.

That Genuine Heddon Dowagiac "Dummy-Double"

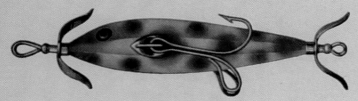

SEE that hook, **looped** instead of barbed! Would we have the nerve to put three years of our time and hundreds of dollars into the perfection of that idea, if we did not **know** it was the greatest forward step ever made in hook manufacture? Would we risk the Heddon name and Heddon reputation by telling you to buy a freak—unless we knew—positively and beyond all doubt—that it would **catch more bass than all the treble hooks** you could hang on a bait?

Admitting that it **looks** all that you want to call it—"crazy", "inefficient", "fishless"—we tell you straight that it belies its looks. By test after test, in every water, we have conclusively proved that fish strike this bait so that the barb **must** be driven into the upper jaw—and to stay! The ingenious method of presentment makes a miss **practically impossible**, and once set, your fish can gain no leverage by which to pry or shake it loose.

And look at its convenience in handling, packing, and in landing your fish. Drag it where you please, it is almost weedless. Use a landing net without fear of tangle, or let your fish run into weeds if it wants to.

A strike means a fish—every time, as is proved by the astonishing records our tests have developed—19 straight strikes without a miss—36 with only one miss and so on —throughout **two seasons of exhaustive experiment.**

The Idea Looks Wrong But It Is The *Rightest* Thing Ever Developed In Hook Manufacture

And believe us, you will get the strikes; for this beautifully finished lure is the most artistic and successful of all the Dowagiac line. The sharp, prismatic surfaces enameled as only Heddon can do it, outrival Nature in flashing brilliancy, and with the polished nickel spinners in full action, you find in this the ideal casting bait. And the most sportsmanlike, for with the elimination of treble hooks the last and only valid objection to wooden minnows is disposed of forever!

This is Jim Heddon's last contribution to the angling fraternity—and his best. Buy it on our say-so that it will make good. Furnished regularly in colors illustrated. Others to special order. Extra hook for tail, though unnecessary, included with each bait. Ask your dealer, or it will be mailed prepaid on receipt of **$1.00**

The Free Heddon Book About Bass Casting

BEFORE you go to your store get the big free book that does so much to clear up the mysteries of this trickiest of all game fishing. It shows you scores of odd kinks and tips, big ideas and little details that will help you to make your fishing hours productive. And it shows you in sumptuous colors all the Heddon tackle, and proves why that's the kind you must make the dealer show. Write for your free book today.

Ask to see the wonderful $1.50 Heddon Rod and the Jim Heddon "Favorite" Split Bamboo Rod at $6.00—the cleanest value your money can buy.

James Heddon's Sons

Box 205, Dowagiac, Mich.
Pronounce it "Do-wah-ji-ack"

CHARLES FRANCIS PRESS, NEW YORK

Toy models of the famous Heddon "Jenny" aircraft were marketed in the 1950s.

This 20" x 26" window display decal is from the 1940s and features a four-leaf clover for good fishing luck.

Heddon's "Fish Flesh" baits, new in 1930, were promoted in this color flyer as "indestructible." We now know they were not.

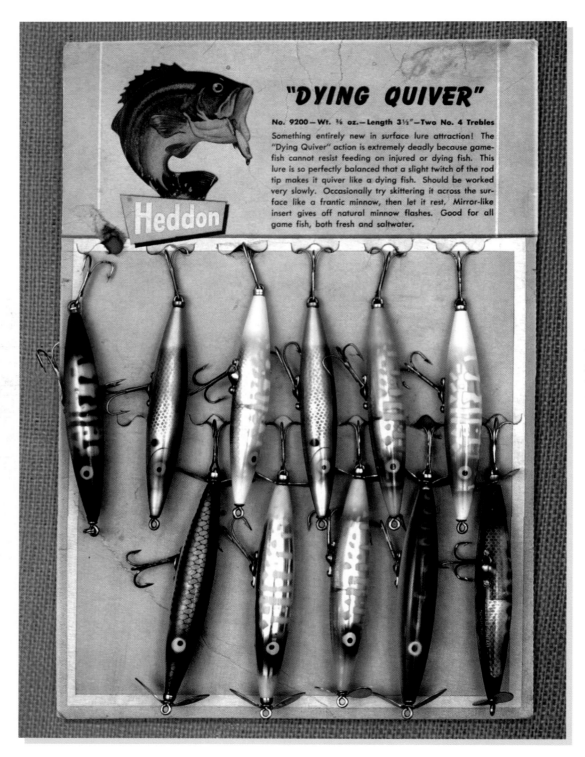

"DYING QUIVER"

No. 9200—Wt. ⅝ oz.—Length 3½"—Two No. 4 Trebles

Something entirely new in surface lure attraction! The "Dying Quiver" action is extremely deadly because game-fish cannot resist feeding on injured or dying fish. This lure is so perfectly balanced that a slight twitch of the rod tip makes it quiver like a dying fish. Should be worked very slowly. Occasionally try skittering it across the surface like a frantic minnow, then let it rest. Mirror-like insert gives off natural minnow flashes. Good for all game fish, both fresh and saltwater.

Heddon

This counter display for the Dying Quiver came complete with lures attached. It dates to 1958.

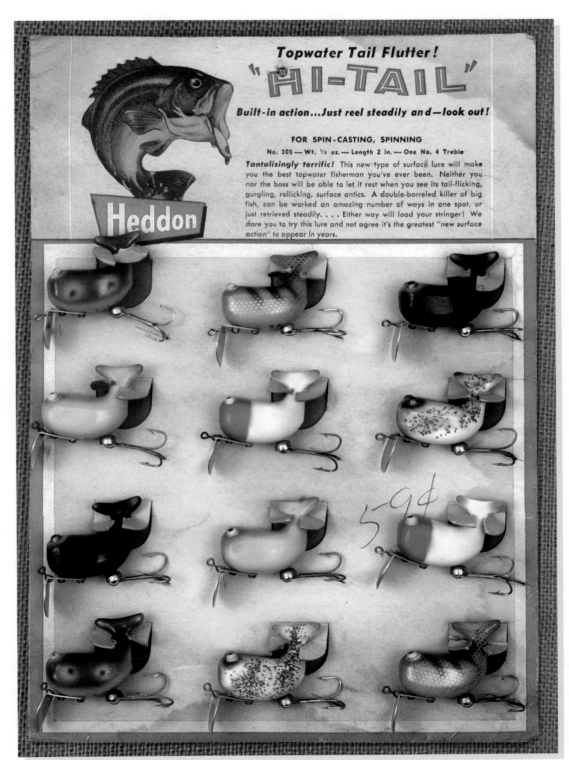

This Heddon Hi-Tail counter display included the cute, whale-shaped baits already attached. This piece dates to 1961.

This color chart for "famous lures" features plastic baits.

This Hep Spinner counter display is from the 1960s.

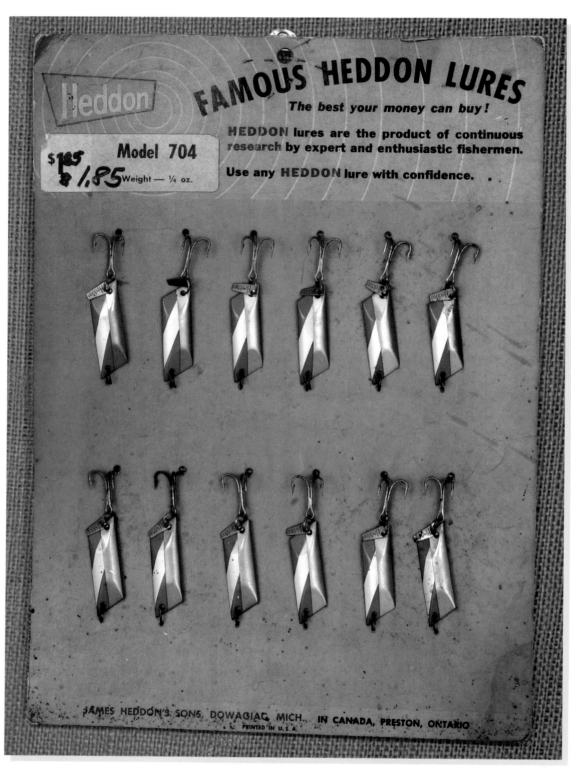

This cardboard display is of "Famous Heddon Lures" that have no accompanying name. They are Model 704 and have an attached bangle with the "Heddon" banner logo.

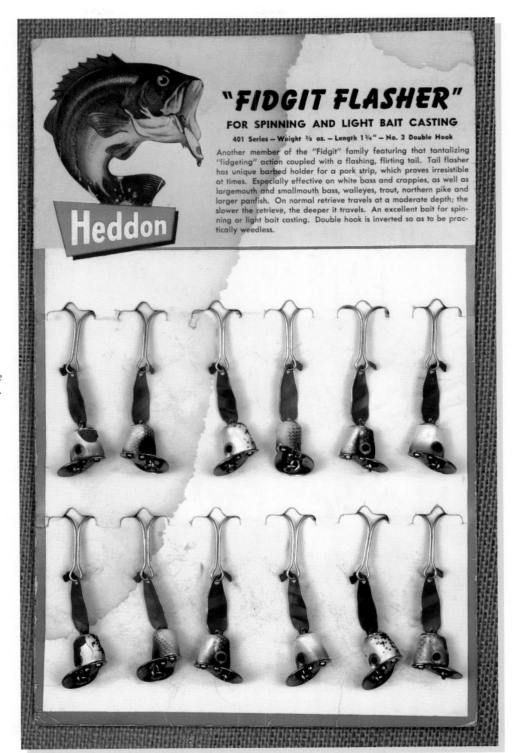

This counter display features the 1960s Fidgit Flasher.

The Sonar is one of Heddon's later lures, shown here in a cardboard counter display.

HEDDON REPAIR SERVICE.

Your Heddon Rod Repaired at Cost.

To purchasers of Heddon Rods, (as well as Heddon Reels),— is offered a complete repair service, which is very prompt and efficient, and its charges are reasonable.

In case of accident, it is a great source of satisfaction to an owner of a Heddon Rod (or Reel) to know that his pet equipment can be quickly repaired; or, that after years of service, it can be overhauled and often made to look and serve almost like new.

TWO Rods Better Than One.

Many fishermen carry extra rods in case of loss, or accident or other emergencies. Your old Heddon veteran should be carried as a "spare". There is a lot of "fight" and "action" in him still, and you will be pleased and surprised when he comes back from our "Hospital", with new winding, guides and a fresh coat of varnish.

Avoid the Season's Rush. Do it Early!

Too many fishermen wait until a few days before the opening season, and then swamp us with rods to be gone over, and rushed back to their anxious owners. We try to accommodate them, but better work and greater satisfaction will be had in avoiding the last minute rush and confusion.

Shipping Instructions.

Be sure to tag your rod, giving your name and address, — and prepay charges. Also write us a note, telling of the shipment and what you want done.

Yours for service,

JAMES HEDDON'S SONS.

Rod and Reel Service Dept.

P.S. Have you used our latest Baits,—
       "Little Luny Frog"
       "Spoon-y Frog"
       "Zig-Wag"
    They're our fish getters!

This colorful illustration accompanied a special 1929 mailout promoting the reel repair service at the Heddon factory.

"SPRING FEVER"

"Your OLD rod repaired?"   "Why, It's as good as NEW!"

Heddon Lure Displays

There are 47 River Runts on this board. How many
different colors can you find?

Here are nine of co-author Bill Roberts's favorite Heddon lures. If you had to pick just one, which would it be?

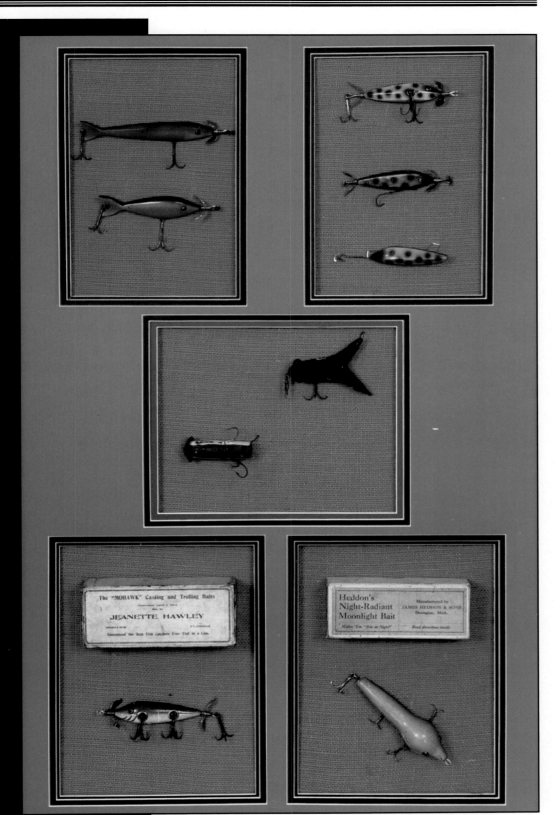

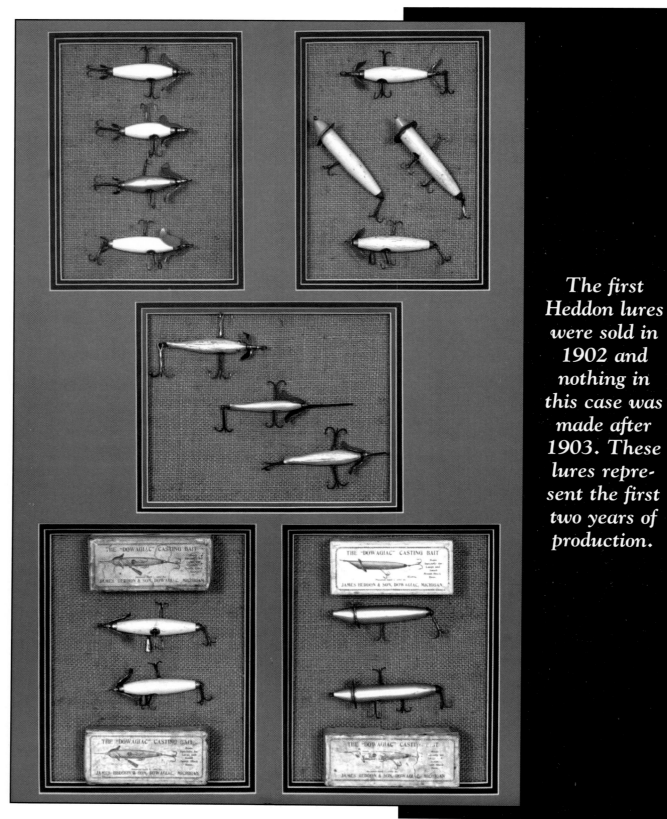

The first Heddon lures were sold in 1902 and nothing in this case was made after 1903. These lures represent the first two years of production.

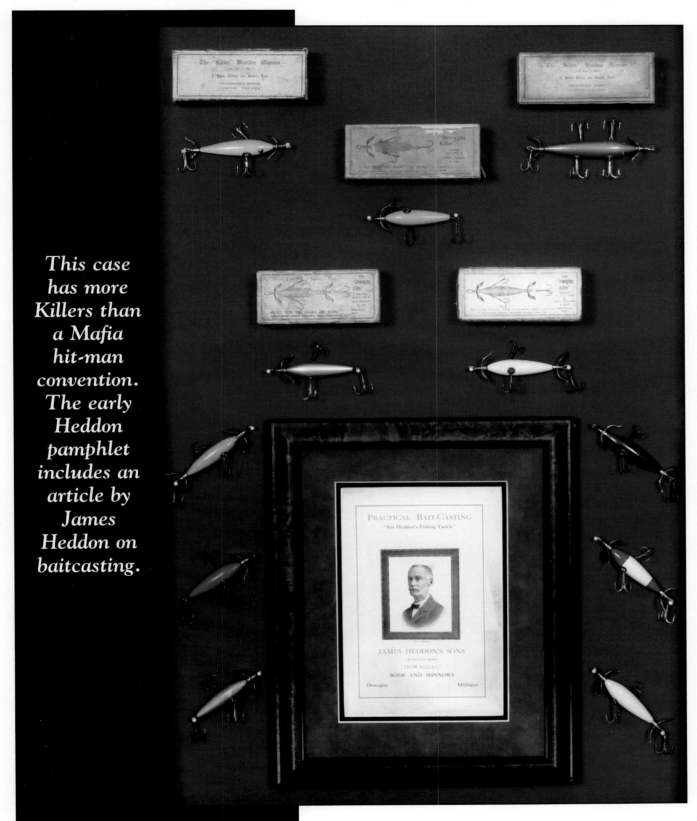

This case has more Killers than a Mafia hit-man convention. The early Heddon pamphlet includes an article by James Heddon on baitcasting.

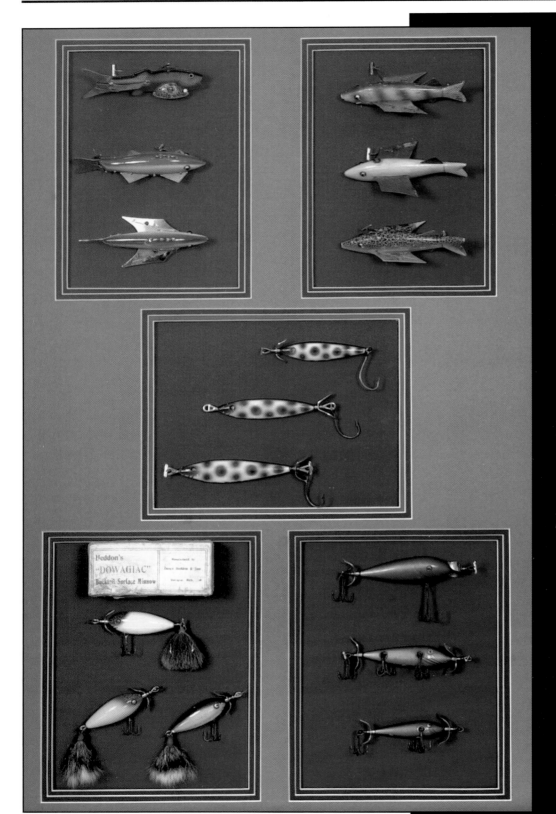

Decoys, Coast Minnows, Bucktail Minnows and some hand-painted gillmark classics in copper finish highlight this display.

Who says size isn't important? Here's a collection of musky-sized Heddons, including 200 Surface lures, Zaragossas, and a few other early classics.

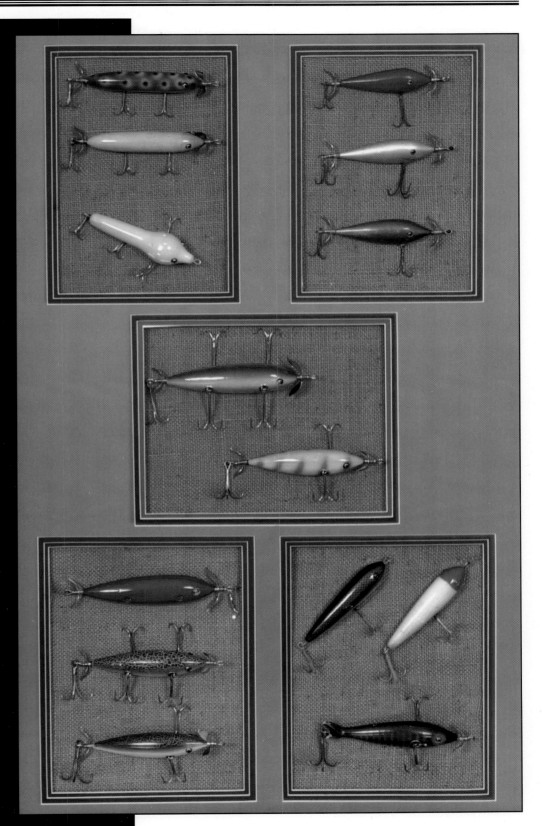

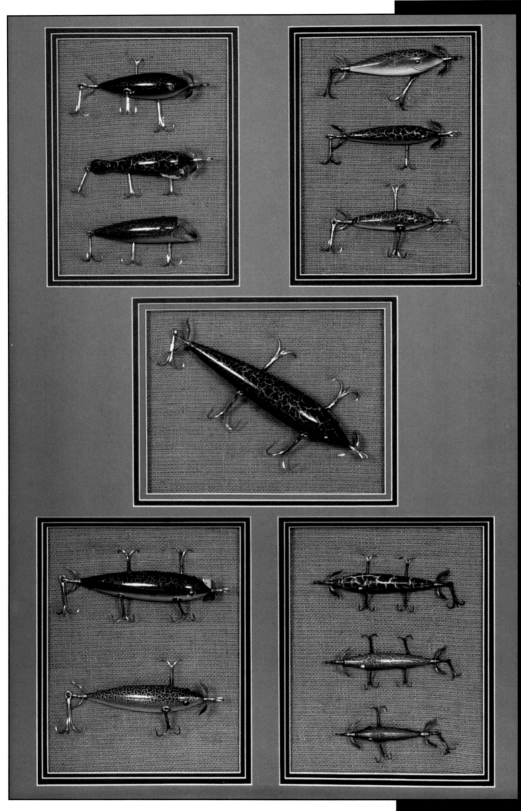

Green crackleback was one of Heddon's favorite paint finishes, and its popularity remains strong with today's collectors.

Surface Minnies, Spindivers, and underwater minnows surround a wide-backed giant.

Dummy Doubles of all configurations surround this wonderful porcelain advertising sign found behind a wall in an old store in New York.

I was caught on a "Heddon's Dowagiac" Rod and Minnow The Best

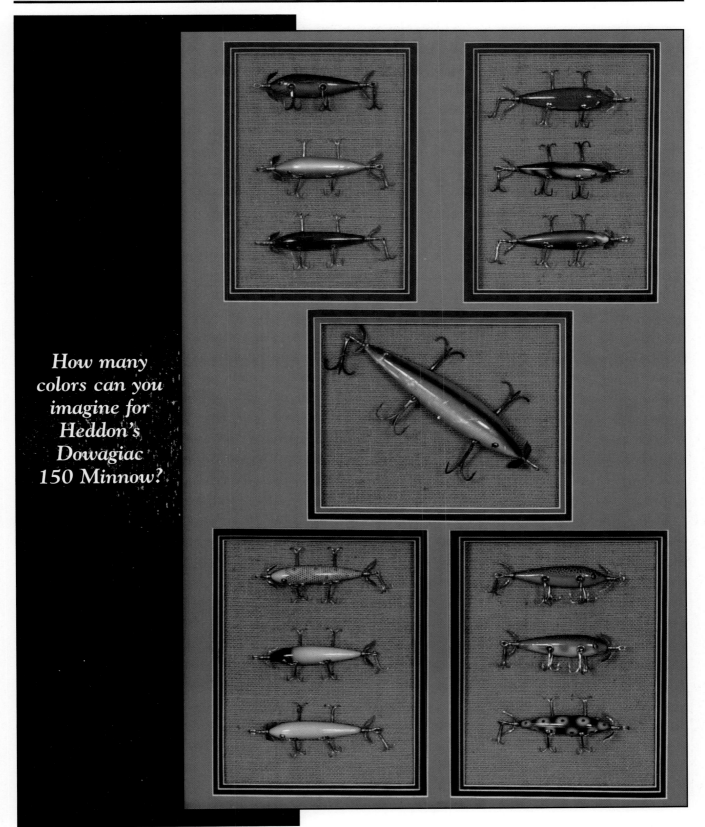

How many colors can you imagine for Heddon's Dowagiac 150 Minnow?

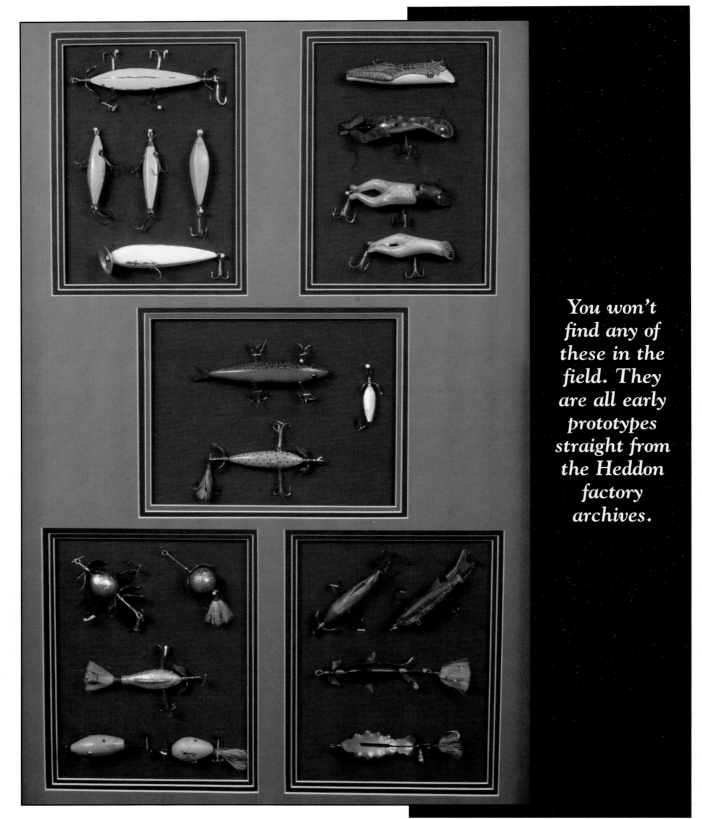

You won't find any of these in the field. They are all early prototypes straight from the Heddon factory archives.

More lures from the Heddon factory collection.

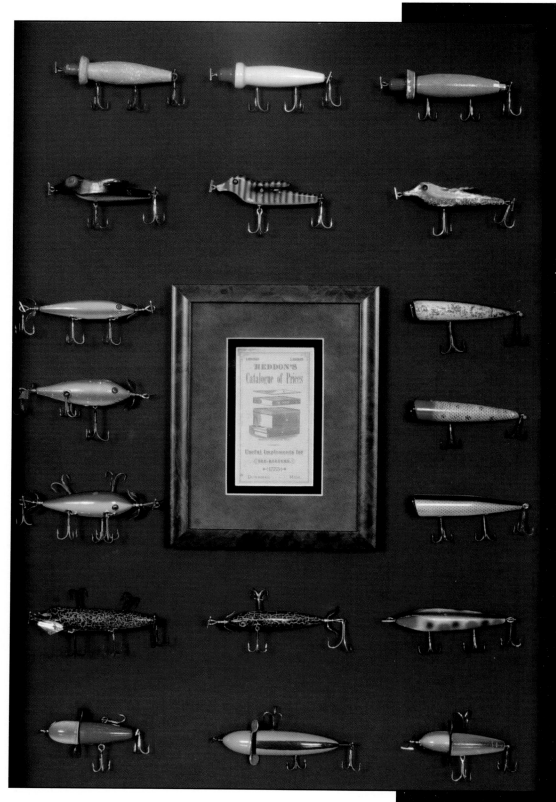

Peckerheads, Kinney Birds, Musky Chuggers, and a few other surprises surround one of James Heddon's beekeeping product catalogs from the late 1800s.

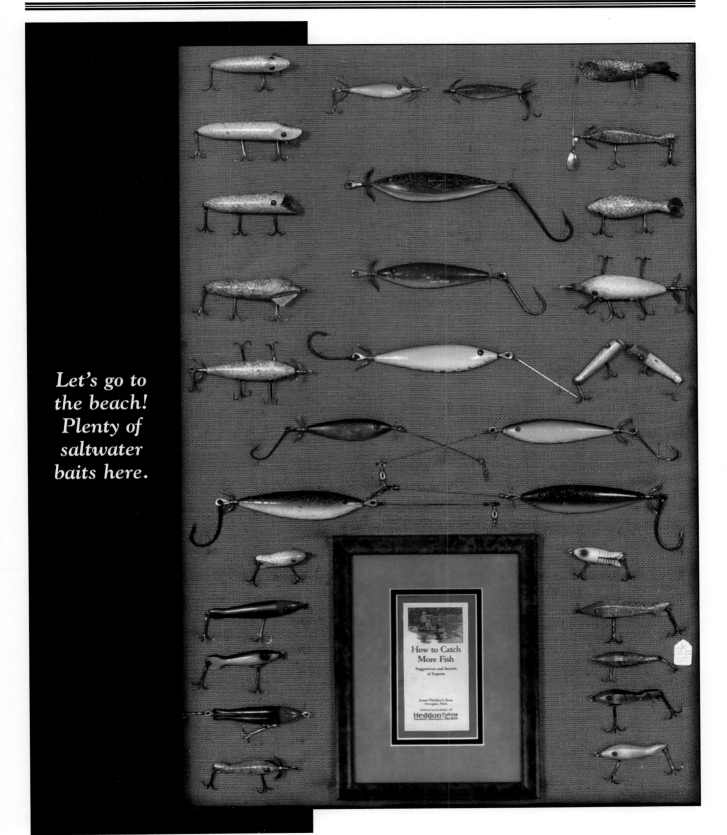

Let's go to
the beach!
Plenty of
saltwater
baits here.

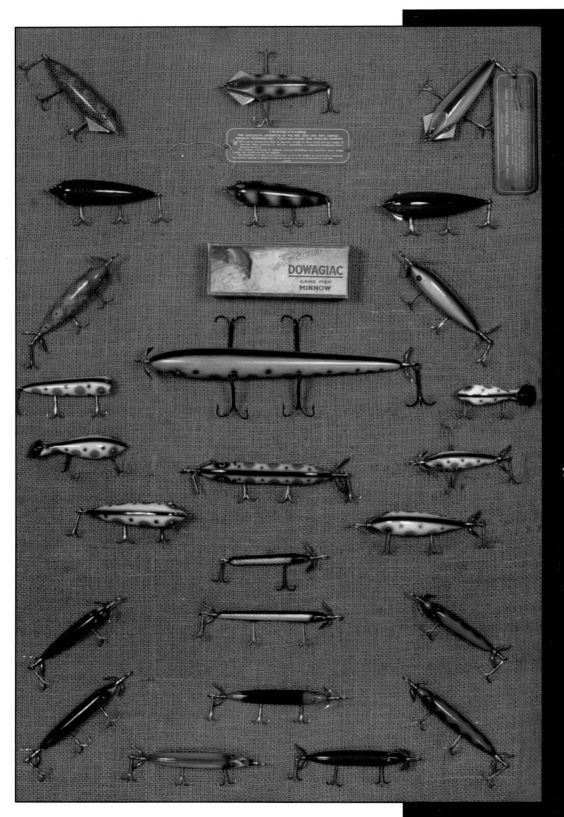

More unusual Heddons, including the longest lure ever made by the company.

The famous
200 Surface
lure in lots of
colors and
variations.

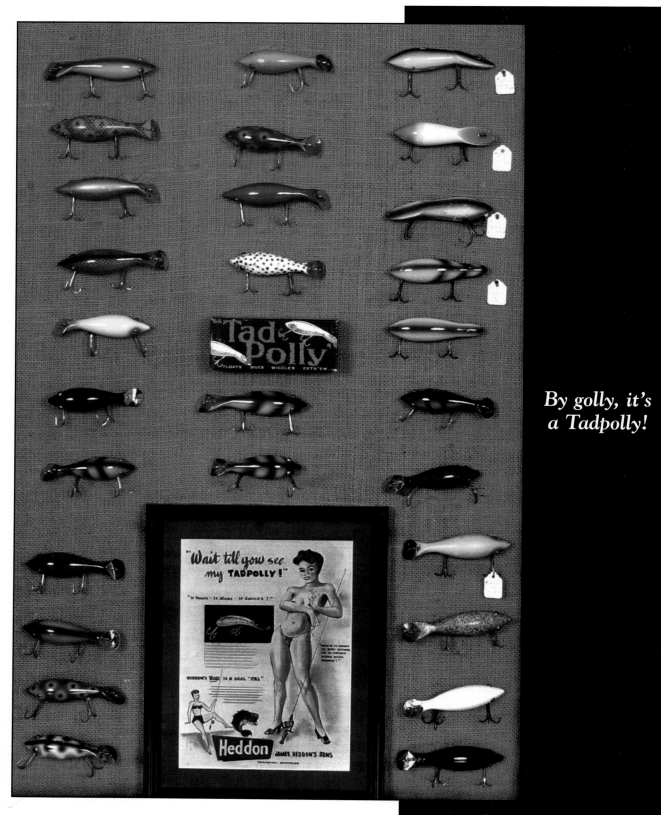

By golly, *it's* a Tadpolly!

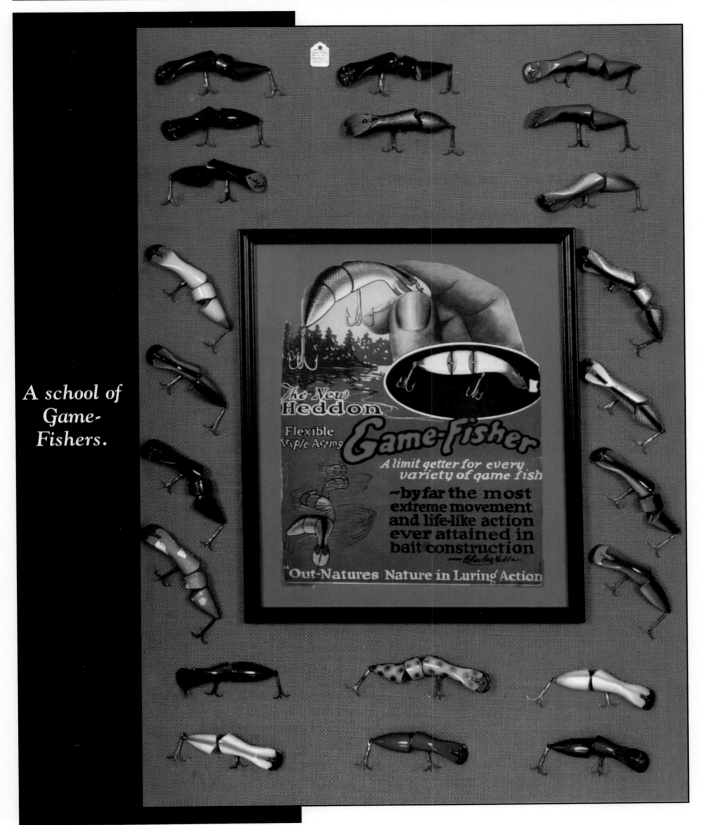

A school of Game-Fishers.

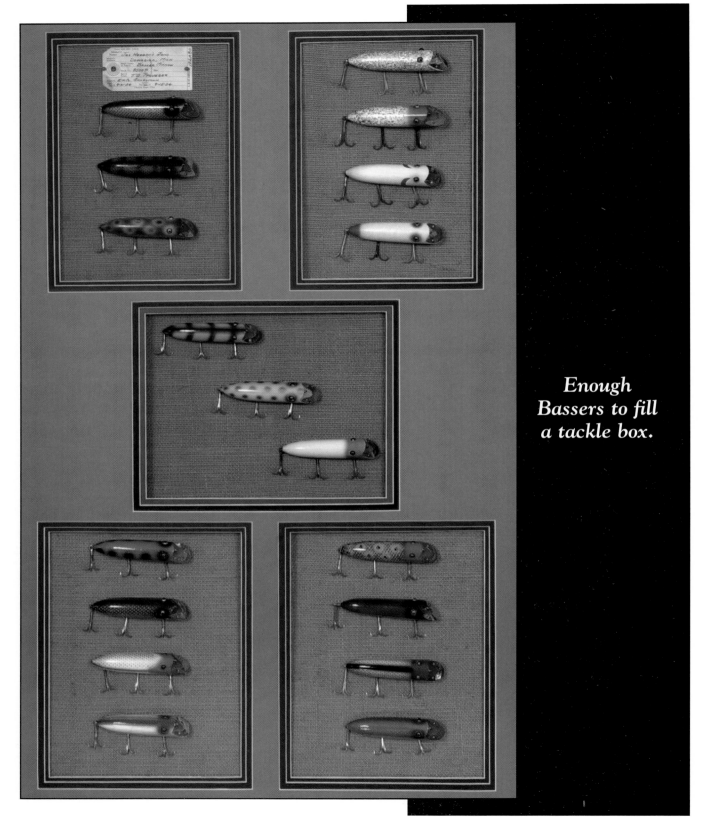

Enough Bassers to fill a tackle box.

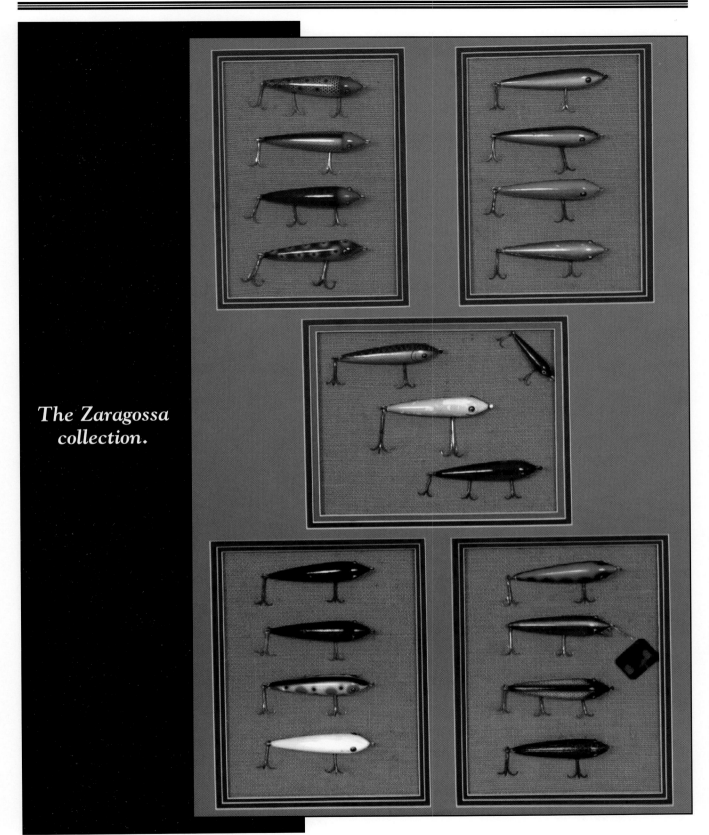

The Zaragossa collection.

The 300 Surface lure came in many colors and configurations.

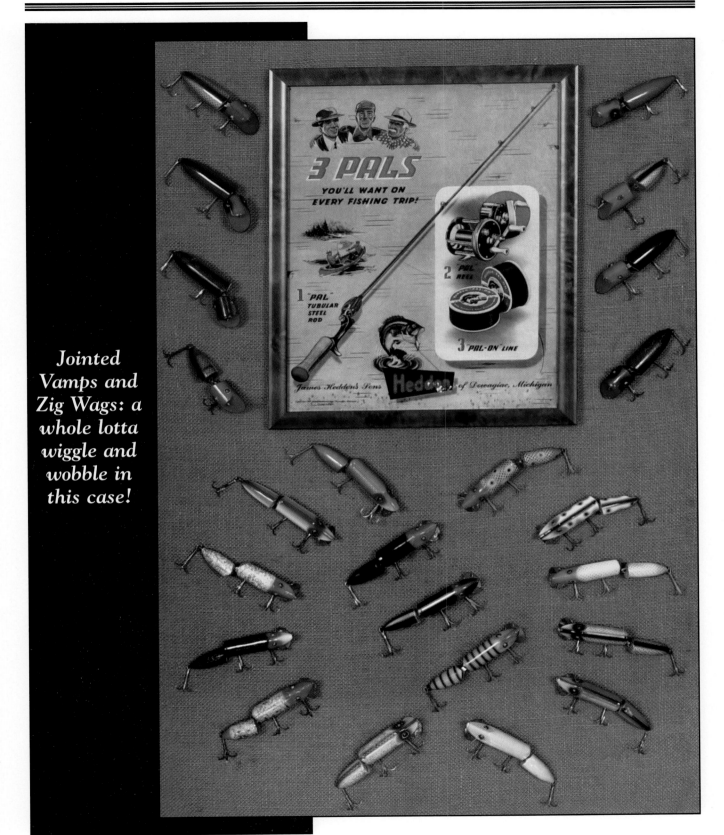

Jointed Vamps and Zig Wags: a whole lotta wiggle and wobble in this case!

Vamps,
Luckys, and
lots of others.

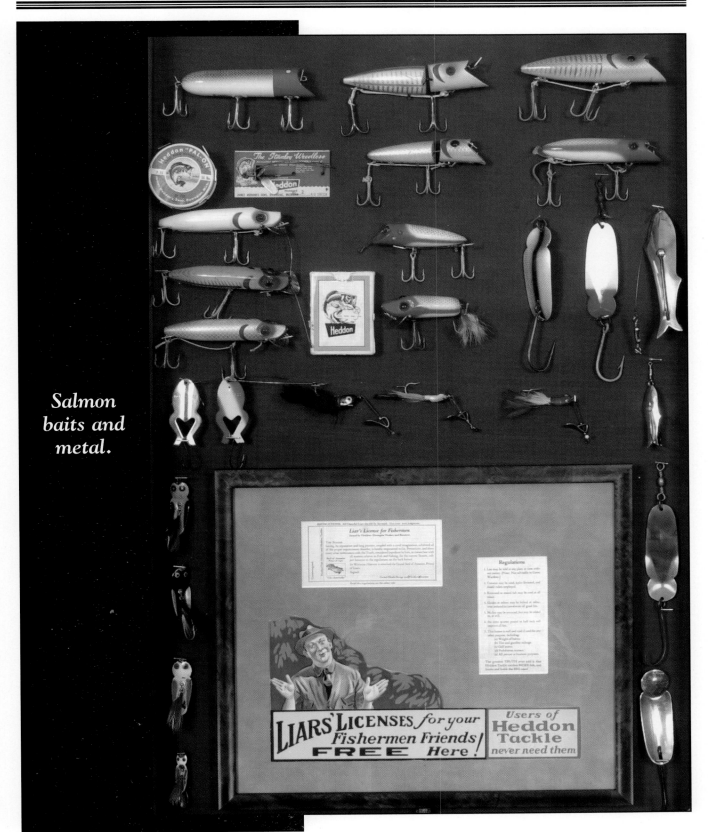

Salmon
baits and
metal.

This case is hopping-full of frog spots.

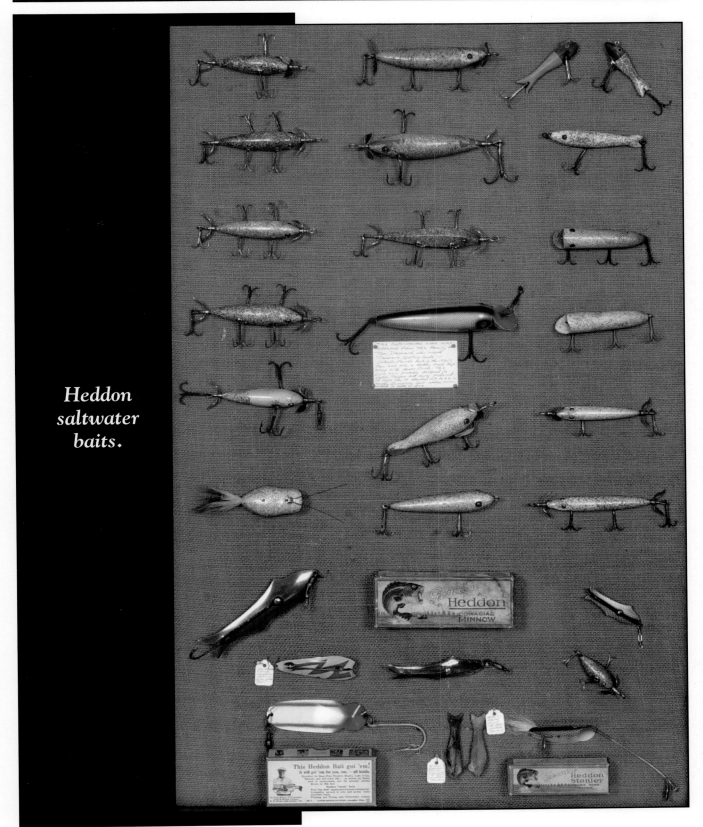

Heddon saltwater baits.

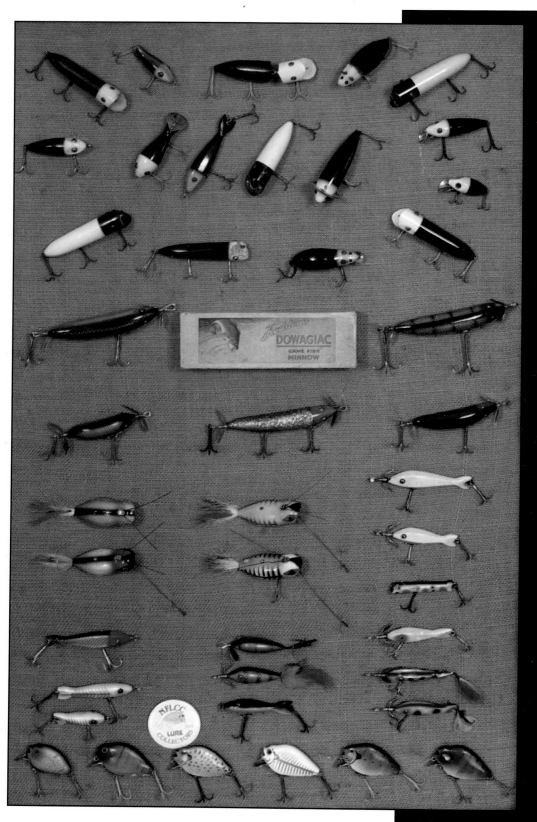

Various Heddons, including lots of black and white.

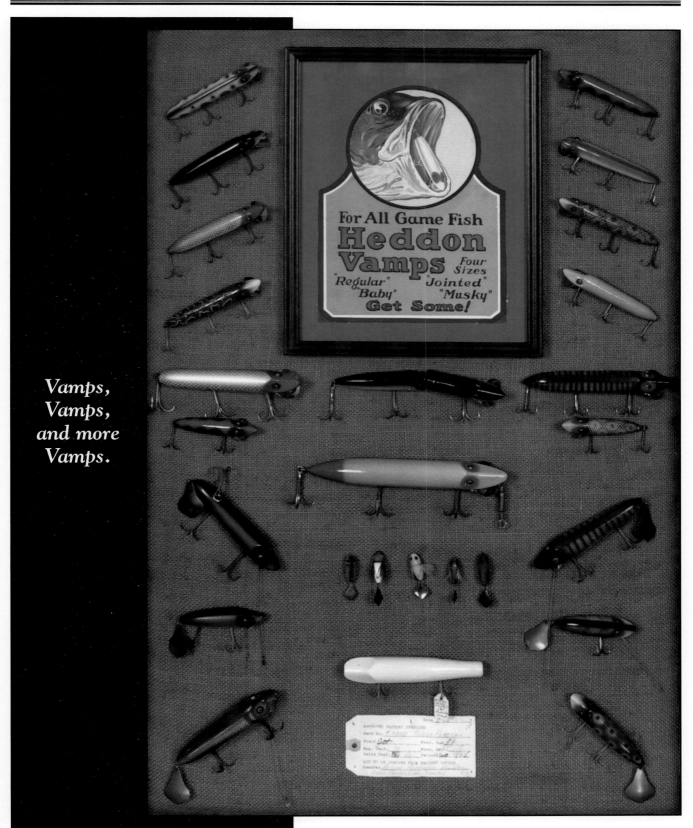

*Vamps,
Vamps,
and more
Vamps.*

*Just when you think
you've found every color of
the Crazy-Crawler...*

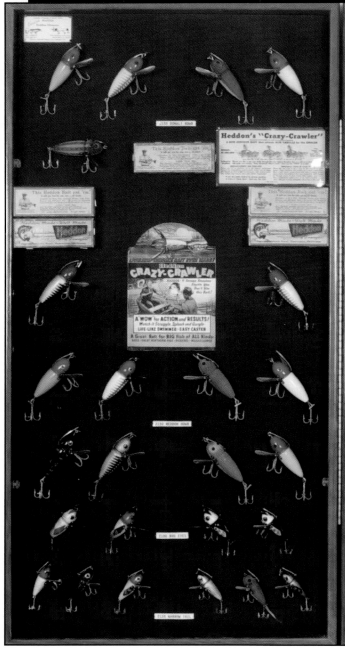

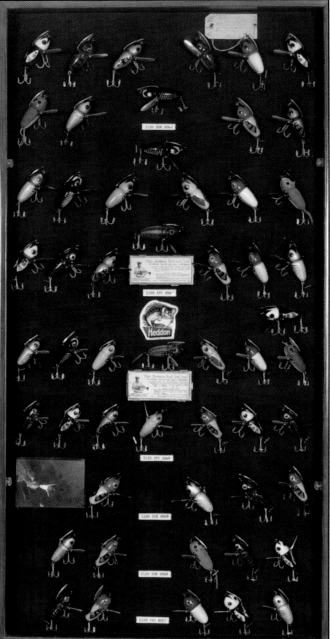

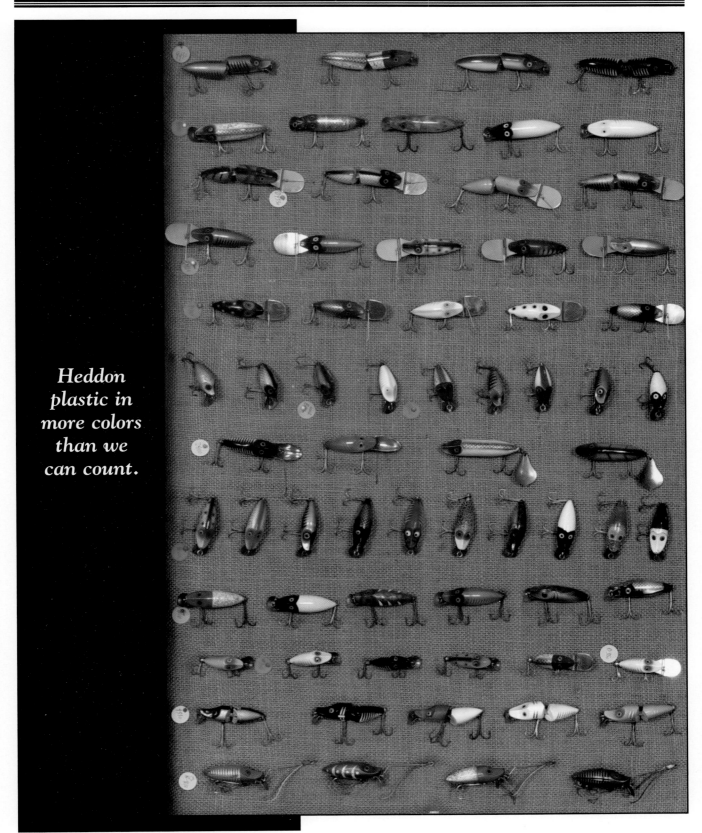

Heddon plastic in more colors than we can count.

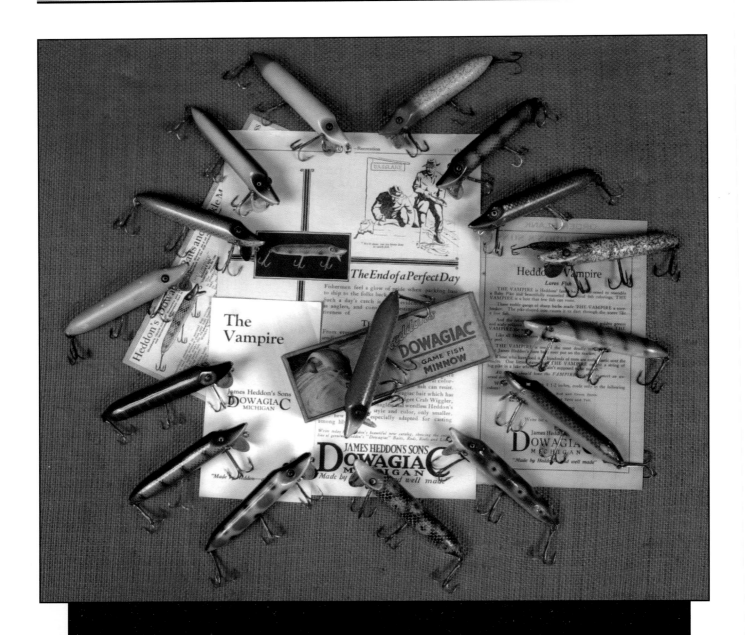

Get out your bat repellent! This
case is "eat up" with Vampires!

**Four Diamond
Submarine baits.**

Mellow Yellow?

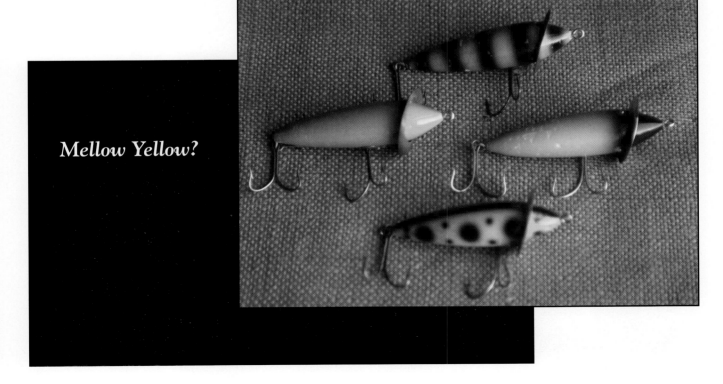

Kinney Bird for lunch?

Zig Wag fever!

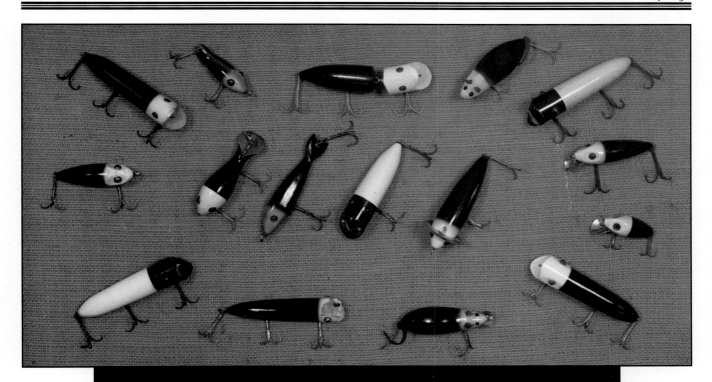

It's a black and white world, isn't it?

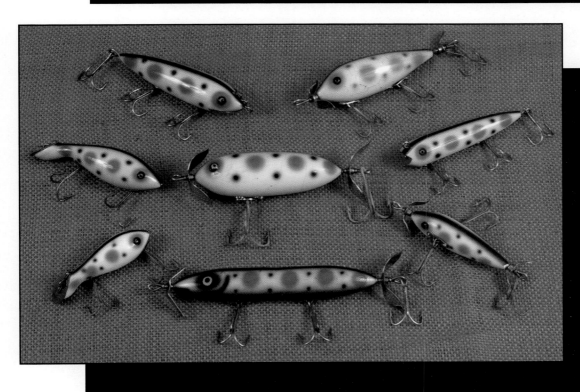

Heddon baits in strawberry spot.

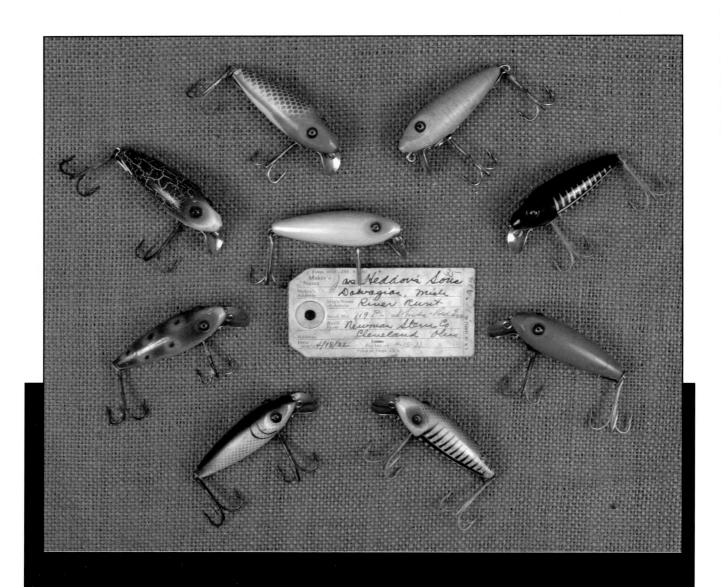

River Runt bonanza!

Crazy Crawlin!

We wuv Wee Willies!
We hope you wuv
them, too.

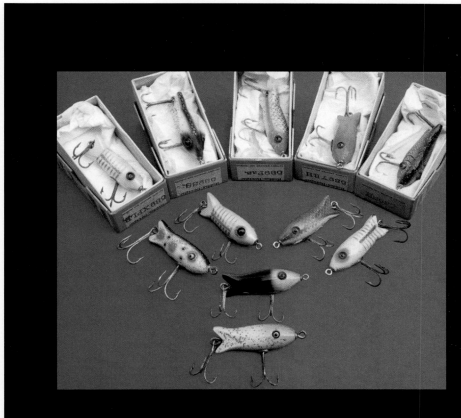

Yours Truly,
Jim Heddon.

About the Authors

Bill Roberts

Bill Roberts, an engineer from Birmingham, Alabama, is one of the nation's leading scholars on Heddon lures. His collection — regarded as one of the world's most complete — traces the evolution of Heddon lures and products from the very beginning. He has been a Heddon collector for 41 years and is an active member of the National Fishing Lure Collectors Club.

Bill got his start in lure collecting long ago — when he was just 14. A childhood friend in his native state of Virginia had an uncle who was a well-known bass fisherman. This uncle had a 14-tray, fold-out tackle box that was packed with — you guessed it — Heddon lures. The seed was planted, and Bill gradually made the transition from an accumulator to a serious collector.

This book is Bill's first foray into publishing, and the research for this project has taken years to complete. He even went as far as casting a 1902 Slopenose into the old mill pond in Dowagiac — just for the experience. He credits the inspiration for this book to his love of fishing — and of old tackle — but most of all to his wife, Margie, and their daughters Rachel and Rebecca.

Bill is always seeking new items for his collection and welcomes any opportunity to examine early tackle, especially Heddon. He can be reached at (205) 980-4677. His e-mail is hednfrog@bellsouth.net, and his website is www.heddonfishinglures.com.

Rob Pavey

Rob Pavey is outdoors editor for *The Augusta Chronicle*, Georgia's second-largest newspaper. He has been a full-time writer and editor since 1984 and has earned awards for feature writing, news coverage, and investigative reporting. His work has appeared in *Gray's Sporting Journal*, *Hunting & Fishing Collectibles* magazine and many other publications.

His fascination with antique lures emerged in the 1980s, when his grandfather gave him a rusty Kennedy tackle box packed with wooden baits. Throughout college, those lures were displayed on a piece of styrofoam in his dorm room. After graduation, the collection continued to grow — and it hasn't stopped yet.

Today, although he enjoys Heddon, his collection focuses on the myriad of smaller companies that thrived from 1900 – 1945. He is an authority on early lures and especially their boxes and maintains an educational website, www.mrlurebox.com, that features photos and background on 227 early fishing lure companies.

Rob is always seeking new items for his collection and welcomes any opportunity to examine early tackle, especially older boxed lures or lure boxes. He can be reached at (706) 860-5316 or via e-mail through his website.

The authors are serious collectors of antique fishing lures and are always eager to discuss or purchase lures and boxes, from any maker, for their collections. Feel free to contact them if you have lures to sell.

365

Index